Another white Man's Burden

SUNY series in American Philosophy and Cultural Thought

Randall E. Auxier and John R. Shook, editors

Another white Man's Burden

Josiah Royce's Quest for a Philosophy of white Racial Empire

Tommy J. Curry

SUNY PRESS

Cover art: Victor Gillam (1867–1920), "The White Man's Burden (Apologies to Rudyard Kipling)" *Judge*, April 1, 1899.

Published by State University of New York Press, Albany

For information, contact State University of New York Press, Albany, NY
www.sunypress.edu

Library of Congress Cataloging-in-Publication Data

Names: Curry, Tommy J., 1979– author.
Title: Another white man's burden : Josiah Royce's quest for a philosophy of white racial empire / Tommy J. Curry.
Description: Albany, NY : State University of New York, 2018. | Series: SUNY series in American philosophy and cultural thought | Includes bibliographical references and index.
Identifiers: LCCN 2017041906 | ISBN 9781438470733 (hardcover : alk. paper) | ISBN 9781438470726 (pbk. : alk. paper) | ISBN 9781438470740 (ebook)
Subjects: LCSH: Royce, Josiah, 1855–1916. | White nationalism—United States. | United States—Race relations. | Imperialism.
Classification: LCC B945.R64 C87 2018 | DDC 191—dc23
LC record available at https://lccn.loc.gov/2017041906

10 9 8 7 6 5 4 3 2 1

Contents

Preface

The Limits of Assimilative Methodologies in the Study of Race in American Philosophy

It is my belief that the integrationist ethic has subverted and blocked America's underlying tendency toward what I would call democratic ethnic pluralism in our society. The ethic has been a historical tendency stimulated both by Anglo-Saxon political ideology, rampant industrialism, racism, and an Americanism whose implied goal has been the nullification of all competing subcultures indigenous to North America. It is my belief that both black and white scholarly rationalization have historically supported the integrationist ethic in pursuit of the ideal American creed. This approach was obviously predicated on an intellectual consensus which held that the political, economic, and cultural values of the Anglo-American tradition were sufficiently creative and viable enough to sustain the American progression to realization of its ultimate potential. But the present internal social and racial crisis we are experiencing proves beyond a doubt the failure of this integrationist ethic. As a result of this failure . . . we have no viable black philosophy on which to base much needed black studies programs.

—Harold Cruse, "The Integrationist Ethic as a
Basis for Scholarly Endeavors," 1969

In Trump's America, poor and middle class whites find unity despite their class differences. This unity is not found in race, but an ideal—the ethnonationalist destiny of whites in the United States for generations to come. The white citizen seeks to sterilize his or her communities of racial and ethnic plurality, because such plurality is a threat to the white community, to white children, to white culture, to the true American ideals that built America. To "make America great again," white citizens are stamping out the presence of different races. Foreigners must be assimilable, or denied entrance all together. The motivation to make America great again does not come from some mythical imagining of Donald Trump's mind; it comes from many of the ideas and ideals promulgated by American philosophers such as Josiah Royce, Joseph Le Conte, and John M. Mecklin in the late nineteenth to the early twentieth centuries. Josiah Royce embraced xenophobia. He believed that it was the trait of the Anglo-Saxon that true Americans possessed to their benefit. Can we deny that the thoughts of white American philosophers have set the stage for the reimagining and reemergence of a white ethnonationalism in America, or must we believe that such ideas were never seriously endorsed or intended by the racist assertions made by early white American thinkers? But history is not usually of any concern to the philosopher. This disciplinary maxim all too often means that whatever one may find that indicts American philosophy, as a project—be it racism, xenophobia, or imperialism—is nothing more than a historical accident and not philosophical. It is assuredly not part of the actual structure or an enduring feature of a figure's thought. This denial should come as no real surprise given the apologetics regarding Heidegger and his Nazism. But what does it mean to think about America, to see America as the testing ground of the world's most insidious anti-Black and genocidal racism? What does it mean to think about America as an American philosopher, or to think about America through a practice that censors that which disrupts the narrative of American exceptionalism, and ignore that which stains democracy?

American philosophy is often practiced as a kind of thinking with a unidirectional relationship to the values (e.g., democracy, diversity, liberalism, freedom, etc.) espoused. Theory mirrors disciplinary consensus much more than the textual impediments to the realization of genuine thought. The discourse of figures in American philosophy often concerns itself with the development, life, and vitality of the democratic ideal, so by consequence of that focus, American philosophers view that intellectual community as more democratic, diverse, and so forth. This is not only to be observed in the figures designated as *the canon of American philosophy*, but also in how the American philosopher is socialized to interpret said thinkers. The American philosophical canon is constructed such that the figures chosen for study emulate the social ethics we desire to suggest are the natural consequence of their thought. Why do we ignore Joseph Le Conte and John M. Mecklin in American philosophy? Joseph Le Conte was an avowed racist and supporter of slavery as well as a teacher of Josiah Royce. John M. Mecklin was an avowed pragmatist and admirer of William James as well as an adamant segregationist. What decides inclusion or exclusion of a figure in the field of American philosophy? These questions are rarely asked or approached in any significant way in the process of thinking through American thought. While racial segregation may be an undesirable political arrangement between Blacks and whites in twenty-first-century America, does the unpopularity of segregation's reemergence negate the justifications and desirability of such arrangements in the various writings and lectures of American philosophers themselves? Segregation is no less American than integration, but the interpretive consensus among philosophers is that segregationist ideas are not only alien to the thought of figures such as Dewey, Royce, or Addams, but simply cannot and does not exist within the American philosophy canon itself. This fiat demands that thinking as an American philosopher displaces the actual centrality that racism, white supremacy, and imperialism occupy in the construction of America. In this way, American philosophy is forced by disciplinary decree to be incapable of destroying the ethos of empire problematized by the racialized outgroups America was constructed upon.

The discipline of philosophy insists that philosophical knowledge tends toward the good. Here the good often presents itself as some constellation of liberal political ideals or goals. Academic philosophers tend to read traditions and figures of those traditions as providing some justification for inclusion, diversity, civil and human rights, or outright political programs, such as feminism, coalitions, and so forth. In other words, philosophy is forced to be a self-justifying appeal to liberal political ends. As I have argued in previous publications, every white philosopher writing in the nineteenth century, for instance, John Dewey, Jane Addams, Josiah Royce, is interpreted to anticipate—and be acting in accordance with—integrationism, despite integration being an unintended program taken up after desegregation. As such, philosophy is never seen to be in the service of slavery, racism, or genocide but the complete opposite of those programs, since slavery, racism, and genocide emerge from the bowels of the unreasoned. Consequently, the effect of philosophy is its prima facia incompatibility with such human evils, despite the fact that every major figure in American philosophy has either been taught by someone who advocated for racist hierarchies between whites and other raced peoples, segregation, assimilation, imperialism, or slavery, or advocated for those hierarchies themselves. The turning away from historical fact is demanded so that all American philosophical thought, no matter its origin or authorial intent, resolves toward democratic inclusion and not the machinations of racist empire—segregation, ethnonationalism, assimilationism, and so on. In other words, those who are victims of the imperial and racist tendencies of the American philosophical enterprise are rewarded not for their identification of these tropes and other ethnological remnants of American philosophers' thought but for their ability to imagine for themselves a place within the thought of these authors.

The thinking of an earnest philosopher is not a fountainhead from which theory and method freely flow, unshaped by the geography of reason and unmolded by the stakes of a people's claim to reality. This account of the origin of theory, as either being given to the world as a function of reason or being formed within the world by rationalizations of human existence, has been contested and conceptualized beyond its usefulness for centuries. These contests, between modernists and postmodernists, anti-essentialists and essentialists, traditionalists and post-colonialists, over questions of race announce a remarkable profundity, namely, that theory and the illusion of philosophical rigor are all reducible to the uncanny ability of political interests to dictate the processes by which seemingly natural moral considerations demarcate reality. Because theory stands in as the formalization of ideology and is itself the origin of methodological justification, disciplinarity requires theorizing to be about something or things, and that theorizing is able to be judged as true by the extent to which there is a conscious social program that consensus deems a worthy accompaniment to inquiry. Rather than theory being evaluated on its ability to explain the relationship between an idea and fact, or the repetition of social or historical phenomena, theory—the generalizations we make to narratively explain reality—is gauged as morality.

When dealing with race, this social program and the philosophical engagement of those *raced* tend toward the post-racial eventuation of American society. Thus, theorizing about racial oppression commits the theorist to endless normative considerations about the world absent oppression, or dare I say a world of equality. Unfortunately, however, this thinking about race happens well before the inquiry and is built into the moral considerations that compel the sentiments of the thinker toward the initial investigation into the race problem to begin with. While this affair between theorization and "theorizing about" is rumored to be speculative and remains unspoken, except in its most exceptional moments, the drive to theorize about Blacks as part of the white imagination's narrative of

American exceptionalism shows that an explicit social program of theory nonetheless exists and resides behind every philosophical encounter with race. As we are now aware, the derelictical crisis of Black philosophy exists precisely because of this treacherous love affair between inquiry and the idealizations that inquiry aims to achieve socially. This book on Josiah Royce's racism is but the first of what I hope to be many new projects by Black, Asian, Brown, and Indigenous scholars that situate the problem of race and racism in the thoughts and thinking of many white American philosophers as more than an accident, or off-handed quip, in their writings. Far too often, the idea of race is approached in its most ideal and abstracted formulation in academic philosophy. Canonical white figures are often thought to be blind to their biases concerning race, not racist or particularly averse toward Black Americans or immigrants. This line of thinking has no actual basis in fact, of course, but is the popular consensus of the majority of the discipline regarding the problem of race in the life, works, and writings of white American philosophers from the nineteenth century forward. This is of course not any earth-shattering revelation regarding the discipline of philosophy more generally or the field of American philosophy specifically, but it is rare that there is in fact a conversation beyond critique in the annals of the American philosophical canon. Black scholars point out the racist idea, and *white philosophers* fix it, explain it away, or render said criticism irrelevant to the core contributions of said thinker.

It is because of this fiat by the masses that I have always found it difficult to love American philosophy. I know for some the works of John Dewey, Josiah Royce, and Jane Addams offer some hope that there can be a conversation about race in academic philosophy, but for me there is a level of denial, a deliberate misrepresentation of the history and ideas these thinkers promulgated, that one must engage in to truly embrace American philosophical thought as a canon. Over the last several decades there have been growing conversations concerning the reality of race as a formative idea in the works of canonical figures such as John Dewey and Josiah Royce. However, these conversations remain at the periphery of philosophical discussions and usually involve apologetics by the white majority of the field. Overt criticisms of white philosophers often result in the labeling of Black philosophers, especially Black men, as ideological or aggressive within the discipline. Consequently, many if not most of the critiques waged by Black, Brown, or Indigenous scholars against American philosophy generally as well as American philosophers often entail a pointing out of or pointing to the particular racist idea in the thought of white philosophers, then proposing a remedy, say, from the corpus of a Black thinker like W. E. B. Du Bois or Alain Locke to fix the racist notions of the canonical figure. In "On Derelict and Method: The Methodological Crisis of Africana Philosophy's Study of African Descended People Under an Integrationist Milieu," I state the problem as one of idolatry.

> Black thinkers function as the racial hypothetical of European thought whereby Black thought is read as the concretization of European reflections turned to the problem of race, and Black thinkers are seen as racial embodiments of white thinkers' philosophical spirits. In this vein, the most studied Black philosophers are read as the embodiment of their white associates; W. E. B. Du Bois is read as the Black Hegel, the Black James, the Black Dewey, and Frantz Fanon as a Black Sartre, or Black Husserl. This daemonization of Black thinkers by the various manifestations of the European logos as necessary to the production of African-American philosophy is a serious impediment to the development of a genuine genealogy of the ideas.[1]

Black figures are introduced into philosophical discussions to reform the thinking of white philosophers, not refute white thought. This orientation is the basis by which nonwhite scholars are deemed to be philosophers.[2] In other words, there is an unstated premise that functions as a criterion of inclusion in American philosophy that remains unchallenged in most of the societies, organizations, and publications of American philosophers: to be an American philosopher, you must love American philosophy. For those of us who *love* the activity of thought and thinking, a *love* that is required for us to do the critical work around racism and the histories of sexual terror and death involved in discussing colonialism and segregation, the love of American philosophy itself is a quality often found lacking. There is a tension between what is found in the thought of John Dewey and Josiah Royce and what the love for those figures creates. In embracing democracy, as the product of the organic individual, there is also the recapitulated child that stands in for the primitive Negro—savage—in the United States.

The effect of these assimilative dynamics is that Black, Brown, and Indigenous philosophers are forced to accept as given the political and cultural assumptions of the white majority and their particular readings of history, even when the descriptions of history offered by the white majority in American philosophy is most politely stated as revisionist. Let me be as concrete as possible here. In American philosophy circles, there is often the practice of asking whether certain Black figures were sufficiently feminist or pragmatist, or can be claimed as feminist, pragmatist, or liberal in their orientation. Consequently, Black male figures like Frederick Douglass or W. E. B. Du Bois are problematized for their maleness and nationalism and for their proximity to feminist ideas, while Black female figures such as Ida B. Wells-Barnett or Anna Julia Cooper are rewarded for their associations. These assertions about race and gender are primarily idealistic in the minds of American philosophers, because the consensus in American philosophy is that feminism is synonymous with equal rights and not its horrid history of imperialism, racism, and anti-Black misandry in the nineteenth century. In other words, while the time period under investigation is the late nineteenth and early twentieth centuries, the conversations about feminism and women's rights is not understood within that timeframe, but what the liberal political ethos of the field asserts should be the meaning of the term. This means that the decades of research most notably found in Louise Newman's *[w]hite Women's Rights: The Racial Origins of Feminism in the United States*, explaining how "feminism, assimilation, and imperialism were historical siblings, the offspring of a marriage between democratic ideals and social evolutionary beliefs [in which] equal citizenship was possible only for those who conformed to the racialized and gendered precepts of (white) civilization,"[3] is not only ignored but rendered unbelievable.

By revising the history of suffrage, feminism, and ethnology, American philosophy not only creates but invests in disciplinary practices that sanitize white supremacist movements. These sanitized movements, such as feminism in this case, then serve as a barometer of Black, Brown, or Indigenous thinkers' writings and theories. Specifically, Black philosophers are either interpreted or problematized within American philosophy based solely on these revisions to the political movements of the late nineteenth and early twentieth centuries, whereby their participation or withdrawal from these idealized movements not only determines their political progressivism and their place but also the alleged blind spots of their thought. The backlash against Black male emancipation by white suffragists involved a widespread propaganda campaign dedicated to showing that newly enfranchised Black men were savages, less forward thinking than white men and ultimately spelling doom for the republic. In "Women and Black Men," Elizabeth Cady Stanton reiterated that giving the vote to Black men only endangers the political power of white women. She explained: "manhood suffrage not only rouses woman's prejudice against the negro, but on the other hand his contempt and hostility towards her as an equal."[4] Restating Lucretia Mott's reports of two Black men named Mr. Downing and Mr. Purvis, Stanton implored her readers to see the misogyny of Black men toward women. "Mr. Downing, a colored man . . . said that in his opinion Nature intended that the male should dominate over the female everywhere . . . [and] young Dr. Purvis remarked that woman was the Black man's worst enemy."[5] Because "this is the feeling among the majority of all colored men," white women were asked to think about and fear the "the enfranchisement of Africans, Chinese, and all the ignorant foreigners the moment they touch our shores."[6] The historian Rosalyn Terborg-Penn explained that "negative reports about black male voters became consistent with the rhetoric of white suffrage leaders after the post–Civil War years, especially among southern suffragists who expediently attacked the black male electorate for failing to support the woman's movement."[7] To discredit Black men and their political presence, white suffragists and suffragettes began a smear campaign to convince the nation that Black men were against women's rights. This was undertaken while white women were actively trying to kick Black women out of the suffrage movement.

By the 1890s, the anti-suffrage movement had gained national prominence in both the North and South, so strategies aimed at white opposition to Negro enfranchisement became most expedient. To make suffrage more attractive, white women and their white male supporters threw their support behind educated suffrage. Educated suffrage was not a novel idea in 1890. The strategy was introduced by Elizabeth Cady Stanton as early as 1867. In an 1868 article entitled "Manhood Suffrage," Stanton wrote, "If the civilization of the age calls for an extension of suffrage, a government of the most virtuous, educated men and women would better represent the whole humanitarian idea, and more perfectly protect the interests of all, than could representation of either sex alone."[8] In the late 1860s, Stanton was interested in unifying the white race into a world power. The white male force was destructive and warlike. To rule successfully, the white race needed balance and harmony. This was the eternal law of nature and of races.

Mid violence and disturbance in the natural world, we see a constant effort to maintain an equilibrium of forces. Nature, like a loving mother, is ever trying to keep land and sea, mountain and valley, each in their place, to hush the angry waves and winds, balance the extremes of heat and cold of rain and drought, that harmony and beauty may reign supreme. There is ever a striking analogy in the world of matter and mind, and the present disorganization of our social state warns us that in the dethronement of woman we have let loose the elements of violence and ruin, that she, only, has power to curb.[9]

Two decades later however, "educated suffrage" became an important argument used to exclude black women from the movement."[10] To make suffrage attractive to Southerners, there was a need to make it explicitly anti-Black. Aimed at gaining white women's support in Southern states, educated suffrage became a national movement directed at limiting the ability of Black men to exercise their Fifteenth Amendment right to vote and excluding Black women from gaining that right altogether.

Southern white women were taking greater interest in the woman suffrage movement. Simultaneously, anti-black woman suffrage arguments developed, not only among those who basically opposed the movement, but among some white suffragists who had spoken on behalf of African American women in the past. Although anti-black suffrage sentiments did not come only from southern white women who believed in white supremacy, some northern suffragists said that it was expedient to ignore black women while wooing support for the movement in the South.[11]

I want to emphasize this point. Black Americans did not have anti-suffrage organizations; white men and women did. While white feminists were actively trying to ensure that Black women did not have the right to vote, Black men and women took to the Black press to write against this racist effort. Black men specifically spoke and wrote in support of women's suffrage and the right of Black women to vote. Rosalyn Terborg Penn noted that of the eighty-three Black American males who commented upon suffrage publicly, eighty of those men supported, advocated for, and participated in pro–women's rights organizations. Contrary to the intersectional mythos, based on public or written commentaries on women's suffrage between 1840 and 1920, only three Black men were opposed to women's suffrage.[12] By accepting the accounts of white gender theory, its history and political narratives, Black and white American philosophers propagate blatantly false historical narratives as the basis of theory and disciplinary coalitions.

Like Josiah Royce, Mississippi suffragettes like Belle Kearney implored Southerners to limit the freedom of Blacks, specifically Black men, to preserve the Anglo-Saxon character of the United States. Kearney, like many of the anti-Black racists of her day, believed that "today the Anglo-Saxon triumphs in them more completely than in the inhabitants of any portion of the United States—the Anglo-Saxon blood, the Anglo-Saxon ideals, continue the precious treasure of 2,000 years of effort and aspiration."[13] Continuing the colonial legacy of her British forebears, she was concerned with the complexion of those who would rule the American republic. For Kearney, the expansion of women's rights and freedoms would ensure the rule of whites over the Black race. She writes:

> The enfranchisement of women would insure immediate and durable white supremacy, honestly attained; for, upon unquestionable authority, it is stated that in every Southern State but one, there are more educated women than all the illiterate voters, white and black, native and foreign, combined. As you probably know, of all the women in the South who can read and write, ten out of every eleven are white. When it comes to the proportion of property between the races, that of the white outweighs that of the black immeasurably. The South is slow to grasp the great fact that the enfranchisement of women would settle the race question in politics.[14]

The complexity of racism—the push of the evolutionary superiority whites (Anglo-Saxons) claimed over other races—pulled all political ideas and social organization toward white superiority. Instead of our supposed liberal ideas resisting the cultural and sociological institutionalization of racism, they are compatible with and in many cases dependent on white supremacy.[15] There was no aspect of white society that was unaffected by the dynamics of racism. In our rush to assimilate Black, Brown, and Indigenous voices into the accepted traditions and thoughts of white

American figures, be they male or female, we lose the experiential breaks racialized thinkers had with the politics and ideologies of domination. Is it necessary to claim Anna Julia Cooper as a feminist? Du Bois as a pragmatist? What urges us to do so? Is it even possible to align these authors with these political or intellectual movements once the origins and goals of these thoughts are ascertained? Even more worrisome is the idea that despite this history of feminism, the racism of American democracy, and the cost white individual rights levied upon racial groups around the world, taken as ideals, the ideas of feminism, American democracy, and liberalism can serve as *theoretical beacons* that should guide and could improve our existing philosophical sensibilities.

Black Americans had to position themselves outside of and within various discourses of American politics. This complexity cannot be captured by the intuitive appeals white American figures or organizations have to academics, be they Black or white, who are not specifically trained in the history of American ethnology or nineteenth-century American politics. To assert as is often done that the racist and imperial history of women's rights should be used either as the measure of Black Americans' political consciousness or the barometer of political progressivism for Black men and women suggests that suffrage, feminism, and the subsequent reformism for women's rights that became the WKKK, or legitimized white women segregationists' support for (male-dominated) Citizens Councils, are absolved of their historical terrors when presented as *theory*.[16] Black Americans had to fight against the domestic rationalizations that justified segregation and concomitantly empowered the logics of imperialism. Black Americans' refutations of white racism were statements about the nature of race itself. They were an attempt to commit to the humanity of all the darker races, and these intellectual discourses are not reducible to one political movement or identity category. In short, white theory (e.g.: feminism, pragmatism, liberalism) cannot be used to fix the history of the white ideas being critiqued.

Because of the ahistorical nature of the discipline of philosophy generally, American philosophers and their writings dealing with racism, gender, and empire are being praised as anti-racist by scholars having no actual knowledge of the debates of nineteenth- and twentieth-century figures deploying various ethnological assumptions, theories, and terms throughout their writings. These terms and references are thought to be inconsequential to understanding the relationship American thinkers, both white and Black, have to the ever-evolving concept of race and the violence of racism in the United States. The force racism exerts on the development of American democracy in its natality is ignored, suggested to be an accident of particular democratic arrangements, not the phylogeny of American democracy itself. The debates in nineteenth-century ethnology, focus on democracy because it was a social system that could control, manage, or repress racial characteristics. These thinkers emphasize America's trajectory toward unity; it was part of its natural evolutionary tract under nineteenth-century ethnology. Because the races were thought to represent streams of civilization, a particular expression of God's intent, the white man's burden was popularly understood to be God's will, his earthly mechanism that hastened unity. The philosophy, politics, and ethnology of the nineteenth century were dedicated to this ideal. As A. H. Keane explains:

> [Ethnology] proceeds by the comparative method, coordinating its facts with a view to determining such general questions as the antiquity of man; monogenism or polygenism; the geographical centre or centres of evolution of dispersion; the number and essential characteristics of the fundamental human types; the absolute and relative value of racial criteria: miscegenation; the origin and evolution of articulate speech and its value as a test of race; the influence of the environment on the evolution of human varieties, on their pursuits, temperament, religious views, grades of culture; the evolution of the family, clan, tribe and nation.[17]

So to suggest that there is a foundation of racial exchange whereby races evolve and share similar knowledge, have a shared culture, was impossible without the eradication of the inferior race's psychology by the more dominant race. All white populations, their thoughts and politics, were understood as a strand of this ethnological lineage. While there certainly were political disagreements, the differences were usually resolved in favor of the unity, superiority, or expansion of the white race's power.

Throughout American philosophy there are assertions that politics, the similarity a Black historical figure like W. E. B. Du Bois or Ida B. Wells-Barnett has with white figures like Dewey or Addams about race or democracy, can and in fact do override the evolutionary trajectory of their day. By displacing the historical meaning and ethnological findings concerning the actual meaning of race, philosophers are able to conflate any position held by a white philosopher that suggests Blacks should not be slaves, or should become citizens, or are not condemned by their biology, as anti-racist. These positions about Blacks by whites are asserted to be compatible with any number of thoughts by Black philosophers. In 1958, Du Bois tells Aptheker that he read his first chapter of the book by the same name "History and Reality" with great interest. Du Bois then tells Aptheker, "For two years I studied under William James while he was developing Pragmatism; under [George] Santayana and his attractive mysticism and under [Josiah] Royce and his Hegelian idealism. I then found and adopted a philosophy which has served me since; thereafter I turned to the study of History and what has become Sociology."[18] So while Du Bois may in fact be quite adamant that he turned away from pragmatism in an effort to find a new way of studying Black Americans, the product of his novel turn makes no actual difference in the interpretation of his works in American philosophy. He is relevant to American philosophy because he represents the accumulative apex of white thinking and mentorship in a Black figure as a pragmatist, not because of his own novel contributions to how we think about and diagnose the recurring ills and crises of the American empire.[19]

In American philosophy, the work by Black philosophers aiming to separate the thinking and theory of Black figures like W. E. B. Du Bois, William H. Ferris, or Alain Locke from the fray so to speak are not routinely embraced by the field.[20] There has been a constellation of writings on Alain Locke, for example, aimed at this very delineation in his thinking.[21] The introduction of William H. Ferris's Black idealism, which posits the de-evolution of the Anglo-Saxon, attempts to provide resources suited to the task of reorienting how the philosopher thinks about race far beyond identity or politics. Ferris believes that race is a core ideal tested and tasked with the weight of a humanity throughout history. Engaging Ferris's philosophy of history problematizes the attempts by Royceans to introduce anti-racist thinking to Royce's racist thought, because Ferris accepts that Anglo-Saxonism was firmly committed to world domination and cultural homogeneity. By contrast, Ferris offers a philosophy of history and community written as a response to the imperial and destructive race trait of the Anglo-Saxon. Whereas Royce sees philosophy as a mechanism to modernize the past strategies of British colonization and the South's racial managerialism toward Black Americans, William H. Ferris offers an idealist philosophy that breaks with the imperial logics of Royce's social philosophy and assimilationist ethics. Despite the accessibility of Ferris's writings and works over the last several years, his insistence that the Black race has the most humanist worldview that does not depend on the destruction of other cultures, but rather the gathering of the spiritual ideals offered by the darker races, has not broadly captured the interests of American philosophers.[22]

Another white Man's Burden is an attempt to orient American philosophy differently. Rather than being simply a book waging a polemic against Josiah Royce, this text is trying to explain and explore how nineteenth-century ethnology—specifically, the meanings, terms, and rhetoric—dictated the thinking of philosophers, and how the theories they promulgated were intimately connected to a vision of empire and the aspiration of white domination. There was no mediation in this thinking. The assumed primitivism of the Negro race took a seemingly infinite number of forms in the discourses of the late nineteenth and early twentieth centuries. This text is a case study so to speak of the problematics race and ethnological theories present in our interpretations of American philosophers' thought. Rather than simply sidestep the race question, a maneuver that also includes deliberately misreading race as an identity or simply a set of individual beliefs or biases, this book wrestles with the contravening thoughts and logics of white superiority. It examines how the aspirations for a white republic extended into the projects for white empire.

Josiah Royce was a racist, but he was not alone in this endeavor. He was not the only American thinker that desired the assimilation of racialized peoples into harmless populations managed by white governance. Authors like John Dewey saw education as the way to accomplish this goal; Josiah Royce saw communities and memorialization as a way to strip foreigners of their culture. This xenophobic and ethnocentric orientation is a mark of American philosophy, and it must be dealt with as an orienting telos rather than an accident of the democratic ethos of the United States. This book demonstrates what a true understanding of race and racism actually involves. The philosopher must be a student of history and become immersed in the language of ethnology to truly understand the projects, resistance, and subtle—but profound—ruptures and challenges waged against the tides of white supremacy. Such an approach would expose scholars to the complexities of Black thought beyond identity. It would reveal resistance and complacence, rupture and alignment, in the thinking of Black American figures. The radicality and refutation of white supremacist thinking was not always a rejection, but as in the case of Ferris, a complete reorientation of how we think of God, history, and the trajectory of race and evolution.

This book is not a testament to the problems in the thought of Josiah Royce; it is a study of the historical gulf—the methodological failures—of American philosophy's engagement with race itself. *Another white Man's Burden* is a challenge to American philosophers that questions how we read, what we believe we understand, and urges us to refine our thinking so that we can better do philosophy.[23]

American philosophy can no longer remain settled with a methodology that produces theory through ahistoricism. The distance imposed upon ideas by the philosopher—their decontextualization under the guise of abstraction—produces concepts that are taken to *the ideas* comprising theory. Valorizing the idea(s) assigned to the American project as philosophy through the process of decontextualization, ideas that are chosen arbitrarily but nonetheless are taken as the products of disciplinary coda and individual proclivity dedicated to formulating what is American, reifies (as method) the sanitizing of America's racist history, its genocidal impulse(s), and the deliberate suppression of the horror that gives context to the concepts of democracy, community, and plurality. In this sense, *Another white Man's Burden* is intentionally an unsettling exploration of American philosophy itself.

Acknowledgments

It is often difficult to recount the number of conversations concerning a specific topic or theme or reference relating to this book. Over the last several years, I have come back to Royce and his philosophy of race because of some denial, some slight against evidence, some misappropriation of Black philosophical thought. It was often the case that my engagement with Royce was driven by what unsettled me about his vision of the world. For years, Dwayne Tunstall spoke with me concerning Royce's shortcomings. I am indebted to his patience and interest in this topic since graduate school. Similarly, I have to thank Randy Auxier for his help in pushing me to develop this theory into a full-length study. I must thank my wife, Dr. Gwenetta Curry, who laughed with me over the obviousness of Royce's racism when it was denied by so many scholars in the field. She listened to endless passages and my reading of sources interpreting Royce during his own day as a Northern imperialist and racist by Southern racists and segregationists. I have to thank Kenneth Stikkers for his reading and support of this project in graduate school, as well as Doug Anderson and Doug Berger for their initial support of this project on Royce. I have to thank Dr. Leonard Harris for his inspiration to persist in an unpopular opinion. Thank-you to countless forums, such as Philosophy Born of Struggle, SAAP, and the Royce Society, for the space to share this work, and to those scholars and audiences who have listened to paper after paper, intervention after intervention on this topic. I have to thank Daniel Brunson, Seth Vannatta, Eric Weber, Myron Jackson, Stephanie Rivera Berruz, Jessica Otto, and David Rodick for their support. I would also like to thank my graduate students: Andrew Soto, who would not let white Americanists forget the debilitating effects assimilation and western expansion had on Indigenous peoples; Dalitso Ruwe, who continues to remind the world of the importance of Black intellectual history; Patrick Anderson, who refuses to go quietly into the night; Rocio Alvarez, who reminds philosophy of what cannot be accounted for; Adebayo Ogungbure for his insistence that the dehumanization of nonwhites is the basis upon which we begin to ask metaphilosophical questions; and Curry O'Day for being the persistent gadfly. Over the years, these individuals and countless more have driven me to complete this book and start another era of anti-colonial criticism and theory in American philosophy. I thank everyone for their contributions, and the staff of State University of New York Press for their support and excitement surrounding this book. To those I did not mention, I am indebted nonetheless.

Introduction

Books that aim to expose the racism of white philosophers are usually of little consequence to the trajectory of disciplines or the interpretive lens of scholars, especially when they are written by Black, Brown, or Indigenous scholars. Often framed as external criticism and irrelevant to the thought of the authors in question, critiques of white philosophers' racism or their endorsement of colonialism are usually described as anachronistic commentaries that are overly concerned with personal predilections, rather than seriously rigorous historical analyses of a given philosopher's worldview. Previous works exposing the centrality of anti-Black racism to the thought of modern philosophers like Immanuel Kant, David Hume, or John Locke have remained as ineffective in changing the intellectual historiography of the discipline as texts demonstrating the rise of modern philosophy to be inspired by and rationalized within the colonization of Africa and Asia.[1] Even sub-specialties like American philosophy that are responding to the dominance of continental and analytic thought throughout philosophy departments in the United States remain obstinate toward works exposing the reliance of Progressive Era thought on scientific racism and colonialism after three decades of scholarship documenting these linkages.[2] Since such investigations are often regarded as verbose ad hominem(s), critiques of white philosophers' racism and indebtedness to colonial projects are deemed creative interpretations of philosophers rather than historically informed exegeses of the terms and concepts that form the basis of a philosopher's work.

So why Josiah Royce? Or more accurately, why write a book on the racism of Josiah Royce, given that he is such a marginal figure in philosophy generally? At one level, I believe it is important to acknowledge that the contention that Josiah Royce was an anti-racist thinker at the turn of the twentieth century is simply false. Josiah Royce was an ardent supporter of British colonization, an adamant racist, and an

1

advocate of American empire. His proposal to colonize Black Americans in the South is an extension of this logic and is especially relevant to how one theorizes his idea of community and the consequence of such ideas on racialized groups like Black Americans today. At another level, while Josiah Royce is a marginal figure generally, the critique of Royce's racism is more accurately thought of as a case study of the gross mis-understanding philosophers, literary critics, and theorists have of the nineteenth century broadly. Philosophers tend to create heroes or heroines when reading historical figures like Royce rather than seriously engaging his thought and its consequence. Important terms like the white peril, or references to the work of Adolf Bastian, are thought to be irrelevant to the philosopher but were central to Royce's own philosophy. In other words, the racial critique raised against Josiah Royce in this book is more accurately understood as a corrective to the historiographic lens deployed by American philosophers who intuitively assert that nonbiological accounts of race are anti-racist and less pernicious than other nineteenth-century theories of race that linked blood to destiny. The assertion that cultural or environmentalist thinking about Blacks, Native Americans, or the Japanese were less racist and indicative of progress in America's racial consciousness ignore the actual debates ethnologists, anthropologists, and sociologists were having about race at the dawn of the twentieth century. By analyzing Royce's theories of race, we gain an understanding not only of the historical meaning or significance of terms and thinkers in the late nineteenth century, but how these concepts actually functioned and were utilized among philosophers as they approached the problems of a new century. Through Royce, the contemporary scholar can gain insight into the assumptions of Royce's peers, such as John Dewey, Charles S. Pierce, and Jane Addams, as well as the milieu of race thinking among American philosophers generally in the early 1900s. Royce simply offers contemporary (American) philosophers an opportunity to observe American democracy and progressivism in the womb so to speak, allowing even the most casual observer to see how the social stability required for American democracy to take root and flourish depended on the subjugation of Black, Indigenous, and immigrant peoples broadly.

Origins of the Project

This book began as a presentation paper on the first chapter of Josiah Royce's *Race Questions, Provincialism, and Other American Problems* in

Randall Auxier's class at Southern Illinois University Carbondale. I was a doctoral student in the department of philosophy in 2005. A decade ago, there was no literature explaining the connections that Josiah Royce had to the white man's burden or colonialism. Ten years ago, the world had not noticed Royce authored "Some Characteristic Tendencies of American Civilization," nor did it care to know. At this time, Royce's philosophy of race was being presented as a multicultural anti-racism. His essays on "Race Questions" and "Provincialism" were the primary source material used to speak of his understanding of American racism, and it was concluded based on these two texts that Royce should be thought of as a racial progressive who was not only sensitive to the racism of American science, but especially attentive to the problem of lynching in the American South. I remember when I presented my paper to the class, there was a staggering disbelief that all the other scholars writing about Royce had gotten it wrong, while this one Black student (studying nineteenth-century ethnology mind you) had gotten it right. My actual knowledge of nineteenth-century ethnology and the debates concerning race at the turn of the century were thought to be inconsequential by many of the students, though Randy Auxier suggested this idea may have some legs and merit further consideration. This disbelief in Royce's racism continued for years, until Dwayne Tunstall assembled a panel at the joint session of the Josiah Royce Society and the Personalist Discussion Group at the Central American Philosophy Association conference on April 19, 2008. I remember receiving a letter from Frank Oppenheim before the conference urging me to remember that Josiah Royce was the most progressive American thinker on race to date. I remember thinking to myself—"by what measure?"

The panel was a discussion of Josiah Royce's racism. It was formative of my approach toward discussing Royce's racism and imperial aspirations, because it was the first time I revealed my knowledge of this wholly neglected article by Royce delivered in 1900 as an address to the Aberdeen Philosophical Society at Aberdeen University. Given my knowledge of this previously unengaged document, I attempted to convince Royceans that Josiah Royce was in fact racially intolerant and fearful of racial and ethnic diversity. I cited passage after passage where Royce demanded Blacks and other alien races to assimilate into America and urged the audience to think of the consequences of colonizing Black people in the American South as the British had done in Jamaica. I demanded a fairer comparison of Royce on race and sought to place him in conversation with the Black scholars of his day. I remember the conviction I had at the time trying to convince Royceans of the ahistoricism and dishonesty involved in claiming Royce as the most progressive American thinker on race based on his writing of "Race Questions" given the ethnological treatises authored by Martin R. Delany, Kelly Miller, W. E. B. Du Bois, or even Black idealists inspired by Royce like William H. Ferris. As a young scholar, just a year out of graduate school, I urged a room of senior philosophers to reconsider their methodology and reading of Du Bois, who seemed to be suspiciously present in every reference to Royce's racial progressivism. I found it ironic that in these debates concerning Royce's racism, Royce was described as agreeing with Du Bois on practically everything, or everything Du Bois suggested about race in the two primary documents analyzed in philosophy—"The Conservation of Races" and *The Souls of Black Folk*.

This panel led to a series of articles being published in the fall edition of *The Pluralist* in 2009 and brought this debate to the public's attention. Dwayne Tunstall's introduction to the series framed the debate on Royce around a central dispute during the panel. Can Royce be an anti-essentialist (cultural) racist? Tunstall concluded, "Because of Royce's cultural, anti-black racism and his (unwitting) perpetuation of white supremacy, I think that Royce is not the person to read concerning race issues."[3] My essay, entitled "Royce, Racism, and the Colonial Ideal: White Supremacy and the Illusion of Civilization in Josiah Royce's Account of the White Man's Burden," argued that the previous articles published on Josiah Royce and racism were decontextualized from the actual meanings and events he believed constituted the crisis of white supremacy and the racialist sciences of his day. I insisted that assimilation was not a progressive racial theory at the turn of the century, that Royce's endorsement of the white man's burden was blatant imperialism, that British administration as a strategy to control Blacks in the South was racist, and while it is true that Royce had rejected a strict biological determinism, his evolutionary accounts of racial plasticity and environmentalism were no less racist.[4] Jacquelyn Kegley's "Josiah Royce on Race: Issues in Context" was also published in this issue of *The Pluralist*. In Kegley's article, Royce was simply well intentioned and naïve of the racism he exhibited. This was a common defense of Royce at the time. For example, Shannon Sullivan argued that "Royce makes every effort to avoid racism . . . and is unaware of the fine analysis of contemporary times about the evils of colonialism and the havoc it wreaked on people's lives."[5] In Kegley's interpretation, Royce is focused on alerting the reader of white privilege, white ignorance, and the dangers of racism. Citing his now famous question, "Is it a 'yellow peril,' or a 'black peril,' or perhaps after all, is it not rather some form of 'white peril' which threatens the future of humanity in this day of great struggles and of complex issues," as evidence of his disavowing of white supremacy, Kegley writes:

> Royce turns tables on white folk who tend to view racial prob-lems as concerning everyone but white people. Indeed, I believe Royce's article is somewhat justified in proposing that white domination and imperialism might be the greatest threat to the flourishing of humankind in the twentieth century. Royce was sensitive, as we see in his history of California, to issues of white domination, imperialist tendencies, and prejudice.[6]

From her reading of Sullivan's introduction to the republication of Royce's *Race Questions, Provincialism, and Other American Problems*, Kegley explains that "Shannon Sullivan and I agree that Royce stands out in the history of classical American philosophy in taking an anti-racist focus on race questions when very few philosophers—especially white male philosophers—took scholarly time to think about these issues."[7] Kegley and Sullivan offer readers no actual proof of this claim. They merely assert that the arbitrarily designed white academic canon chosen by white male and female philosophers in the mid-twentieth century to be "American philosophy" is in fact representa-tive of the significant voices at the turn of the century concerning race. If one expands the canon even slightly based on philosophers dealing with ethnology, or America's first school of sociology at Atlanta University, or the research at the University of Chicago, then such a statement would become vastly inaccurate, if not silly. The debates concerning race were much more complex than the figures American philosophy has selected for study. Because American philosophy chooses to imagine history as a tale of white ignorance to racism, and then white benevolence and virtue upon discovering it, white figures like Royce are interpreted as exceptions because they engaged racism in America at all. This disciplinary disposition in American philosophy makes the standard of anti-racism embarrassingly meager, since it suggests not that a white American author is in fact anti-racist in his or her original work, but that said author can be interpreted as anti-racist because he or she was not blind to the existence of racism. This has been the underlying premise behind the neglect of some of Royce's most adamantly colonial and racist writings to date.

When lost or neglected essays or writings of authors are discovered, there is usually some consideration, in many cases celebration, of the meanings found within the unearthed gem. Such was not the case with introducing Royce's Aberdeen speech, "Some Characteristic Tendencies of American Civilization." There were no deliberations on this discovery, nor was there a panel over the last several years to ascertain the meaning this speech has for Royce's larger corpus. While Royce's other reflections on race have become canonical in many respects, this last talk, despite being listed in Ignas Skrupskelis's "Annotated Bibliography of the Publications of Josiah Royce" in 1968, remains relegated to the periphery of Royce's philosophical thought.[8] The question of why must be addressed. For older generations of Royce scholars, who would have known about this speech and known of its contents from Skrupskelis's annotated summary, why was it not engaged or mentioned as relevant for the study of Royce's social political ethics, specifically that of race? For younger Royce scholars, why was it simply avoided; designated as irrelevant? One could only guess at the motivations Royce scholars had in neglecting this work, but the effect was the same—it was to some extent deliberately ignored.

Ideo-Racial Apartheid as Method and Paradigm: How American Philosophers Read Royce into Anti-Racist Discourse by Ignoring the Work of His Black Contemporaries

Despite the scholarly advancements in other fields like sociology, American studies, and Africana philosophy—and the proliferation of critical works in these fields concerning the problems of race, whiteness, and color-blindness in texts produced by historic white thinkers—philosophy has adamantly enforced an "ideo-racial apartheid" whereby white thinkers are praised for any attention given to the question of race, regardless of the extent to which their ideas are assimilationist, culturally depraved, or firmly rooted in colonialism. Under this ideological apartheid, Black thinkers' contributions are categorically excluded from philosophical conversations concerning race. This exclusion is in itself racist, because it not only assumes that Black scholarship, despite its lifelong attempts to understand, cope with, solve, or at least educate people about the American race problem, does not contribute to "philosophies of race." This segregationist logic reinforces the idea that whites set the standards of racial responsibility in American society, while Blacks are merely examples of the failings of said standards. The consequence of such a system is that white thinkers are only accountable to other whites on the issue of race and cannot and should not be compared to the philosophical outlooks of Black thinkers on the very same questions.[9]

My survey of Royce's racial bibliography so to speak places him squarely within the debates and sensibilities of his time. Starting with the views of race presented by Black thinkers like W. E. B. Du Bois in the Atlanta Sociological Laboratory, I show that Royce is behind the ball in many regards. While it is not uncommon for American philosophers to mark Josiah Royce's reflection on race as exceptional, often suggesting that "except for W. E. B. Du Bois and Jane Addams, no other major figure associated with pragmatist philosophy substantially addressed issues of race and racism in their written work, nor did anyone so early as in the twentieth century as did Royce,"[10] the earnest scholar must probe perhaps the most fundamental question, "In comparison to whom?" Nineteenth-century Black thinkers, be they philosophers, educators, historians, or political activists, have long acknowledged and engaged the ethnological assumptions that Royce attempts to question. Yet their work and texts, which remain for our use, are thought to be without relevance for the debates surrounding race and racism in American philosophy. Why does Royce enjoy the luxury of being elevated within the canon when the basis for comparison is segregationist? He emerges as "a little less racist" than other turn-of-the-century white racists who believed in biological determinism, and on that basis—his comparison to other whites—he is elevated and lauded as being anti-racist. I find this historiography woefully inadequate; a kind of ideo-racial apartheid that must be dismantled.

Today, it is this type of thinking that frames contemporary Roycean debates over the race question and regards Royce as an anti-racist thinker, because he may have been a little less racist when compared to his white counterparts. American philosophy, and the inordinate number of white philosophers who comprise this area, has not begun the arduous task of assessing the gap between their romantic revisions of historical white philosophers and the historical moment in which these thinkers were writing. Because philosophy assumes a literal access to meaning whereby the reading of works is assumed to be intuitive and mediated hermeneutically (only distorted through personal bias or inclination), there has been somewhat of a methodological aversion to historicizing American philosophers. Consequently, the canon is drawn arbitrarily around white figures whose writings resonate with particular disciplinary debates already established as relevant. Black thinkers, despite writing in the same time, are made invisible despite contesting the meanings and challenging the same audiences the white American philosophers engage. Since the 1850s, Black Americans have deliberately engaged the myth of Black racial inferiority. In *The Condition, Elevation, Emigration, and Destiny of the Colored People of the United States*, for instance, Martin R. Delany argued that the idea of Black inferiority is "mere policy, nature having nothing to do with it."[11] Crediting the scholars in the National Negro Conventions of the 1830s with the role policy has in defining Blacks as inferior, Delany adamantly held that "colored people were selected as the subordinate class in this country, on no account of any actual or supposed inferiority on their part, but simply because . . . they were the very best class that could be selected."[12]

By the 1880s Black anthropologists and theorists around the world sought to refute the claims of white pseudo-science maintaining the inequality of the races. The Haitian anthropologist Antenor Firmin's *The Equality of the Human Races* (1885) concludes: "after reviewing all the possible arguments put forward in support of the doctrine of the inequality of the human races, we realize that none seems to resist the most superficial examination."[13] Firmin continues, "As we recapitulate the various objections raised in order to destroy the very foundations of every method used to rank the human races, we find that we are justified in asserting that all the races are naturally equal."[14] Unlike the inclinations of white American philosophers who disagreed with the biological theories of racial inferiority, while maintaining that nonwhite races were savage and consequently inferior, Black scholars during the same time period insisted on the equality of the races. Martin Delany argued in his *Principia of Ethnology: The Origins of Races and Color* that the Black race was as historically formidable as the white race. In 1879, he wrote that "the white and black, the pure European and pure African races, the most distinct and unlike each other in general external physical characteristics, are of equal vitality and equally enduring."[15] Absolute equality was insisted upon by Black scholars throughout the nineteenth century. Firmin for example was equally adamant: "Proven by science and confirmed by increasingly numerous, eloquent, and indisputable facts, the principle of the equality of the races is the true basis of human solidarity."[16] These works are just a couple of examples of the work Black scholars were doing in the mid-nineteenth century that far surpassed the supposed progressive attitudes of white American philosophers like Royce. Edward

Blyden, Kelly Miller, Alexander Crummell, James McCune Smith, and John E. Bruce are just some of the authors who wrote multiple works arguing for the equality of the Black race.

American philosophy, historically and in the present, evaluates the racism of particular white authors by their endorsement of now popular political ideas and their personal relationships with accepted, canonical Black figures of their time. John Dewey, for example, celebrated the vocational training of Black students in segregated schools, but his relationship with the National Association for the Advancement of Colored People trumps his belief of racial inferiority and Black primitivism.[17] No matter the offense, be it the discovery of Dewey's segregated schools, his use of recapitulation theory, or his evolutionary thinking regarding pedagogy, he is affixed canonically as a theorist of education despite what education scholars have shared with philosophers.[18] Even progressive white feminists like Jane Addams, who still believed in the inferiority of the Black race and held firm to the belief in the Black male rapist, is thought to be absolved of her racism because she had personal relationships with Ida B. Wells and W. E. B. Du Bois and wrote against lynching. Bettina Aptheker explains that Addams

> comprehended the symbolic relationship between the alleged property crimes of the so-called "lower classes," and the woman-as-property psychosis. Yet she failed to appreciate the dialectics of a racial and sexual oppression with common roots in the ownership of private property which sanctified the lynching of the former slave by maintaining the woman's status as a male possession. Furthermore, to concede that rape was the cause of lynching made effective opposition to it impossible because it concealed the real class origins of the racist assaults.[19]

In "Respect for Law," Addams does argue that Southern lynching often "rises to unspeakable atrocities" and "is complicated by race animosity." Nonetheless, she believes "brutality begets brutality, and proceeding from the theory that the Negro is undeveloped and therefore must be treated in this primitive fashion is to forget that the immature pay little attention to statements but quickly imitate all they see. The under-developed are never helped by such methods . . ."[20] According to Addams, by implication, it is not that lynching is unjustified, it is that lynching is ineffective in teaching the primitive Black male rapist the moral disposition to prevent rape. Maurice Hamington's "Public Pragmatism: Jane Addams and Ida B. Wells on Lynching," makes no effort to analyze this specific racist misandrist logic and the ethnology behind it, but he nonetheless concludes that Addams is insightful for her time and progressive for associating with a Black woman like Ida B. Wells-Barnett and speaking on a controversial issue like lynching.[21] Hamington neglects to mention however that the debate at the turn of the century was between what progressives termed the barbaric practice of lynching and the more humane alternative of castration.[22] American philosophers often emphasize the personal relationships white thinkers had with Blacks as evidence of their anti-racism. The racism of their actions as well as their philosophy is absolved in the minds of many American philosophers if one can suggest that these white thinkers associated personally or had an intellectual overlap with nonwhites.

At the dawn of the twentieth century, the shift from biological determinism revolved around a primary question: Could backward peoples, when placed in contact with civilized races, acquire the lessons of civilization? This debate between biological determinists and social Darwinists and progressive environmentalists drove theories about race beyond the presumption that those born a race were irrevocably fixed by their phenotypical and evolutionary station. In American philosophy however, any liberal (meaning environmentalist) explanation by white American figures in the nineteenth century and dawn of the twentieth century that entertains the possibility that Blacks could learn, embrace, or imitate white culture is taken by contemporary (white) scholars to be an anti-racist philosophy. Nothing could be further from the truth. Biological determinism was quickly replaced with cultural deprivation theories that maintained Black and other alien races should be assimilated or left to die for the advance of human civilization.[23] Whereas Royce is praised for rejecting the ethnological fixation on predetermined racial temperament and capacity, his work pales in comparison to even early nineteenth-century Black thinkers much less the work of twentieth-century Black figures specifically addressing scientism. Despite this vast gap between the actual work of Black figures and those of white American philosophers like Royce, the texts and debates about race by Black scholars remain not only absent from any discussions and literature concerning race thinking at the turn of the century in American philosophy, but denied as having any actual relevance to debates undertaken by canonical white figures. Perhaps the greatest irony is that Black race theory had already made the shift toward environmentalist accounts of races by reading the research of other prominent European scientists well before Royce's engagement with the work of Adolf Bastian and James Frazer. In Edward Blyden's *African Life and Customs* (1908), he quotes liberally from Jean Finot's *Race Prejudice* (1901), which argued that

> the Negroes, regarded as occupying the last rung on the human ladder, have furnished us with proofs of an unexpected evolution. Within the space of 50 years, they have realized as much progress as white peoples have in five or six centuries. . . . After all, we have seen the impossibility of attributing immutable psychological qualities to certain peoples or races. Their virtues and their vices are only the effects of historical circumstance or the influence of milieu.[24]

This is just one instance of Black thinkers at the turn of the century being years, if not decades, ahead of white theorists in the United States on race theory and the decline of ethnological accounts of Black inferiority by reading other white thinkers outside America condemning the racialist sciences of the early twentieth century. In an effort to refute the racist biological determinist theories of extinction established from authors like Thomas Huxley in the late 1890s, Black sociologists and anthropologists, like W. E. B. Du Bois, Caroline Bond Day, and W. Montague Cobb, separated the moral, spiritual, and psychological adaptations of the Negro in America from the allegedly inferior biological traits passed down from African ancestry.[25] In short, these Black thinkers asserted the mental and spiritual elevation of Black people in America—their ability to adapt and create genius in the world as a response to the inferiority associated with their skin color.

W. E. B. Du Bois's work as a sociologist reacting to the biological determinism within ethnology during his time at Atlanta University is completely ignored in American philosophy. As early as 1894, Du Bois had already established a functioning school of American sociological thought dedicated to the scientific study of the American race problem—several years before the Chicago School founded by Albion Small was up and running.[26] While the Chicago School is usually credited with popularizing the anti-essentialist work of Franz Boas in the 1920s and 1930s, Du Bois's Atlanta Sociological Laboratory had already understood that race was a historical and cultural artifact, not biologically causal, well before the insights of American sociologists. For example, Du Bois published Atlanta Sociological Paper No. 11 on *The Health and Physique of the Negro American* (1906) as a critique of contemporary ethnological conclusions and craniometry, where he maintained that "it is doubtful if many of the persons in the United States who are eagerly and often bitterly discussing race problems have followed very carefully the advances which anthropological science has made in the last decade. Certainly the new knowledge has not yet reached the common schools in the usual school histories and geographies."[27] Drawing heavily from the work of Italian anthropologist Giuseppe Sergi, *The Mediterranean Race* (1901), and William Z. Ripley's *The Races of Europe: A Sociological Study* (1899), the eleventh Atlanta University Publication argued that there is no one white race that can claim ownership of civilization. This conclusion is far more radical that anything theorized by Royce at the same time, because Du Bois and the various Black scholars participating in the Atlanta University Conferences in fact maintained there were no natural racial hierarchies and only suggested that the spiritual and physical equality of the races should translate socially into full democratic citizenship. Take Herbert A. Miller's contribution to this Atlanta University Publication entitled "Some Psychological Considerations on the Race Problem" for example. In this section Miller boldly argues:

> To conclude, from the manifestations of immorality among the Negroes, or from their failure to recognize certain social conventions, that the Negro is incapable of morality or of adaptation to the social demand, is a conclusion based upon inadequate evidence. Morality and social adaptation are the result of the interpretation of the value of a situation, and not a necessary development of inherent capacity. Therefore, not until different races have had exactly the same history can any valid conclusion be drawn as to their relative psychophysical capacity if mere observation is used. This does not mean that there is no such a thing as race characteristics, but that there are elements in interpretation that are independent of race. This, however, is a philosophical question. My point is that there is something that cannot be put to empirical test in all practical activity.[28]

Miller's analysis is suspicious of the basis for, the theoretical foundation of, psycho-physics, a branch of ethnology interested in the common mental states and spirituality of the races that outlined the psychological stages of civilization.[29] Like the alleged benefits some philosophers claim they receive from reading Royce, Du Bois's decade-long Atlanta University Publications prove concretely that Black sociologists and anthropologists were at least a decade ahead of Royce's conclusions and reached the same conclusions about biological determinism with the added insights of not believing the white race or any race owned or was charged with the progress of civilization, or that any psychological measure could tell one about the potential or possibility of civilization within a race.[30] Philosophers writing on Royce without any real engagement with the Black thinkers of his time are asking disciplines and scholars alike to imagine Black thinkers without having scientific and philosophical insights into the social relations that problematized their existence.

These philosophers are encouraging disciplines and scholars to continue to ignore Black contributions to civilization, philosophy, and history so that Royce appears to be a forerunner of an argument that had been articulated by Black thinkers in several iterations throughout the 1800s. The "racial apartheid" ideology that sustains the invisibility of Black thought in the historical debates of those times and our own is what allows American philosophy to thrive as a field within the disciplinary geography of philosophy. Written as a valorization of turn-of-the-century white thought, American philosophers are able to suggest a particular social consciousness and awareness concerning democracy, community, and experiential knowledge against much of the transcendentalism and intuitive assertions of analytic and continental traditions. Such approaches however ignore that the aspirations and historical grounding of such positions at the dawn of the twentieth century were not only imperialistic but insidiously racist. In order to maintain the pretense of progressivism, American philosophers elide history. A peculiar practice given that much of the work designated as American philosophy defines itself as a particular set of social and philosophical problems that originated geographically and historically upon American soil, or the irony that one of the earliest texts penned by Royce was on the history of California.

While there is often a lip service paid to the idea that American philosophy is attempting to diversify the thinkers available for study, this gesture is often made to the detriment of efforts attempting shift the narrative of the American philosophical endeavor from one of white exceptionalism to one grounded in its actual history of imperialism, recapitulation, and nativism. Confronted with the vast treatises and texts of late-nineteenth-century Black thinkers, American philosophers are forced to assert that while the progressiveness of Black research during the late 1800s and early 1900s far exceeds that of its chosen white idols, such works by Black thinkers are ultimately irrelevant for how scholars should designate and weigh the thinking of white scholars concerning race in *American philosophy*. To maintain the idea that figures like Royce, Addams, or Dewey have resources to deal with the problem of racism, there is a refusal to compare their actual texts with that of the Black thinkers in their own time. In lieu of direct comparison to what Blacks, Asians, or Mexican thinkers are writing or saying during the same time period, Black intellectual giants like W. E. B. Du Bois or Ida B. Wells-Barnett are made into the disciples of white traditions like pragmatism, or they are tokenized as associates (students) of white philosophers who are robbed of intellectual independence and consequently beholden to the thought of canonical white idols. This is not an external concern but a serious indictment of the methods employed in retrieving Royce as well as other white American thinkers as philosophers with resources for America's racial problems. In other words, Royce only emerges as a progressive thinker by eliminating Black schools of thought like the Atlanta University project, and over a half century of writings where Black thinkers were already utilizing cutting-edge ethnology, anthropology, and sociology from scholars the world over.

The Debate concerning Josiah Royce and Racism

As with most historic white figures in philosophy, their repopularization and reintroduction into contemporary circles commits their works, regardless of its initial silence, to speak to the problem of anti-Black racism in America. Josiah Royce is no different in this regard. Over the last decade, philosophers, like Jacquelyn Kegley, Shannon Sullivan, and Scott Pratt, have introduced revisions to Royce's thought that make him appear to be the premier multicultural and anti-racist thinker at the dawn of the twentieth century. While this declaration has influenced the philosophical framing of Royce's work over the last decade, there is a grave anachronism in such a contention given the history of racism and racialist sciences in America. Generally speaking, Jacquelyn Kegley's early essays on Josiah Royce and race are considered to be the first attempts to ground Royce's philosophy of race. In "Is a Coherent Racial Identity

Essential to Genuine Individuals and Communities? Josiah Royce on Race"
(2005), Kegley emphasizes Royce's rejection of biological determinism as
evidence of his anti-essentialism and racial progressivism. According to
Kegley, "Royce believes, as others in the contemporary scene, that 'race'
as a concept cannot be eliminated, [because] it plays too crucial a role,
both positive and negative, in self and social identification."[31]

In order to bolster this claim of Royce's progressivism, Kegley
makes use of a wealth of contemporary Black philosophers' views on
race and racial identity. While Kegley's article is correct in suggesting
that contemporary Black scholars like Lucius Outlaw and Cornel West
had adamantly defended the importance of race as a social and cultural
entity, her claim that Royce also agreed with racial eliminativists like
Anthony Appiah and Alain Locke presents something of an insurmount-
able problem. It is quite difficult to agree with racial conservationists and
eliminativists simultaneously.[32] In short, upon Kegley's reading of Black
philosophical traditions, Royce maintains several irreconcilable positions
at the same time. While it makes perfect sense for Kegley to try to put
Royce in conversation with contemporary Black thinkers in race theory,
her work is indicative of a trend aiming to gain currency for historic
white thinkers in current race debates at the expense of historical accuracy.
Black scholars who studied under Royce and applied his theories to the
race problem from the mid-1900s onward, like William H. Ferris[33] and
William T. Fontaine,[34] are ignored by many white philosophers because
the first application of Roycean philosophy supported assimilation. It
is only today with the political and ideological ethicizations of racial
diversity and multiculturalism that Royce's work is interpreted as *criti-
cally conserving race*.[35]

The republication of *Race Questions, Provincialism, and Other
American Problems* in 2009 marked a decisive racial *epochē*—a subtle
suspension, a refusal to become involved in the implications of Royce's
racist commitments—asserting, almost axiomatically, that Josiah Royce's
advocacy of racialist sciences, white supremacist imperialism through his
moralization of the white man's burden, and Southern colonialism in
the form of British administration, are indeed irrelevant to the growing
canonical enterprise dedicated to the preservation of his philosophy.[36] In
Scott Pratt's introduction to the republication of *Race Questions, Provincialism, and Other American Problems*, he argues that Royce's essay on race
questions "raises significant ways in which race is understood and how
race prejudice can be addressed."[37] Pratt argues that "Royce presents two

examples of good responses to race conflict, one from Jamaica and one from Trinidad."[38] Rather than centering the violence and poverty British colonialism imposed on Black populations, Pratt sees each case as evidence that "Royce holds that the key to fostering tolerance and peace is the development of a sound administrative and legal system that includes full participation by non-whites."[39] Pratt's interpretation of English colonization is woefully inaccurate. To understand this point does not actually require one to conduct the kind of historical research into Jamaican colonization undertaken throughout this book; Royce, himself, is in fact quite clear in "Race Questions" that administration places Englishmen above Blacks on the island. Royce writes that the Englishman

> organized his colony; he established good local courts, which gained by square treatment the confidence of the blacks. The judges of such courts were Englishmen. The English ruler also provided a good country constabulary, in which native blacks also found service, and in which they could exercise authority over other blacks. Black men, in other words, were trained, under English management, of course, to police black men. A sound civil service was also organized; and in that educated Negroes found in due time their place, while the chief of each branch of the service were and are, in the main, Englishmen.[40]

Royce sees the Englishman as an efficient ruler and British administration as a system offering the Negro self-respect and value. The Black man only has authority over other Blacks. He in no way dictates the behavior or constrains the practices of his English rulers. His task in such a system is service to whites, not authority over them. Even educated Blacks find their place to be under the authority of Englishmen. Royce in fact writes, "For the Englishman, in his official and governmental dealings with backward peoples, has a great way of being superior without very often publicly saying that he is superior."[41] Black Jamaican inhabitants were British subjects not citizens and certainly not Englishmen according to Royce. Race, more specifically Blackness, delineates the subjugated from the free for Royce. This is but one example of how race serves to demarcate the relationship between the white citizen of empire who has the duty to bring civilization to the world and the Black primitives who are to be colonized in the name of civilization. How an administrative system recognized for its proficiency in conveying the superiority of the Englishman to backward people becomes a system of full participation for Blacks encouraging tolerance and peace in philosophy can only be explained as the product of the liberties philosophers engaging race can take with history regarding Blacks the world over.

While Pratt does acknowledge that one could possibly surmise that although Royce does not accurately understand the depth of American racism, especially in the American South, in light of his administrative proposal, he nonetheless believes this is where Royce's philosophy of loyalty to loyalty offers solace to the critic. Pratt writes that "loyalty to loyalty is a commitment to one's causes in ways that foster the loyalty of others. . . . Administrative relations provide a formal context in which the boundaries of communities can intersect, come into conflict, and promote ways of resolving conflicts that preserve and foster others' loyalty."[42] The irony of Pratt's introduction is that it praises Royce's reflections on American race relations in 1905 and 1906 with the presentation and publication of "Race Questions," while simultaneously acknowledging the imperialism Royce supports in "Some Characteristic Tendencies of American Civilization" in 1900. Even more surprising is that this essay (which I tracked down a year earlier) was in fact republished in Pratt and Sullivan's edition. Pratt admits that Royce concludes "Some Characteristic Tendencies of American Civilization" with "recommendations for how the Empire might be maintained . . . [such as] the development of a stronger central government that can enforce a uniform education system and the affirmation of a kind of 'manifest destiny' for Anglo-American culture," but he argues that "it is important to note, however, that these recommendations came to be challenged in Royce's later work."[43] Pratt explains to the reader, "rather than finding nations (empires) as the ideal, the Beloved Community introduced in the *Problem of Christianity* provides a framework that will undermine causes that seek to dominate others."[44]

Pratt, however, is not attentive to the actual development of Royce's thinking of community in this regard. First, Royce's *The Problem of Christianity* was not published until 1913, so it is difficult to understand how this would affect his ideas about imperial aspirations and colonial administration argued for in 1905 in "Race Questions." Second, in the preface to *The Problem of Christianity* Royce writes "since 1908, my philosophy of loyalty has been growing. Its successive expressions, as I believe, form a consistent body of ethical as well as of religious opinion, and teaching, verifiable in its main outlines, in terms of human experience, and capable of furnishing a foundation for a defensible form of metaphysical idealism."[45] Given Royce's reflections on the shifting of his thought, and Pratt's own urgings, Royce simply could not have imagined loyalty to loyalty as separate from empire in 1900 with his publication of "Some Characteristic Tendencies of American Civilization," in his delivery of "Provincialism" in 1902, or in 1906 with his publication of "Race Questions and Prejudice." In fact, since many of these essays were published practically unchanged in Royce's 1908 publication of *Race Questions, Provincialism, and Other American Problems* as testaments to his philosophy of loyalty to loyalty, it is safe to conclude that Royce's shift did not include an incompatibility between his notion of the beloved community and empire but instead rearticulated his earlier imperial aspirations through religious and idealist doctrines.[46]

In the second introduction to this republication entitled "Royce's Race Questions and Prejudices," Shannon Sullivan focuses on Royce's resources for contemporary whiteness studies. Sullivan begins her essay suggesting that "the centrality of the race essay to Royce's thinking is all the more significant since, with the exception of W. E. B. Du Bois and perhaps Jane Addams, no other major figure associated with pragmatist philosophy substantially addressed issues of race and racism in his or her written work, nor did so as early in the twentieth century as Royce did."[47] Unlike Pratt's previous essay, Sullivan does recognize that Josiah Royce's call for British administration is rooted in white supremacism. She observes quite accurately that "what Royce admires about the English is the way they dominated people of color through imperialism and colonialization. Such domination need not rely on rifles and cannons. In fact, it is all the more effective, as Royce understood on some level, if it is internalized by those who are dominated rather than forced on them with arms."[48] Though Sullivan admits that Royce actively perpetuates racism and the deliberate domination of Black people in the American South, she apologizes for Royce, suggesting that he was ignorant and ultimately naïve concerning the consequences of his proposals. Sullivan explains, "Writing before the worldwide post-colonial struggles that generally began after World War II, Royce did not see that imperial colonialism was part of the violence of global race problems . . . he did not recognize that the English type of social pedagogy . . . could be a deceptively polite way of making Black people the enforcers of their own subordination."[49]

In Sullivan's reading of Royce, white ignorance has a double meaning, so to speak. It both justifies Royce's mistakes concerning the evil of colonization while simultaneously describing what Sullivan takes to be the greatest insights of Royce's thinking concerning the American race problem, namely, his identification of white ignorance. Sullivan reads Royce as criticizing white civilization for its ignorance about whiteness. She believes that Royce offers a searing indictment of whiteness as the ownership of the earth, speaking a truth about the lie of white benevolence, charity, and exceptionalism that most white people do not want to know.[50] Sullivan's engagement with Royce begins with the premise that "Royce's condemnation of civilization reveals the disloyal ignorance of civilization's actual effects that is required of its members."[51] She emphasizes that Royce concludes that "no one knows with certainty how different racial groups are from one another, nor how fixed or changeable the traits of any particular groups are. Perhaps there are significant differences and perhaps also there are fixed traits that future science will uncover. But 'we are at present very ignorant regarding the whole matter,' and that ignorance should not be treated as if it were knowledge of white supremacy."[52] In Sullivan's reading, loyalty to loyalty is a means to demystify the white supremacism of white communities.

These aforementioned views of Royce's racial corpus have been largely apologetic. In the cases where Royce is admittedly racist, imperialist, or colonialist, he is ultimately excused as being ignorant and unknowledgeable of the effects of his beliefs. In the cases where Royce can be read as somewhat reflective about race or the racialist sciences of his day, he is critical, and a precocious thinker and philosopher of America's racial legacy and history. In other words, it seems a philosophical analysis of Royce makes him inculpable and without sin regarding matters of race. Royce becomes a figure whose insights are intentional, but whose faults are accidental. He, like many others handled by the current theories of white ignorance, is presumed to be innocent—an ultimately good and virtuous turn-of-the-century white man. He is thought to have meant no harm to Blacks, where any detriments inflicted upon nonwhites came from his inability to anticipate the consequences of his thought. As is often the case, the practitioners of American philosophy can imagine an early twentieth-century America defined by the white man's burden, Jim Crow segregation, and lynching as racist, but somehow cannot fathom that many if not most of the canonical figures of American philosophy actively contributed to, participated in, and intimately desired this world. In other words, in the practitioners' current narrative, America had racism, but there were no American philosophers who were racist. The American philosopher is thereby conceptualized as distant and outside this world, not constituted by it.

In contrast to the contemporary works dealing with Josiah Royce and race, which conflate Black thinkers who used his terminology or ideas with his actual character or projective social perspectives as being anti-racist, this book evaluates the legitimacy of the current arguments for the relevance of Royce's thoughts in contemporary debates about race and racism in America based on his actual texts dedicated to race questions and problems. Royce only appears to be an anti-racist thinker if he is taken out of his historical moment and revised as gesturing toward the political ideal that defined the latter half of the twentieth century. While such (poststructural/-modern/-colonial) readings are now the bread and butter of many scholars' repertoires, the historical context of late-nineteenth- and early twentieth-century thought simply do not allow Royce to gain much distance from the imperial and anti-Black racism of his explicitly stated ideas on race and the racialist sciences he manifestly endorsed and even practiced at the dawn of the twentieth century. If scholars actually place Royce in his historical context, it becomes quite easy to demonstrate that Royce's essay entitled "Race Questions and Prejudices" is an unapologetic extension of his 1900 essay entitled "Some Characteristic Tendencies of American Civilization," where Royce adamantly champions British colonialism and assimilation as the remedy to the burgeoning race problem both at home and abroad. These two foundational essays not only articulate his thinking about race but also serve as the basis of his thinking about provincialism.

As with any attempt to expose the racism of a canonical white figure, the road is especially hard and fraught with attacks from defenders of the status quo who seek to establish the virtue of the alleged racist. It is often the case that accusations concerning the failings of canonical white figures are intuitively denied, so the real failing must therefore lie in the character of the accuser. In the face of such narrowness, every citation of actual textual evidence contrary to the favored narrative becomes "irrelevant to Royce's philosophical project," or "merely histori- cal"—common code words for "not worthy of *our* philosophical con- sideration." Comparisons to Black thinkers become "a political agenda," and disputes concerning the meaning of race and racism is "ideology." Despite establishing a clear-cut historical and textual account of Josiah Royce's racism and colonialism in my previously published article entitled "Royce, Racism, and the Colonial Ideal: White Supremacy and the Illusion of Civilization in Josiah Royce's Account of the White Man's

Burden" (2009), there remains a strong insistence upon disregarding the dangerous suppositions of Royce that support the white man's burden, the colonial administration of Blacks in the South, and the assimilation of alien races into white (Anglo-Saxon) culture. For many Roycean scholars and the larger American philosophical community, racism, imperialism (the white man's burden), and colonialism are thought to be irrelevant to the "American philosophical project," despite the cultural resonance these ideas had through turn-of-the-century America. This book is an attempt to contextualize the origins and theories that served as the basis of Josiah Royce's race theory. It aims to capture the world Royce looked upon when he cast his thinking forward and projected his philosophical sensibilities into social consciousness and political theory. Royce was deeply concerned for the future of America. His work reads as that of an anxious man who saw the uniting force of the Civil War but worried about a future fragmentation of society. Behind these thoughts was the fear of racial plurality, the seemingly unending problem of racial, ethnic, and cultural difference, in the United States.

Hiding Behind Blacks: The Historiographic Problem of Interpreting Josiah Royce Based on Black Associations

Despite the voluminous works of Black thinkers at the turn of the century, American philosophers have not attempted to situate Royce's thinking in relation to Black philosophers working on race in the first decades of the twentieth century.[53] Instead, Black scholars are used as placeholders for Royce, idols used to insinuate that Royce was a supporter of the Negro because his work was mentioned by Black scholars around the turn of the century. For example, in *Loyal Subjects: Bonds of Nation, Race, and Allegiance in Nineteenth-Century America*, Elizabeth Duquette suggests to readers that Royce agrees with W. E. B. Du Bois that "the problem of the twentieth century is the problem of the color-line."[54] In order to convince her audience of Royce's racial progressivism, she also mentions that *Race Question, Provincialism, and Other American Problems* was mentioned by Alain Locke in *The New Negro* (1925).[55] In Locke's *The New Negro* he composes a bibliography of books written about "The Negro Race Problem" from the sociological perspective wherein he does list Royce's *Race Questions, Provincialism, and Other American Problems*,[56] but the bibliography is comprised of some blatantly racist texts as well as some friendly to the cause of the Negro. For example, Jerome Dowd's

The Negro in American Life argues that the extrovert temperament of the Negro "i.e. his pronounced emotionalism, predisposes him more to a crime of person than of property."[57] Thomas Nelson Page's *The Negro: The Southerner's Problem*, which advocates the lynching of Blacks, is also listed. Duquette insinuates that Royce's inclusion in Locke's bibliography of the sociological aspects of Negro race problems is evidence of his progressivism without explaining why it is on a list with blatantly racist texts or why Royce's work could be considered one of those blatantly racist texts as well. Taking advantage of the disregard for Black works, Duquette offers readers a symbol, being included on a list about the Negro by Alain Locke, as evidence of Royce's regard among Black thinkers in the early twentieth century without giving any context to the actual books comprising the list. She gives the illusion that Royce and Black authors were of the same mind on issues of race, racism, and imperialism, but nothing is further from the truth. In reality, most of the Black authors that we have established read Royce's works only cite his dismissal of biological determinism. In other words, Black authors use Royce as a white philosopher arguing against biologism, not a race progressive as many contemporary authors suggest.

These Black scholars did not actually cite Royce for his theories about race, lynching, or race frictions in the American South, or the ethical and moral theories Royce believed should guide Americans more generally. In the works of nineteenth-century Black thinkers, Royce's loyalty to loyalty does not appear once, nor does support for his proposals for the managing of Blacks and other nonwhites in the United States. Black scholars, like W. E. B. Du Bois, cited Royce primarily for his criticism of biological determinism. In a short editorial paying respect to Josiah Royce after his death in *The Crisis*, W. E. B. Du Bois writes, "In the death of the great teacher, Josiah Royce, at Harvard University, the Negro race in America and indeed all races lose a fine-fibred friend. His book, 'Race Questions and Other American Problems,' published in 1908, should be in every Black man's library."[58] For a scholar who was an ex-student of Royce, Du Bois is surprisingly short in his regard for Royce's work. In fact, he only cites two paragraphs of Royce's whole book, and only those paragraphs that show that the Negro is not biologically doomed to inferiority. Du Bois says Royce "writes in the wise":[59]

> For man, whatever his race, is an animal that you unques-
> tionably can debase to whatever level you please, if you have

power and if you then begin early enough and devote yourself persistently enough to the noble and civilized task of proving him to be debased . . . I doubt not, then, that some races are more teachable than others. But I do very much doubt our power to estimate how teachable a race is, or what can be made of them, or what hereditary mental powers they have until we have given them centuries of opportunity to be taught. . . . Let their descendants not boast unduly until they, too, have given to other races not indeed the opportunities of conquerors, but some equal opportunity to show of what sort of manhood they are capable.[60]

Du Bois concludes his citation of Royce by saying, "How clear and just is this reasoning and yet how seldom it is applied."[61] The rest of Du Bois's tribute to Royce focuses on how the university "must stand for intellectual freedom"[62] and "strike off the fetters of prejudice."[63] Philosophers have simply asserted that Du Bois's thinking in *The Souls of Black Folk* was compatible with Josiah Royce's notions of loyalty, yet in the only citation of Royce in Du Bois's almost century-long corpus, Du Bois only quotes Josiah Royce's criticism of racial biologism. Remember *The Crisis* was a propagandist organ edited by Du Bois under the auspices of the National Association for the Advancement of Colored People.[64] Its editorials appealed to the liberal agenda of social equality and distanced it from radical socialist or anti-colonial positions.[65] The only other mention of Royce's "Race Questions" by Du Bois comes at the end of his 1915 book *The Negro* in a section on suggested readings concerning "The Future of the Negro Race."[66]

Dr. Du Bois was not alone in this approach to Josiah Royce's *Race Questions, Provincialism, and Other American Problems*. In Dr. Charles Victor Roman's *American Civilization and the Negro* (1916), he also only quotes Josiah Royce's book for its criticism of craniometry and the biologism of the previous ethnological era. Roman appreciates Royce's attempt to de-biologize the inferiority of the Black American, but little more.[67] As we will see in chapter 4 ("On the Dark Arts"), Royce believes in evolution (albeit non-Darwinian) and the eventual assimilation of the Negro. For this to be possible, the Negro race must be impressionable, or somewhat plastic. This premise was central to both the uplift ideology of the aspiring Black middle class and Black social scientists and physicians like Roman who aimed to prove that Black solidarity could tend toward improvement and civilization. Roman cites Royce saying, "to live in filth; to persecute; to resist light; to fight against progress; to be mentally slothful, dull, sensuous, cruel; to be the prey of endless foolishness; to be treacherous; to be destructive—well, these are the mental traits of no one or two races of men."[68] Roman affirms the fact that a white philosopher is saying there was nothing innate in the Negro race that makes them wretched. In fact, he quotes Royce's text again to dismiss the idea that physiognomy and craniometry can in fact indicate something about the psychology and spiritual possibility of the races. From Royce he quotes, "We know too little as yet about the natural history of the human mind, our psychology is far too infantile a science, to give us any precise information as to the way in which the inherited, the native, the constitutional aspects of the minds of men really vary with their complexions or with their hair."[69]

It is important to notice however that neither Du Bois or Roman, nor any other Black thinker I have been able to find who was not an advocate of cultural assimilation like William H. Ferris, cited Josiah Royce's *Race Questions, Provincialism, and Other American Problems* beyond his criticisms of biological determinism. Black thinkers had little to no regard for Royce's actual proclamations concerning loyalty (to loyalty) or the colonial projects that emerged from them. Research into the corpus of Black intellectuals reveals quite a lot about their positions and intellectual relationships with white canonical figures. It is simply no longer adequate to utilize Black figures as the racial daemons of white philosophers.[70] Because Black philosophers and political thinkers were undervalued and dismissed as inferior within the intellectual culture of America for almost two centuries, these Black scholars were forced to speak through the authority and visibility of whites. This means that many Black intellectual giants, like Frederick Douglass or W. E. B. Du Bois, often gained the attention and respect of white individuals and institutions by framing Black liberation projects under the insights of whites. As such, the reader must carefully attend to the actual proximity white thinkers have to how Black figures like Du Bois actually thought versus the pragmatic uses Black scholars had in excising the rhetoric or gestures made by white philosophers like Josiah Royce that aided their specific cause. Said differently, the race theories of Royce simply did not garner the kind of mass support among Black intellectuals of the succeeding generations, not even Du Bois, to the extent that many philosophers and literary theorists of today claim. Du Bois's Atlanta University papers do not list Royce as an attendee or resource for the debates in the organization at the turn of the twentieth century. In short, the philosophical kinship claimed to exist between Du Bois and Royce specifically, as well as the recognition of Royce's social ethics among Blacks, is simply adventitious.

Royce's provincialism, his ideas of loyalty to loyalty, and his assimilationism were not held in high regard by Black thinkers generally. In fact, it is not until William T. Fontaine's "Josiah Royce and the American Race Problem" that we see a Black philosopher specifically taking up Royce's philosophy of loyalty as a justification for desegregation, and as a philosophical warrant for the Supreme Court's recent *Brown v. Board of Education* decision in 1954.[71] Fontaine reads Royce's *Race Questions, Provincialism, and Other American Problems* as specifically addressing what was "the intensified in the United States by a series of history-making events: emergence of the United States as an imperial power; racist responses to Japan's defeat of Russia in 1905; continuous mass immigration of European peoples of various stocks, and the rigorous, brutal implementation of 'white home rule' and legalized segregation of Negroes in the South."[72] It is relevant to mention here that Fontaine understands Royce as responding to the events of his time that motivate his engagement with race problems. Though Fontaine will read Royce as supporting desegregation, it is crucial to understand that Fontaine is concerning himself with the cruel system of Southern segregation, not Royce's specific racial theories in general.

Fontaine considers integration as the complete opposite of South segregation. He reads Royce specifically in service of this opposition and as fundamentally against the idea that the Negro should stay in his place. For example, Fontaine writes,

> A more complete survey of Royce's writings on social philosophy reveals four major arguments against this "in his place" social philosophy of the segregationist: (a) It assumes that the individual is first and foremost a member of a particular race and secondarily a member of the human race; (b) it assumes that the mental and moral traits of individuals are determined by "racial" inheritance, an assumption both scientifically unfounded and fatalistic; (c) it excludes Negroes totally from the administration of government; thus depriving them of the opportunity to learn; (d) it bipolarizes the groups in such a way as to produce the following results: relations remain

fixedly dyadic, accompanied by dangerous tensions; there is neither a common objective, nor a mediating interpreter, nor dialogue of any sort; segregationists achieve only a spurious self-realization since they commit the cardinal sin of ethics, viz., disloyalty to loyalty.[73]

Fontaine's primary concern here is segregation, not Royce, but his choice of philosopher is interesting, since Royce is among the few philosophers explicitly writing against Southern segregation. In Fontaine's *Reflections on Segregation, Desegregation, Power and Morals* (1967), he is adamant that integration stands opposed to Black Power and Black self-definition.[74]

Understanding the historical context of Fontaine's concerns and comments is necessary here. Integration was thought to depend on the eventual assimilation of the Negro into American life and culture in the 1960s. There had not yet been scholarly work to determine the extent to which Black Americans could in fact maintain their cultural distinctiveness as a Black community among a dominant white culture. Political movements like Black Power or multiculturalism, which come to mind quite readily for thinkers in the twenty-first century, had not yet occurred to substantiate the idea that minority populations both be part of a white society and still resist assimilation into the dominant group. E. Franklin Frazier affords substantial remarks to this problem confronting Black intellectuals in his now seminal essay "The Failure of the Black Intellectual." There was no question for most Black intellectuals in the 1960s that Black Americans had to be integrated into the America community following the mandate for desegregation in *Brown v. Board of Education*, but what would happen to the Black community during this process remained a real question for scholars of the time. According to Frazier, "integration involves the acceptance of Negroes as individuals into the economic and social organization of American life, [and it would] imply the gradual dissolution of the Negro community, that is, the decline and eventual disappearance of the associations, institutions, and other forms of associated life in what constitutes the Negro community."[75] Consequently, Fontaine desires in the 1960s the assimilation and hopefully the removal of the stain of race by taking on the dominant white culture that Royce proposed in 1900s.

W. E. B. Du Bois was of a similar mind as Frazier on the matter. For Du Bois, integration posed perilous questions for the Negro: "what will be our aims and ideals, and what will we have to do with the selecting of these aims and ideals. Are we to assume that we would simply adopt the ideals of Americans, and become what they are or want to be?"[76] Du Bois feared that integration meant "that we would cease to be Negroes as such and become whites in action, if not completely in color. We would take our culture from white Americans—doing as they do and thinking as they think."[77] Not to be misunderstood on this point, Du Bois continues:

> Physically, it would mean that we would be integrated with Americans, losing first of all the physical evidence of color and racial type. We would lose our memory of Negro history, and of those racial peculiarities with which we have been long associated. We would cease to acknowledge any greater tie with Africa than with England or Germany. We would not try to develop Negro music, and art, and literature as distinctive and different, but allow it to be further degrading—as it is today. We would always, if possible, marry lighter skinned people so as to have children who are not identified with the Negro race, and thus solve our racial problem in America by committing racial suicide.[78]

Du Bois suggests that the effect of integration is the destruction of racial specificity, the destruction of Negro cultural traits and history. Du Bois, like many mid-twentieth-century Black intellectuals, feared the consequences of integration for the cultural and historical life of the Negro in the United States. Already physically removed from Africa, the Negro in the United States was now threated with the spiritual severing of ties with darker races following desegregation. The question now confronting the Negro was whether he would in fact be a Black race in America or American.

The idea that integration was superior in kind to the segregationist epoch of American society misses the complexities facing Black Americans in the mid-twentieth century. Contrary to the argument that Royce was anti-racist because he was against segregation, these debates between Black scholars show that while a possible reading of Royce can be stretched to make such a case, the real fear among Black intellectuals was the assimilation and destruction of Negro culture. In other words, Black intellectuals feared the assimilation and loss of Blackness, the very program Royce thought necessary to cultivate peace in the South and stability throughout the nation.

Paradigms of Anti-Blackness:
Interpreting Racism in Its Historical Context

Historically, and this is no different in our contemporary moment, white and Black scholars have differed fundamentally in how they articulate and describe the idea of racism. Whereas Black scholars from the dawn of the nineteenth century to our present time have described racism as structural problems, the work of systems' and individuals' reification of the actions and ideas of these systems and the practices they give rise to, white scholars tend to focus on racism as attitudinal and malleable—a definition that points to symbols of social and attitudinal change among the white group itself rather than the actual arrangements or concrete indicators of change in the economics, political power, or mortality of the oppressed racialized group in the society in question. Often white philosophers attempt to demonstrate the precociousness of nineteenth- or twentieth-century thinkers by linking them to the ideas and policies that emerge from the civil rights movement. Every white pragmatist from John Dewey to Jane Addams anticipates integration and full civil rights for Blacks. Viewing racism in this way allows white philosophers to be excused from their actual writings and views about Blacks choosing to emphasize the personal (read political) associations these figures had with Blacks during their lifetimes. Taken to indicate the attitude of the white figure toward Blacks, these philosophers take an overly segregationist view of racism. They suggest, since said white philosopher interacted with, taught, or advocated on the behalf of Blacks (e.g., against lynching or against race as a biological idea) when other whites endorsed segregated distance and disassociation, these philosophers are simply not racist. Notice how this understanding is attitudinal and celebrates the willful violation of segregated space as liberating. Because whites felt a sympathy for or associated with Blacks, it is assumed they did not believe in the inferiority of Blacks. In other words, the accused white figure really did have *Black friends.*

Describing racism's evolution in the nineteenth century from the theories of racial inferiority under slavery to its development as a ratio- nalization for colonialism and the white man's burden is a complicated task far beyond the intentions of this text. Suffice to say, Black thinkers from the early 1800s forward have continued to insist that racism is much more than the mere negative attitudes or stigmas toward Black peoples. In Hosea Easton's *A Treatise on the Intellectual Character, and Civil and Political Condition of the Colored People of the U. States; and the Prejudice Exercised Towards Them; with a Sermon on the Duty of the Church to Them* (1837), racism is described as a malignant prejudice, or "principle which calls into action the worst passions of the human heart."[79] Malignant prejudice intends injury toward Black Americans because it has the purpose of injury. Unlike prejudice, which can be based on common misperceptions or biases that discriminate against individuals, malignancy of racism socially determines Black peoples to be of an inferior caste to the whites of the society. Easton explains that the racism directed toward Black Americans is injurious at both the national and personal level. In describing racism as national in function Easton means that [Blacks] "are lineally stolen from their native country, and detained for centuries, in a strange land, as hewers of wood and drawers of 'water. In this situation, their blood, habits, minds, and bodies, have undergone such a change, as to cause them to lose all legal or natural relations to their mother country . . . they sustain the great injury of losing their country, their birthright, and are made aliens and illegitimates . . . outcasts."[80] The condition of slavery transformed Black human beings into perpetual aliens and laborers unable to be citizens and forever stained by the color of skin that indicated their servitude to whites.[81]

Easton argues that the institution of slavery birthed the concoction of the Nigger among whites. To call a Black person a Nigger indicated the debasement of the race—"It makes the colored people subserve almost every foul purpose imaginable."[82] "Negro or nigger, is an opprobrious term, employed to impose contempt upon them as an inferior race, and also to express their deformity of person," writes Easton.[83] The term is meant to create terror among young whites and inspire the white race to never devolve to the level of Niggers in behavior or civility. "The first lessons given are, Johnny, Billy, Mary, Sally, (or whatever the name may be), go to sleep, if you don't the old nigger will carry you off; don't you cry Hark; the old nigger's coming—how ugly you are, you are worse than a little nigger."[84] The fears that whites are taught, the idea that Black men will kill and rape your women, are instilled from the infancy of whites. The idea of the Nigger is meant to separate the world of the civilized whites from that of the savage Blacks. It socializes white children to understand that they are always threatened as victims of the savage Black beast. This delineation is also used as a deterrent to bad behavior, because to act badly is to degrade whiteness to the level of Niggers. Easton writes: "To inspire their half grown misses and masters to improvement, they are told that if they do this or that, or if they do this and so, they will be poor or ignorant as a nigger; or that they will be black as a nigger; or have no more credit than a nigger; that they will have hair, lips, feet, or something of the kind, like a Nigger."[85] After emancipation this idea evolved into a terror that made the free Black man synonymous to the rapist.[86] Slavery confined the sexual perversion of the Nigger, the end of slavery freed his *furor sexualis*, or his racial instinct to rape.[87] These ideas justified the need of Blacks to be managed and ruled by the racial orders of the South. Often the notion of the savagery and barbarism of primitive peoples was used as a justification for colonialism, especially the idea that primitive women needed to be rescued from the violence and abuse of their savage men.[88] They could not truly enjoy freedom because their savagery made them more fit for labor and the rule of civilized peoples. They simply were unfit for the duties of democracy.

W. E. B. Du Bois explains that the 1800s were a times in which popular opinion held that "labor was fundamentally degrading and the just burden of inferior peoples."[89] This racial mythos held that "the white people of Europe had the right to live upon the labor and property of the colored peoples of the world."[90] As Du Bois explained of America at the dawn of the twentieth century, "America wanted to believe in the failure of democracy as far as darker peoples were concerned . . . she established a caste system, . . . and conquered tropical colonies."[91] "She stands today shoulder to shoulder with Europe in Europe's worst sin against civilization."[92] In America's desire to emulate Europe's civilization, she took on Europe's racial disposition toward the world's darker peoples. The idea of racial superiority became a cornerstone of how America would come to encounter the lands of the darker races. The imperial endeavor of America was in part her aspiration to "sit among the great nations who arbitrate the fate of the lesser breeds without the law."[93] In America, part of the racial mythos that served as the foundation of their empire was their ability to assimilate new white populations toward the hating of Blacks. America "trains her immigrants to this despising of niggers from the day of their landing, and they carry and send the new back to the submerged classes in the fatherlands."[94] The invention of Negro inferiority, the need of the Negro to be ruled and the efficiency of the exploitation of his labor as a means to his civilization, was the cornerstone of early twentieth-century racism.

What Is Racism?

Racism is white supremacy—it is an architecture of dehumanization that conceptualizes distinctions between humans who possess rationality, morality, and civilization, and nonhumans, who are irrational, deviant, and uncivilized as a consequence of their racial origins outside of Europe. As an architecture through which whites create, sustain, and materialize the division between whites/humans and those lesser than—negations of—(white) humanity, racism creates systems that normalize the practices of institutions and individuals that manage, control, and exterminate racialized populations that pose threats to the economic, political, or societal superiority of the dominate white racial group. The most peculiar aspect of racism is its transubstantiating property, whereby the erroneous ideas of white superiority and Black inferiority that have framed the perception of the world have the ability to transform from ideas into concrete social processes that enforce the inferiorization of racial groups in actual societies. At the individual level, racism is aspirational in that individual actions or behaviors that seek to injury, degrade, or exterminate the lives of racialized people are thought to have some resonance with the existing societal order. Stated differently, the individual racist's actions against nonwhites are rationalized as being able to be supported or endorsed by other white individuals and the dominant institutions (legal, political, or social) of the society.

According to philosopher Charles Mills, white supremacy is "an unnamed political system that has made the modern world what it is today. . . . [It is] the system of domination by which white people have historically ruled over and, in certain important ways, continue to rule over nonwhite people."[95] Within actual societies, legal scholar Frances Lee Ansley suggests that white supremacy would manifest itself as "a political, economic, and cultural system in which whites overwhelmingly control power and material resources, conscious and unconscious ideas of white superiority and entitlement are widespread, and relations of white dominance and non-white subordination are daily reenacted across a broad array of institutions and social settings."[96] In societies imbued by white supremacism the social organization of a particular society will give rise to social stratifications that reflect the prior conceptual bias of the dominant racial group throughout the whole. As sociologist Eduardo Bonilla-Silva explains: "The race placed in the superior position tends to receive greater economic remuneration and access to better occupations and prospects in the labor market, occupies a primary position in the political system, is granted higher social estimation (i.e. is viewed as smarter or better looking), often has license to draw physical (segregation) as well as social (racial etiquette) boundaries between itself and other races, and what Du Bois called a psychological wage."[97]

To say then that Josiah Royce is racist is to mean that Josiah Royce's theories and thinking about the bodies of Black populations should be managed by colonialism—as in the case of his advocating for the administration of Blacks in the South based on British strategies in Jamaica. Royce believed that Blacks, Negroes, were alien populations who were inferior in part because of their racial origins. Royce's theories of assimilation viewed Blacks, Asians, and Native Americans as inferior racial groups, which indicated to him that these groups should be treated as lesser persons—inferior humans—that have a need to be civilized by white culture. The racism of Josiah Royce is spoken of throughout this book within the colonial rationalizations described by Du Bois, which were common throughout the end of the nineteenth century and popularized by various ethnologists in the early twentieth. Negrophobia, the dangers whites believed Blacks posed during Reconstruction and beyond, affected how Royce saw the race problem and the programs he believed would arrest it. At the most basic level, Josiah Royce may have believed that Black people may evolve beyond slavery, but he still maintained that they did not warrant the full citizenship rights promised to them after the Civil War that would put them on par with whites. Blacks and nonwhite foreigners remained social problems for America and its local communities. It is necessary however to clarify a point. To say that Royce was racist does not mean that he had to support biological determinism, or slavery. It is to say that as ideas evolved and America's society changed, Royce endorsed the more current science of his day all of which still maintained the inferiority of nonwhite peoples as a general rule.

Power relations in a racialized society are often thought to be most overtly racist in policies like segregation or apartheid, which mark proxemics with the bodies of nonwhites thought to be inferior to whites. However, the socialization effect these racial proxemics have—and the prior racist conceptualizations of Black peoples that organized society such that these barriers to interracial contact demand—survive beyond the disaggregation of the formal structures that mark the presence of racism in a society. For example, while Americans may no longer practice Jim Crow segregation or, as in the case of Royce, reject strict biological determinist theories that suggest racial inferiority and destiny is dictated by birth, it simply is not true that the absence of such policies or scientific theories mean the society is less racist or has progressed beyond the time at which these policies or views were held. Suggesting for example that de facto (residential) segregation that confines Black bodies to impoverished communities exposed to toxic wastes or impoverished public housing plagued by toxins and other pollutants are less racist—and less morbid—than Jim Crow segregation identifies only the *idols of racism in the society* (e.g., segregation, apartheid, etc.) as the epitome of the *practice of racism*, and all other social arrangements that are not these idols as differing in kind, hence not racist, or a lesser degree of racism than the previous arrangement.[98]

Perceived as a debate about white identity, where all white figures become whipping posts of these racial historiographies, instead of a concrete system endemic to American society, white philosophers attempt to focus on the identity and actions of the white philosopher accused as the main issue of contention—suggesting either that the philosopher was merely the product of their time, or that other identities like maleness or femaleness either absolve or implicate the speaker(s) waging the criticism against the white author. These interpretive tropes err in making identity equitable to systems of social organization and the thinking that propagated such arrangements. The historian Barbara J. Fields explains this reaction: "Racism—the assignment of people to an inferior category and the determination of their social, economic, civic, and human standing on that basis—unsettles fundamental instincts of American academic professionals who consider themselves liberal, leftist, or progressive. It is an act of peremptory, hostile, and supremely—often fatally—consequential identification that unceremoniously overrides its objects' sense of themselves."[99] In order to deal with the dissonance of reading and writing about racism, the coping mechanism of the liberal academic conflates race, understood as one's identity, with the structures and exercise of power that have always defined racism. Fields continues, "That is why well-meaning scholars are more apt to speak of race than of racism. Race is a homier and more tractable notion than racism, a rogue elephant gelded and tamed into a pliant beast of burden. Substituted for racism, race transforms the act of a subject into an attribute of the object. And because race denotes a state of mind, feeling, or being, rather than a program or pattern of action, it radiates a semantic and grammatical ambiguity that helps to restore an appearance of symmetry, particularly with the help of a thimblerig that imperceptibly moves the pea from race to racial identity."[100]

Perhaps the greatest irony is that while white figures are usually absolved of nineteenth-century and early twentieth-century racism by appealing to the policies of the mid-1960s, Black scholars critiquing historic white figures for racism are often accused of anachronism. This is to say that the commonly accepted charge of anachronism offered by many philosophers and theorists accuse Black scholars of reading our present understandings of racism (as white supremacy, unconscious bias, anti-Blackness) unfairly into the thought of whites centuries prior to these understandings while nonetheless absolving white figures based on our present day understandings of racially progressive ideas. The charge of anachronism is often waged as a deflection meant to distract scholars from understanding the complexities of white supremacy, while socializing upcoming scholars and graduate students negatively toward considerations of race and racism in American philosophy. American philosophers generally know very little, if anything, about race in the nineteenth century. Ethnology is not taught as part of the intellectual history or discursive milieu of American thinkers. This blindness applies to white figures such as John Dewey and Josiah Royce, as well as Black figures such as W. E. B. Du Bois and William H. Ferris. This disciplinary ignorance however is disingenuously manipulated when race is concerned. Black, Brown, and Indigenous scholars are often attacked by white scholars for critiquing white canonical figures based on mid-twentieth-century understandings of racism that were not present in the late 1800s or early 1900s, while those white scholars nonetheless defend white figures by suggesting their personal relationships with Blacks during their lifetimes, or any discussion of race or racism is evidence of their forward thinking and anticipates civil rights era agendas toward the integration of races. In other words, white figures are defended by anachronistic associations with or anticipation of integrationism, while Black, Brown, and Indigenous scholars are dismissed for even suggesting that race, racism, and xenophobia were central motivations behind the works produced and grammars used in the thought of pragmatists, American idealists, and sociologists at the turn of the century. Given the historic tendency of Blacks to understand racism as a structural dehumanization—a systemic violence toward supposedly inferior racial groups—such accusations ring as manifestly false, an apologetic meant to distract from serious analyses of racism and colonialism rather than a demonstrable charge of revisionism, or comparative assessment of the charge against the white figure and the position of the Black, Brown, or Indigenous scholars of the relevant time period.

On the Amendment of Categories: The Problem of Racist Concepts Being Revised as Anti-Racist Philosophy

The often-accepted assertion within philosophy is that racist theories by anti-Black thinkers can be used for anti-racist work. This claim depends on an unstated but presumably shared premise—namely, that integration, in this case of the categories or concepts presented as racist, is both desirable and analogous to the moral aim of its societal version. For many liberals, the idea of segregation is made synonymous to racism. Integration, because it is not segregation and rests on the presumption of a shared humanity or reason, is asserted to result in less racism and a mutual, more democratic culture between whites and Blacks. While Black lawyers who worked on *Brown v. Board of Education*, various sociologists, and psychologists have shown that racism continues and thrives under the post–civil rights ethos of colorblindness and integration—since these ideas do nothing to arrest the power and maintenance of white supremacy—the traditional appeal of similitude between whites, who have historically been considered human, and Blacks, who have been depicted as nonhuman, continues to hold ideological sway over many theorists.[101] Though scholars admit there is a political faux pas committed when one says Blacks and whites are culturally similar, since this contention makes light of the contributions of multiculturalism, there is at a very basic and intuitive level a belief and practice among philosophers and theorists more broadly that asserts that assimilating Blacks into the categories and traditions of whites is in fact humanizing, since it suggests at the most intuitive level that they (Blacks) share in the humanity of the white race. In short, let's just include Black or Brown or Indigenous peoples into the (white) definition of humanity.

However, the amendment of categories that presume white humanity are not so easily changed. If we begin with the idea prevalent during the writing of many of these ideas, namely, that white races were the standard of civilization and, consequently, the only ones that possessed humanity and Blacks were savage lesser beings who had not yet attained humanity, then what occurs when we seek to conceptually assert sameness or equality between these two beings marked as different if not contradictory. Often such arguments begin by stating that race is not biological or real; hence, the division between Blacks and whites on that basis is false. This premise while accepted as true by most scholars does not in itself explain how Blacks and whites separated by race in the theories of white authors automatically become similar enough to be included within the (white) subjects the theories of white philosophers presuppose. For example, it is true that race does not really separate groups of people biologically or genetically predetermine their mental capacities; however, it does not follow from admitting these arguments that white authors who asserted philosophies based on said distinctions can be amended to include racial groups previously deemed inferior based on an acknowledgment that the scientific assumptions are false. Stated differently, while it may be true that Blacks are not morally or intellectually inferior to whites, accepting this proposition in no way says that Blacks are morally or intellectual similar or the same as whites. Likewise, showing that Blacks are not inferior to whites does not reveal a shared humanity or sameness among groups that can be read backward into previously racist texts that excluded Black, Brown, Asian, or Indigenous peoples. There is no assurance that the capacities described as belonging *solely* to whites when they were assumed to be *racially superior* to all other groups are in fact capacities that all other (racial) groups previously thought *to be inferior to whites* actually possess in ways similar to how the racist white philosopher in question describes these capacities in the superior white race of their time. Such arguments assert a nonsensical proposition—while white supremacy that holds theories of white racial superiority in intelligence, civilization, evolution, and culture are false, the very same ideas emerging from white supremacy are true if they are not thought to be the exclusive capacity of whites but in fact are the natural capacities of all humans. As such, the argument rests not on the actual belief that white supremacist ideas are wrong but that they are erroneously thought to be exclusive to whites.

At a more practical level, the inclusion of presumed inferior racial peoples into the philosophy of white thinkers presumes a monocultural viewing of the world, or a view that supposes that other racial, ethnic, or cultural groups would tend to see the same problems encountered by white Western philosophers in the same way that these white thinkers do. Such inclusions of Blacks and other racial groups into the thought of white philosophers assumes that Black, Brown, Asian, or Indigenous people would view that world, the problems of the self, and community through the monocular of whites. The problem of loyalty in Royce for example is not a universal problem; some cultures simply do not have the same distinctions between communities and the self. The perception of problems in the world emerges from the position of the group, and the individual—their position in relation to the world and others.

Colonizing peoples see the world from a different perspective than the colonized. The group suffering from genocide sees the world differently from the group committing genocide. How does the Black subject, now taken to be enough like Royce to engage his ethics, understand their existential position in relation to a philosophy that says that Blacks are an enduring social problem? The conceptualization of Blacks, or Asians, or foreigners as participants in Royce's ethics would assert that they accept themselves as alien. To this the philosopher would no doubt say, "But Royce was wrong about that"; yes, but he was also wrong about every racial distinction he made, every claim about immigration, colonization, and the efficiency of British administration in the South. What would be left of what Royce *actually* thought about race in America but some ambiguous gesture toward inclusion—a gesture more fully grasped by W. E. B. Du Bois, William H. Ferris, or Dr. Martin Luther King Jr.

Consequently, we see that the price of the allegedly inferior racial group's semblance to the white theorist not only supposes a monocultural purview but requires the excision of the aspects of the world white thinkers generally took to be reality at that time. There was colonialism, racial contact, and perils in the day of Royce. He like other white Americans assumed a rightness if not divinity to the colonial project and the triumph of the white race in racial contact with inferior peoples. It is usually asserted that such views and historical contexts are not central to the text, or the real philosophy of the (white) thinker under scrutiny, yet every argument made in favor of a white philosophy being useful as an anti-racist resource insists upon white philosophers' political stances or their views toward slavery, colonialism, or lynching. In short, when the white philosopher's theory is suggested to have remnants of racial differentiation or racism attached to it and are placed within the philosopher's historical context, the common retort is "the philosopher is merely a product of their time." When their stances on race, or protests of lynching, or their involvement with the NAACP or Blacks are part of the activism of white philosophers in such a way that it aligns with the liberal racial politics of the twenty-first century, then historical context, personal attitudes, and politics are relevant. Suddenly, these beliefs and actions are the consequences of the white philosophers' philosophical outlook and evidence of their philosophy's relevance to real-world problems like racism.

When the racist assumptions of white philosophers align with their times, their social philosophy and political programs are said to be irrelevant and dismissed as not central to their actual thought. The

fickleness of this response—how it is asserted without an actual literature or proof demonstrating its plausibility—suggests that it is merely a
retort asserted with the rhetorical force of a political ideal, but it shows
little evidence of actually being a methodology. This response is merely
what is said, not an actual account of the relation racist ideas have to a
philosopher's actual theory.

Generally speaking, philosophers do not want to admit that anti-
Black racism is structural to, or a problem with the metaphysics of, the
texts of white philosophical authors. The text and character of whites
may be mistaken but never malicious or of ill intent. If I could use the
work of my past professor, Emmanuel Eze, who explored Kant's racism
back in the 1990s, as an example. When Eze pointed out Kant's racism,
white scholars immediately rushed to say that Kant's racist anthropology
was not central to his philosophy or was merely his personal bias. These
two ideas meant that his actual critical philosophy remained unscathed
and could be used to problematize his other works. For the last several
years of his life, Eze fought to prove that racial delineations based on
physiognomy were created by nature and hence categorical in Kant. I
would argue white philosophers have done something similar with regard
to Royce. Mainstream philosophy continues to define racism in liberal
terms as a matter of personal bias and attitudes, despite the work of
Black scholars as far back as the 1800s showing racism to be cultural,
cognitive, institutional, and structural mechanisms that materially enforce
white superiority and Black inferiority. At the core of Royce's metaphysics
there is the ideal of the Anglo-Saxon. Assimilation is merely the means
by which communities, and the individuals in those communities, move
toward that *ideal* through unity.

What would be required to repair Royce? Do we merely assert that
Royce's generalized language describing humans and their ethico-religious
capacities should include Blacks and other races originally excluded? Often
the methods by which one appeals to the idea of the philosopher in question is not specific or clear. If one imagines Royce without the idea of
race or savagery, do we now assume Black people who were thought to
be culturally inferior now share in the civilization of the white Americans
who raped, lynched, and castrated them? Blacks seem then to have no
cultural specificity; they would appear as whites—literally, the philosophical anthropology of whites becomes applicable to them. In such efforts
there is no need to know anything about Blacks—how they thought,
their culture, their a priori concepts—it would simply be asserted that

they are like white enough to be welcomed into the bosom of God and Reason. In our efforts to *include* Blacks, do we ignore the barbarism of the white race? Do we insist on giving Blacks reason for the purposes of the philosophical project and ignore that we are also talking about cultural idealizations of the white man's burden? Arguments suggesting that we can appeal to the metaphysics, or less pretentiously, the universal claims proposed by philosophers, often revise the categories that serve as the basis of the exclusion. Blacks have been excluded from humanity, often confined to categories like the nonhuman, the savage, or what Charles Mills often understands the sub-persons, or "an entity which, because of phenotype, seems (from, of course, the perspective of the categorizer) human in some respects but not in others."[102]

The idealized starting point of many philosophers holds that humanity begins with a universal equality epitomized by the West's concept of the rational human. Blackness has however never been formulated on the graciousness of this concept. As Mills contends, sub-personhood "captures the defining feature of the African-American experience under conditions of white supremacy (both slavery and its aftermath): that white racism so structured the world as to have negative ramifications for every sphere of black life—juridical standing, moral status, personal/racial identity, epistemic reliability, existential plight, political inclusion, social metaphysics, sexual relations, aesthetic worth."[103] While I prefer nonhuman or inhumanity, which is often utilized by ethnologists who described Blacks as savage, Mills correctly points out that Blackness is the existential rupture to the universal claim. The reality of racism and its exclusion from the category of the full white human-citizen-person is "a more illuminating starting point than the assumption that in general all humans have been recognized as persons (the 'default mode,' so to speak). In other words, one would be taking the historical reality of a partitioned social ontology as the starting point rather than the ideal abstraction of universal equality, qualified with an embarrassed marginal asterisk or an endnote to say that there were some exceptions," says Mills.[104]

I am always left with the question, "If we say Blacks are considered by Royce to be inferior and savage, but that was wrong, are we now just saying Blacks and whites are basically the same?" Do we assume Africans had the Anglo-Saxon ideal as well, or that Africans could understand the rightness of apartheid? What do we have to leave out of Royce's vision of the world if we attempt to include Black people in it? Where would the Chinese fit given that Royce believes they have no culture to contribute to America? What do we pick to represent the cultural contributions of Chinese people to these shores? Does the philosopher who extends Royce's metaphysics know enough about Chinese culture to assert such subjectivities accurately or do we just guess, or worse substitute our personal stereotypes as the basis of their subjectivity in the text? To suggest that we can just appeal to the larger metaphysics of the human, the individual, or the rational-religious subject would thereby force us to rewrite history and most egregiously make the oppressed be ideally fixed upon the subject and inclinations of their oppressors. It merely argues by analogy that the alien-nonwhite race is enough like whites to be considered white for the purposes of a philosophical experiment, despite the failure of this ideal humanism to be expressed in reality. In my view, this is revisionism and a creative rendering of ideas one might attribute to Royce but are not part of Royce's actual thought.

The Organization of the Book

The first chapter of this book, "Royce, Racism, and the Colonial Ideal: white Supremacy, Imperialism, and the Role of Assimilation in Josiah Royce's Aberdeen Address," begins with a thorough analysis of Royce's 1900 Aberdeen lecture, "Some Characteristic Tendencies of American Civilization." This chapter aims to establish the major trends and themes found in this speech regarding assimilation, provincialism, and Royce's peculiar fascination with the British colonial legacy. Chapter 2 focuses on Royce's "Race Question and Prejudice" essay first delivered in 1905 but published in 1906 in the *International Journal of Ethics*. Chapter 2, "Race Questions and the Black Problem: Royce's Call for British Administration as a Solution to the Black Peril," takes great pains to uncover the nuances within the debates that Josiah Royce was not only having with Thomas Nelson Page over *The Negro: The Southerner's Problem*, but the alternative Royce proposes in lieu of lynching, namely, British administration. Royce's proposal was not well received by Southern segregationists, and not for the reasons one might initially think. Southern philosophers like Edgar Murphy and John M. Mecklin believed that Royce was advancing a project dedicated to the promotion of white racial superiority and the destruction of the gains Blacks had achieved politically and socially under Reconstruction. While Murphy and Mecklin both supported segregation, they adamantly rejected racial assimilation and the deliberate expansion of America's empire, which was advocated by Royce. This chapter offers not only a testament to the diversity of thinking by Southern philosophers, but a call for more attention to the specific theories and debates concerning the conditions newly freed Black Americans found themselves in during the early 1900s.

Chapter 3, "No Revisions Needed: Historicizing Royce's Provincialism, His Appeal to the white Man's Burden, and Contemporary Claims of His Anti-Racism," focuses on Royce's provincialism and his philosophy of loyalty. This chapter argues that Royce's focus on America's national unity and stability was an unending worry. Royce fears the division and chaos exemplified by the Civil War.[105] His philosophy is driven by this worry, so much so that he creates an ethics—loyalty to loyalty—to rationalize the subservice of the individual to the larger national ideal. This chapter takes great care to engage those thinkers who believe that Royce's loyalty to loyalty can rescue his social ethics and practical suggestions concerning the race problem. Because Royce believes "Race Questions" is a concretization—the practical manifestation—of his ethics, it is my belief that such abstractions tend toward redundancy and revision. In short, Royce does not have a concept outside of loyalty that corrects the cultural homogeneity he desires. While philosophers of course have the liberty to create any number of versions wherein loyalty to loyalty can be envisioned as synonymous with twentieth- or twenty-first-century political ends, it still stands that these are anachronistic revisions to Royce's thinking about race, not Royce's actual vision and motivations concerning race at the turn of the century.

Chapter 4, "On the Dark Arts," is somewhat different is composition and tone. This chapter concerns itself with Royce's evolutionary theories, specifically his intellectual indebtedness to the work of Joseph Le Conte. The evolutionary position of Josiah Royce requires the acceptance of a certain capacity for races to change, to be malleable to their environments. The use of this capacity for colonial advance was first developed by Adolf Bastian, a pivotal figure for Royce. Le Conte's theories only supported the ideas of Bastian, since Le Conte insisted upon a social program to drive racial development and determine the milieu of the society. This is why Royce refers to assimilation as an "especial art." Racial organization and provincialism is an aesthetic idea that transcends the materiality of the present. Royce anticipates a future engineered by the proficiency of

Anglo-Saxon culture. He imagines a society ordered by the aspirations of the backward races to be like—to imitate—the moral character and persona of the superior white race.

This book will be challenging to many American philosophers because it engages materials and figures not routinely encountered in the discipline. There will be a tendency, as is often the case in philosophy, to explain away new evidence as irrelevant to one's already existing thinking or defer to the established disciplinary consensus on the matter. This strangeness, the unsettledness that will accompany the reading of this book, however, offers a rich opportunity to not only critique Royce for his shortcomings but expand the perspectives and voices that have been of some consequence to the development of race theory in American philosophy at the dawn of the twentieth century. This book makes a genuine effort not only to critique but to diagnose the methodological and historical erasures of American thinkers, both Black and white. It requires more than reading for the American philosopher who is captivated by the ideas and exceptionalism of the American social and conceptual project. It requires divestment in the dream and allure of Americanism. It is a paradigm of examining America as historically constituted, not fallen but ideal. It is to understand that freedom, democracy, individuality were ideas in history, not ideals that necessarily directed history. They were birthed in time and shall expire similarly. Part of the lure to the idea that there is a uniqueness thought to be captured by the diversity of America—its democratic experiment—depends on the belief that there was something exceptional about the ideas, peoples, and problems that define America that indicate the *possibility and hope of resolution*. This progression of civilization was not measured by civility and democracy as these tells often suggest. America's concern for democracy entailed the power of citizens to rule themselves, but also expanded their power to rule over others both domestically and abroad. The power of individuals to determine their own course of action, to sacrifice their life, or accumulate power from the lives of others to their own cause(s) had to be curtailed by the ideal. Communities, racial communities, became a way for many white American thinkers to not only explain the internal racial dynamics between whites, Blacks, and Asians in early twentieth-century America, but also provided the basis of how America would relate to the larger communities of the world.

The study of Josiah Royce's thinking concerning race undertaken in this book tells a story of inheritance—how *America* now matured beyond its previous eighteenth-century status as a British colony sought its birthright as an empire alongside its Anglo-Saxon predecessor. This book historicizes philosophy by pointing out the assertions made under the guise of race theory vastly misunderstand the struggles and contentions that defined America's geopolitical consciousness, and the aspirations of the American mind in relation to the world in the first few decades of the twentieth century. This is a reflection on the contingency of the American empire, its racial vulnerabilities from within, as much as a reflection on the decisions proposed by white ethnologists and philosophers to stabilize the republic against the instability posed by different races through the managing of different local publics, or communities. This book takes issue with the ongoing scholarship and discourses that aim to convince philosophers of Josiah Royce's precociousness as an anti-racist thinker and resource for philosophers, because such writings deliberately ignore the actual meanings of terms, deny the historical substance of racial programs, and revise debates to make colonial and racist tropes appear separate and distinct from the racist theories of its time. This is a journey through a history of ideas and the social endeavor philosophers undertook over a hundred years ago. I hope this is a journey the discipline can reflect upon in earnest.

1

Royce, Racism, and the Colonial Ideal

white Supremacy, Imperialism, and the Role of Assimilation in Josiah Royce's Aberdeen Address

Introduction

Josiah Royce has come to have a peculiar currency in American philosophy as an anti-racist figure. Far too often critical race theory attempts to correct *already canonized* white historical figures' racism, but in the case of Royce, this debate about his racism is occurring *during the attempt to canonize* a racist, anti-Black thinker—an adamant supporter of imperialism, the white man's burden, and racialist sciences—as a racial progressive. Royce worried that the recent measured freedom of Blacks during Reconstruction and the rise of alien populations in the country at the turn of the century were ultimately destabilizing and dangerous for the unity and imperial aspirations of white America. Because America was destined to be an imperial power like its British ancestor, Royce argued that America needed to embrace its particular "cultural art of assimilation," and learn more efficient methods of repressing these nonwhite (non-Anglo-Saxon) populations, especially in the South. This chapter is both a historicizing of the arguments and texts, including the previously neglected and still not engaged lecture entitled "Some Characteristic Tendencies of American Civilization." Royce's speech was delivered at Aberdeen University during the period when Royce was in Scotland to deliver the Gifford Lectures. These were the same lectures that came to comprise *The World and the Individual* in 1901. One may find it strange that Royce's philosophy of assimilation and empire accompany what is considered to be his defense of his idealist metaphysics. Why does Royce's

45

philosophical exegesis of empire remain so peripheral to his work when it appears next to what is now considered to be his canonical work on metaphysics? Building from my previous publication, "Royce, Racism, and the Colonial Ideal: [w]hite Supremacy and the Illusion of Civilization in Josiah Royce's Account of the [w]hite Man's Burden," I maintain that the consequence of Royce's imperial reflections is not only philosophical in regard to his actual conceptualization of racial difference but disciplinary, in that it exposes the revisionist project engaged upon by American philosophers who insist, despite the evidence of Royce's white supremacist imperial loyalties, that Josiah Royce is a resource for the amelioration of anti-Black racism and white supremacy.

Despite Royce's "Some Characteristic Tendencies of American Civilization" being first engaged as a call for US imperialism and the valorization of its kinship with Britain's colonial legacy, and anthologized (hence, publicly available) since 2009, there has been no philosophical engagement with this speech or its relation to Royce's racial reflections at the turn of the century.[1] This chapter improves upon my previous discovery of, and my initial reflections on, Royce's speech at Aberdeen University. This chapter begins with an analysis of Royce's history of California in the mid-1800s to better understand his ideas of community and what he will inevitably propose as assimilation in his later works. Royce constantly points back to California as an example of assimilation, provincialism, and the materialization of loyalty to loyalty. While many works on Royce's philosophy of loyalty and community have ignored the significance of his 1886 work to his overall philosophy of race, I am of the belief that his historical account of California and xenophobia reveals what he takes to be the process and aim of a wise provincialism.

Royce's engagement with the major racial theorists and popular ethnological terms in his writings show that he was familiar with the racial theories of his day. He is adamant that social irritation and foreignness were dangers to the cultural and social cohesion of the United States. How then to remedy the danger of racial and ethnic diversity was of great importance to him. To deal with these problems, Royce was drawn to racialist theories that were anything but progressive and exceptional. Unlike many of the segregationists in the South, Royce merely chose cultural strategies of colonization to outright violence. After giving a genealogy of the thinkers named by Royce in "Race Questions and Prejudices," I discuss the influence these figures had on his philosophy of race, specifically how he envisioned the processes involved in race contact. Royce is not uncharacteristically white and American in his 1900 essay "Some Characteristic Tendencies of American Civilization." The challenges, or more accurately fractures, of white racial superiority throughout the world at the dawn of the twentieth century impacted both America and Europe. In handling this text, it is necessary to understand that Royce is speaking to a moment that arises from the contact and absorption of alien (nonwhite) races. He is dealing with "race problems," many of which are beyond the purview of the categories and political sensibilities exhibited by scholars in the twenty-first century. The terminology and taxonomies deployed in Royce's writings cannot be grasped intuitively. Understanding that the ethnological orders of races and the context that authors Royce cites are writing during the late nineteenth century is central to how we interpret what is actually being said by Royce. The debate over Royce's racism is not an issue of personal predilection or perspective. In other words, Royce is not racist because he does not display twenty-first-century attitudes toward Blacks, Indigenous, or Asian peoples. Royce's racism is assessed within his own time and evaluated by his turn-of-the-century allegiances to empire and his urging of colonization as a plan of action and control over nonwhite populations the world over. This chapter attempts to capture what Royce actually said about race without apology or revision to his original thinking. By doing so, it establishes a historiography through which Royce, and other American philosophers, can be better understood and more accurately engaged.

California Dreams: Royce's Nostalgia for the Coercion of the Foreigner

Much of Royce's philosophy of community reaches back to the experiences of his youth in California. As a young boy, he saw how the provincial community dealt with foreigners and outside races, and the behavior of the community inevitably made an impression on his ethical outlook and by effect his overall philosophy of loyalty. Royce holds a peculiar nostalgia for California and how he tells the history of this place—it's coming to be—is instructive for how he sees the unassimilable foreigner within a provincial community. In 1886, Royce pens his first history of California, entitled *California: From the Conquest in 1846 to the Second Vigilance Committee in San Francisco: A Study of American Character.* Royce is not offering a mere record of events as told by physical evidence.

He is offering readers a narrative of the community—the story of its becoming. He explains: "the social condition has been throughout of more interest to me than the individual men, and the men themselves of more interest than their fortunes,"[2] but these details do not obscure the purpose of his study, which is an inquiry into California's national character. California is the model of provincialism that conditions his later philosophy of loyalty. In the preface to *California*, Royce is clear: "Through all the complex facts that are here set down in their somewhat confused order, I have felt running the one thread of the process whereby a new and great community first came to a true consciousness of itself."[3]

Royce begins his history of California with a notable description of the land and the American people who came to occupy it. He writes, "Nowhere else were we Americans more affected than here, in our lives and conduct, by the feeling that we stood in the position of conquerors in a new land."[4] The American people who first occupied California were a precarious bunch. They lacked a complete vision of the community and the visitors who came to share the land with them. Royce explains, "We exhibited a novel degree of carelessness and overhastiness, an extravagant trust in luck, a previously unknown blindness to our social duties, and an indifference to the rights of foreigners, whereof we cannot be proud. But we also showed our best national traits,—traits that went far to atone for our faults."[5] There was a certain violence to early life in California. Conquest, lynching, and mining labor become the fabric of the community over time. Despite the cruelty of these practices, Royce believes the provincial spirit born of these tragedies outweighs the costs and lives lost in the process, because the cruelties of pioneer and mining life sensitized the Americans. The tragedies of living in California created common cause and disgust such that communal ideals were born. During the 1830s, Royce describes multiple battles waged for the seat of governor in California. What is as peculiar as it is interesting is that Royce deliberately marks in his text a California contested by battles that were almost bloodless except for "three horses and mules," as in 1845, when it was a Mexican province, and civilized warfare was "introduced into California through the undertakings of our own gallant Captain Frémont."[6] Royce makes sure to note, "For in civilized warfare, as is well known, somebody always gets badly hurt."[7]

With rare exception, "we Americans have seldom been conquerors."[8] Due to the efforts of a few men, however, California became an example of what Royce believed was our national qualities and had a lasting effect on "the life and character of our people in California in the subsequent days."[9] California was to be colonized, but America's national government realized that such a process was slow, hence, "natural colonization would need to be assisted."[10] Despite the American government's complex plans to seize control of California, Royce credits one man, "the gallant young Captain Frémont,"[11] with the gaining of California for America in 1846. Captain Frémont, "with his armed force, [was] to seize for ourselves without warning upon an unprotected Department [of California], and so in time of peace to gain for our country the prize of war."[12] While on this mission, Frémont was alerted to a plan by Governor Castro that intended to "drive all Americans out of the country, to lay waste their farms, to raise the Indians against them, to destroy them altogether."[13] As hostilities ensued between Castro and Frémont, a small band of Americans stationed themselves in Sonoma awaiting the inevitable charge of Castro to rid the land of them and hoping for the arrival of their ally in arms, Captain Frémont. These men, preparing for the worse, chose officers and a flag—"and on it they painted with berry-juice something that they called a Bear."[14]

The Bear-flag heroes, as Royce calls them, exemplified the national character of America. Of particular interest was a statesman by the name of William Ide. As Royce explains, "Providence evidently meant this man to typify for us, even more than Dr. Semple could do, our national talent and mission for civilizing the benighted Spanish-American peoples of this continent."[15] Mr. Ide was the successor to Dr. Semple, a man Royce deemed "the Thucydides of the Bear War."[16] Hearing of Castro's immediate plans to attack, Mr. Ide appealed to Captain Frémont for help. Frémont wanted Mr. Ide to provoke an attack by Castro by stealing his horses. In this way, claimed Frémont, he could intervene without breaking the appearance of America's neutrality in California. Though he hated Frémont's policy of neutral conquest, Ide obliged the leader. After successfully capturing Castro's men, Mr. Ide addresses the crowd in an effort to decide these prisoners' fate. "What were they there for? Was it not for some truly worthy object, namely, after all, independence? Nay, said he: 'we are robbers, or we must be conquerors.' "[17] While Mr. Ide attempted to govern the Bear flag republic as a somewhat islanded democracy, Captain Frémont was forced to act to save the country. According to a senator, Captain Frémont was made aware that "three great operations fatal to American interests were then going on and without remedy if not arrested at once. These were: (1) The massacre of the Americans, and the destruction of their settlements, in the valley of the Sacramento. (2) The subjection of California to British protection. (3) The transfer of the public domain to British subjects."[18] Frémont allegedly had no choice but to pursue dark tactics to seize California and use armed force and violence to prevent the loss of this territory.

There is a long discussion in Royce's *California* concerning the justification for Frémont's tactics: Were they orders from the government or simply his personal predilection for war? In either case, Royce explains that Frémont's actions secured California but indicated a peculiar dissonance throughout the American's character and what that suggested about Americans more generally. According to Royce,

> The American as conqueror is unwilling to appear in public as a pure aggressor; he dare not seize a California as Russia has seized so much land in Asia, or as Napoleon, with full French approval, seized whatever he wanted. The American wants to persuade not only the world, but himself, that he is doing God service in a peaceable spirit, even when he violently takes what he has determined to get. His conscience is sensitive, and hostile aggression, practiced against any but Indians, shocks this conscience, unused as it is to such scenes.[19]

Americans are forced by their conscience to pursue benevolence in public despite the maliciousness of their actual intent. Royce explains that "Semple and Ide, and the cautious secretary of state, and the gallant captain, and the venerable senator, all alike, not only as individuals, but also as men appealing for approval to their fellow-countrymen at large, must present this sinful undertaking in private and in public as a sad, but strictly moral, humane, patriotic, enlightened, and glorious undertaking."[20] Because the American is not a natural conqueror, outright bloodshed and killing does not naturally fit within his moral calculus—it must have moral legitimacy to the constituency. The American must pretend there is morality in his barbarity. Having secured California as an American republic, partially due to the deceit of Frémont, Royce seems unsettled by the brutality of direct conquest and appears to shun "going abroad as missionaries, as conquerors, or as marauders, among weaker peoples."[21] By the turn of the century, however, the increase of race contact between peoples and the discovery of "soft imperialism" offers Royce a more *humane and civilized* alternative to the brute force of conquest. Royce is dissatisfied with the brutal history of California, insisting on more refined methods by which order can be attained.

By 1847, California was still considered an occupied Mexican province. The conquerors of this land began to assert their Americanness within the territory, affirming American community values and renaming the small village of Yerba Buena—San Francisco. These changes affixed a sense of America within the local places occupied by Americans throughout California. By 1848, with the discovery of gold throughout California, there was an influx of foreigners that not only presented physical challenges within the newly acquired territory, but philosophical challenges concerning the character of the communities the foreigners sought to occupy. Royce was clear that foreigners were neither welcomed nor understood in the communities they came to inhabit. He writes,

> The effective majority in all the chief communities was formed of Americans, and here, as everywhere else in our land, the admixture of foreigners did not prevent the community from having, on the whole, a distinctly American mode of life. The foreigners as such had, of course, no political powers, made no laws, affected the choice of no officers, and had no great tendency to alter the more serious social habits, the prejudices, or the language of Americans. The mass of the Americans in California never grew to understand the foreigners as a class, any more than we have elsewhere understood foreigners.[22]

Foreigners were subjugated within the communities of California. These American strongholds did not bend to the will or wants of the foreigner. They remained alien in California—a separate class—just as these groups do throughout America. Because foreigners had no political power or ability to alter the language, prejudices, or habits of Americans, they could not live within these communities as equals. They were culturally, ethnically, racially marked as distinct from Americans. This observation by Royce is extremely important to his subsequent philosophy, since he is adamant that we should look to California as both an example and model for wise provincialism.

Royce is adamant that any appearance of multiculturalism and cross-cultural understanding was illusory. While some casual observers may remark that the miners spoke "a language half-English, half-Mexican,"[23] Royce insists one understand that "this tradition must be understood to mean simply that the majority of these pioneers mispronounced a large number of Spanish proper names and several of the commoner Spanish words and phrases."[24] Royce breaks with the tone of the first two hundred or so pages to communicate to the reader just how strongly he feels about the uniqueness and cultural immunity California has to foreigners. His word choice and phrasing is personal. He moves from using a general description like Americans or Californians to personal pronouns like *we*. He speaks as someone who knows the real California and insists the reader understand the intimate connection and authority his words carry because he is Californian. "No one who has grown up in California can be under any illusion as to the small extent to which the American character, as there exemplified, has been really altered by foreign intercourse, large as the foreign population has always remained," writes Royce.[25] "The foreign influence has never been for the American community at large, in California, more than skin-deep."[26] While foreigners might provide some amusements like music or theater, bullfights, and gambling, in time these enjoyments were outgrown and the (white) American culture and practices continued.

The conquest of California transformed it from a Mexican territory to a piece of America. It became American through processes of cultural imposition, violence, and ostracization. It was to be ruled by Americans and measured not by the masses of foreigners who came to occupy it, but by the national character it projected against foreign influence. In other words, Royce celebrates the ability of Americans to remain stolid and unaffected by the presence of foreigners within their communities. Quite to the contrary of the depictions offered by philosophers in which California becomes a democratic melting pot, a romantic amalgamation of diversity and equality, Royce values the cultural impenetrability of the American national character. Royce also intimates that the national tendency of the American psyche eschews public demonstrations of aggression and violence. He suggests that it is the natural tendency of America to hide behind moral language and prefer to secure its ends without violence if possible. Royce offers a very compelling description of the birth of assimilation and why provincialism is the preferred means of dealing with alien races than outward aggression. The history of California is extremely relevant to how Royce comes to conceptualize and articulate the characteristics of a wise provincialism in his later works.

The Lynching of a Woman:
The Catalyst of Wise Provincialism

Before we leave Royce's *California*, I am peculiarly struck by his account of the Downieville lynching in 1851. The lynching in Downieville in July 1851 was typically brutish for its mob mentality and displays of violence, but atypical in that the victim was a woman. There is a tendency among civilized men to view the public offenses of women with leniency. "A man who gravely transgresses against order is necessarily viewed first of all as transgressor, and only in the second place do his fellows remember that considerations of mercy, of charity, or of his own personal merit, may enter, to qualify the sternness of justice towards him. But a woman, however she transgresses against law and order, is necessarily regarded first of all as a woman, and only in the second place does one remember that even in her case justice must have its place."[27] On July 4, 1851, a drunken American named Cannan breached the front door of a beautiful Spanish American woman's home. He leaned against the front door, which could not support him, and "fell half inside"[28] this woman's home. Cannan could speak Spanish, and the next morning Cannan went to apologize to the woman along with his companion from the night before. The companion of the woman was the first to dialogue with Cannan, at which time the conversation seemed to be growing hostile. While it is maintained that Cannan's tone remained civil, when the woman arrived and spoke to Cannan, the conversation escalated. The woman in fact "grew constantly more excited at his words, whatever they were, and erelong drew a knife, rushed quickly upon him, and stabbed him to death at a stroke."[29] The woman and her lover testified that Cannan insulted her and "that it was his abuse, used in the course of the quarrel, which drove her to the act, in an outburst of fury."[30]

Upon hearing the news of this incident, the town organized a popular court with a judge and jury already decidedly set on a lynching.[31] When the woman and her paramour appeared before the court, the crowd could be heard shouting, "Hang them . . . Give them a trial . . ."[32] The *Great American Mind* settled on a compromise: "Give them a fair trial and then hang them."[33] The Great American Mind is a practically oriented guiding conscience according to Royce. It is the excitable racial instinct—the nativism of the American—that is wakened by disorder. Royce describes the Great American Mind as petulant as it seeks recompense for trespass despite fact. During the trial of the woman, a physician by the name of Dr. Aiken testified that she was three months with child.[34] Much to the dismay of the mind, this news complicated and delayed the verdict in support of lynching the woman. Because Dr. Aiken seemed in support of the woman, the mind demanded a "consultation of physicians" to determine the accuracy of Dr. Aiken's diagnosis.[35] As the mind grew impatient, it "induced the crowd who represented it to threaten fiercely, and in no whispers, the offending Dr. Aiken, and to fill the air with shouts of 'Hang her.' "[36] The meeting of physicians was influenced by these threats, so much so that the consulting physicians stated that Dr. Aiken was in fact in error to guarantee both their safety and his.[37]

The jury verdict of guilty "quieted the tumult of the Great American Mind."[38] In a matter of hours, she was hanged by the neck until dead. The local paper of the town, *The Star*, expressed regret, but gladness in this verdict. The paper declared that "it cannot very heartily approve of this hasty lynching of a woman, but that it expects the moral effect of the act to be on the whole good. Downieville had been much troubled with bad characters, and a necessity existed for some action."[39] The belief by the paper and the people was that they were trying to do right. Royce cannot move himself to condemn the actions of the lynch mob completely. He believes the outward displays of violence are ineffective, but necessary for the spiritual growth and unity of communities. As he himself admits, "the effect of these outbursts of popular fury was indirectly good. . . . The good effect lay in the very horror begotten by the popular demoralization that all this violence tended to produce."[40] As the result of lynching a woman, the community realized "their stay in California was to be long, their social responsibility great, and their duty to devote time and money to rational work as citizens unavoidable. They saw the fearful effects of their own irresponsible freedom."[41]

In Royce's California, the foreigner was managed through violence, but over time the community became ashamed of its outward displays of aggression and brutality and chose to modernize its techniques of preserving social order. It cannot be denied that Royce was not a fan of the brutality displayed by lynchings. Lynchings enrage the public and

> lynch law, as we now know it, through certain too familiar newspaper items from a number of rural districts in our South and West, is sudden in its action, creates no true precedents, keeps no records, shuns the light, conceals the names of its

ministers, is generally carried out in the night by a perfectly transient mob, expresses only popular passion, and is in fine essentially disorderly.[42]

These towns like Downieville began to form stable governments that condemned mob violence and built up institutions within the community that Royce will later explain in his essay "Some Characteristic Tendencies of American Civilization" are necessary for the assimilation of foreigners. As Royce explains: "The coming of women, the growth of families, the formation of church organizations, the building of school-houses, the establishment of local interests of all sorts, saved the wiser communities from the horrors of lynch law."[43] These transformations made the community readier to peacefully accept and adjust, and assimilate foreigners who came to live within its borders.

Royce recognizes that the unassimilated foreigner is a threat to the established order that communities find necessary to their very being. This is not a regional phenomenon but the national characteristic—"our American intolerance towards the unassimilable foreigner is not a sectional peculiarity, however often it may appear somewhat more prominently in one section of our land than in another,"[44] says Royce. The hatred of foreigners is a natural nativism of the American people. This is not to deny that Royce remarks that he is regretful of these tendencies in himself and Californians, but it is something they innately possess—an instinct. Royce asks: "For this hatred of foreigners, this blind nativism, are we not all alike born to it? And what but reflection, and our chance measure of cultivation, checks it in any of us?"[45] Royce provides no answer as to how one eliminates this allegedly natural tendency toward xenophobia and racism; he only expresses the desire to control its brutality through community and the establishing of social order. The violence that follows from such instincts is not exceptional, but the reaction of the community—as a self-conscious whole—to disloyalty.

Like nativism, the social order was instinctual in that Americans naturally desired it, but it was created through the agency and free will of the individual. The social order is, however, something that instinct must make in its essential elements, by a sort of first intention, but that only voluntary devotion can secure against corruption.[46] Because this was a cause one dedicates oneself to within the community, the costs for violating the established order was disastrous and facilitated the barbarous practice of lynchings. Royce is careful to explain that lynchings are not simply the aversion of the populace to order, but a means toward securing it. Royce explains: "we may then say that the well-known crises and tragedies of violent popular justice during the struggle for order were frequently neither directly and in themselves crimes of the community in each case of the past popular crimes of disloyalty to the social order; they were social penalties, borne by the community itself, even more than by the rogues, for the treason of carelessness."[47] The community then awakens to exact vengeance for the violation of its creed and trust. The public mind is swayed, or more accurately directed in Royce's view, to eliminate the threat to the sacred ideals of the community. In Royce's view, the barbarous fury is born of the necessity of the community itself and exhibits such control over the public that "a sentimental speech in a prisoner's favor would have done nothing save, possibly, to endanger the prisoner's life yet more, or even to endanger that of his advocate."[48] These were communities that utilized violence against foreigners for their difference and scapegoated Mexicans for pleasure.[49]

The American communities Royce comes to describe as wise in California are never free of their hate for alien races and foreigners. The nativism of Americans is thought to be natural, a race instinct acquired from birth. While the Anglo-Saxon spirit of compromise and the American national trait of public good humor generally avoid outward displays of violence and aggression toward foreigners, the native race instinct could make brief and impromptu expressions in any condition.[50] When this race instinct does emerge, it does not necessarily doom the community. In fact, it serves as a means to improve it according to Royce. Following the lynching in Downieville, Royce observed:

> despite all their sins, they showed such a skill also; but that the moral elasticity of our people is so great, their social vitality so marvelous, that a community of Americans could sin as fearfully as, in the early years, the mining community did sin, and could yet live to purify itself within so short a time, not by a revolution, but by a simple progress from social foolishness to social steadfastness. Even thus a great river, for an hour defiled by some corrupting disturbance, purifies itself, merely through its own flow, over its sandy bed, beneath the wide and sunny heavens.[51]

It is important to remember that Royce sees the history of California—from its becoming a state through conquest to its establishing of order through provincialism—as a dialogue between sin and providence. The conquest of Frémont to establish the state and the social order instinctively established by the communities are reflections concerning the toil of settlers. "We are all but dust, save as this social order gives us life," writes Royce.[52] The social order created by community—inherent in the relations of man to one another—is the ideal communities should serve. It is the aspiration individuals who are part of communities strive toward, or as Royce says, "what we are serving is simply our own highest spiritual destiny in bodily form."[53] The social order is "never truly sordid or corrupt or unspiritual; it is only we that are so when we neglect our duty."[54] Royce admits he "toiled for a while over the sources, to see in these days a process of divinely moral significance,"[55] but came to understand communal order as the foundation of one's human pursuit toward salvation.

As will be shown throughout this chapter, California serves as a model—the template—of provincial communities throughout Royce's social philosophy and ethics. His childhood experiences and the history he writes of California's founding and establishing of social order offers readers so much insight into his program of assimilation and even disagreements with Thomas Nelson Page concerning lynching. Royce insists that foreigners assimilate to prevent the outward expressions of violence we found in the mining communities in California. Lynching only excited the mob, it awakens the Great American Mind—that fear and hatred Americans carry with them of foreigners. For this to be avoided, social unrest and irritation must be kept at a minimum. This is why Royce warns the Southerners against the outward displays of violence against Blacks. This is why we should build institutions of administration that civilize and assimilate alien races. It is not from compassion or worry about those races themselves, but a fear of the consequences that befall the community if brutality is outwardly displayed.

There is a great irony in the work of Royce and the scholarship that is written about him currently. Royce is adamant that American communities do not become culturally plural from the presence of foreigners, since to do so would be disloyal to the order established by the community. The violence directed toward the unassimilated is more divine than the betrayal of the idea that binds the community, since the unassimilated seek to change the substance of the community itself. The race instinct and nativism of Americans protect communities from outsiders. They are what drives these communities to work as vehicles of the ideal, and what guards them from cultural diffusion by outsiders. Royce believes that California is the example par excellence of American conquest.

Royce's Ethnological Assertions in Context: Situating His Utilization of Frazer and Bastian Next to Chamberlain's *The Foundations of the Nineteenth Century* (1899)

Because essentialism (understood as biological determinism) is demonized to such a great extent in philosophy, there is an erroneous assumption that anything anti-essentialist (meaning environmentalist, i.e., culturally or socially determined) is not racist. This contention, while popular, is grossly inaccurate, and it makes confronting this mythicization of anti-essentialism immensely important in our consideration of Royce's racism, given the weight many scholars place on Royce's nonbiological explanation of race. In his book *Rethinking Race: Franz Boas and His Contemporaries*, Vernon J. Williams, Jr., reminds us that even the most ardent supporters of environmentalist explanations had not separated themselves from the myth of Black racial inferiority.[56] While the introduction of environmentalist explanations in the late 1890s did stand in sharp contrast to the dominant biological determinism advocated in works by social Darwinists, like Thomas Huxley's "Emancipation—Black and [w]hite" (1865) and Frederick Hoffman's *The Race Traits and Tendencies of the American Negro* (1896)—this newly emerging thinking did not advocate or suppose the equality of races, only the potential evolution of backward races from their current degeneracy (primitivism) toward some higher degree of civilization through race contact.[57] In other words, philosophers are working under the mistaken presumption that a move away from ethnological explanations and biological determinism necessarily meant that the newly emerging environmentalist accounts that were being suggested by some thinkers in disciplines like sociology or anthropology were also a move from racism to anti-racism.

We can see an example of this emerging shift between ethnology and environmentalism, as well as the still enduring anti-Black racism of the times, in Royce's "Race Questions and Prejudices" published in the *International Journal of Ethics* (1906). In looking to the theories of Adolf

Bastian (the mentor of the young Franz Boas and Edward B. Tylor) and Scottish anthropologist James Frazer, it is undeniable that Royce was deeply committed to the newly emergent social theories of anthropology that stressed the importance of racial psychologies. However, it should be made clear that these were racialist endeavors that aimed to find out the mental, spiritual, and psychological states of primitive peoples, not humanist sciences, which assumed cultural or racial equality as a starting point. Royce genuinely believed that it was only through inquiring into the mental states of races that anthropology could hope to distinguish what really belongs to the "mind of a race of men, as distinct from what belongs to culture."[58] In "Race Questions and Prejudices," Royce is explicit in his support of this dawning era in racialist sciences. He remarks:

> If you study the thoughts of the various peoples, as the anthropologist Bastian has loved to mass them together in his chaotic and learned monographs, or as Frazer has surveyed some of them in his *Golden Bough*, well, these primitive thoughts appear, in all their own chaos, and in all their vast varieties of detail, to be the outcome not of racial differences so much as of a few essentially human, although by no means always very lofty, motives. These fundamental motives appear, with almost monotonous regularity, in the superstitions, the customs, the legends, of all races.[59]

Royce is pointing to a very important and nuanced distinction in the dawning anthropology of his day. Primitive thoughts are not fixed and unchanging due to racial differences. His view, expressed in this essay and others, is that primitive thoughts are manifested at various stages of human development and are accumulated in certain racial groups due to their environment and contact with civilization. An all too common mistake in reading Royce is attributing to these sorts of comments a nascent humanism that sees civilization and/or primitivism as a capacity belonging to all of humanity rather than limited to specific racial peoples and their environments. Situating Royce's rejection of Chamberlain is of the utmost importance. Royce rejects the biologically determined nature of Houston Stewart Chamberlain's *The Foundations of the Nineteenth Century* (1899). Chamberlain was a Pan-Germanist and believed that Teuton blood not only birthed civilization, but that only the Teutons can lead the world to a higher humanity.[60] This superior racial stock argument based in blood is what makes Royce suspicious of current *Rassentkeoretiker,* especially Chamberlain's. This is not because his race theories are in themselves futile. Royce admits that in reading Chamberlain he learns that "the concept of race is the key to the comprehension of all history, [and] if you only form a clear idea of the important types of men, you can then determine with exactness precisely who ought to rule and who ought to yield."[61]

From Chamberlain, Royce understood the impetus behind attempting to predict and anticipate the various forms of civilization, or the weltanschauungen—the worldviews or what Bastian calls the elementary ideas of a people—as well as other types of racial characteristics that endure over time with these groups. Royce does not reject Chamberlain's work completely, as if from some absolute aversion to Chamberlain's attempts to ground philosophy in the study of racial types. What Royce is at odds with in *The Foundations of the Nineteenth Century* is that the race Chamberlain choses to be the leader of the world, the Bible's "the salt of the earth," is decided by Chamberlain's personal bias rather than racial psychologies that dictate which European peoples or spirit should in fact lead civilization forward. Royce is in fact quite clear on this point: "when I observe . . . that the *Rassentkeoretiker* frequently uses his science to support most of his personal prejudices, and is praised by his sympathizers almost equally for his exact knowledge and for his vigorous display of temperament, I begin to wonder whether a science which mainly devotes itself to proving that we ourselves are the salt of the earth, is after all so exact as it aims to be."[62]

It is generally assumed that Royce's rejection of the dominant racist theories (which argue for superior racial stocks of men) as well as his suspicion as to the biases of such theories place Royce on the side of racial equality. Such assumptions tend to err in privileging the dogmas of twenty-first-century academic thinking about race (biologic/essentialist vs. environmental/anti-essentialist), while overlooking the actual racialized hierarchies at work in the thought of James Frazer and Adolf Bastian—the authors of theories Royce himself favored and advanced as the cutting-edge thinking about racial variations and the move of civilization during his time.[63] Royce is still committed to the existence of racial psychology and open to theories making progress in unearthing these spiritual elements of racial life. So while Royce may insist that "no race of men . . . can lay claim to a fixed and hereditary type of mental life such as we can now know with exactness to be unchangeable,"[64] and he conceded that "we do not scientifically know what the true racial varieties of mental type really are,"[65] he nevertheless concluded that there can be "no doubt there are such varieties."[66]

In Adolf Bastian's "Ethnology and Psychology" (1881), he describes the relationship between ethnology and ethnography, where ethnology attempts to "transform psychology into a natural science,"[67] while ethnography seeks to "order the variations of mankind according to geographic areas."[68] The problem that arises for Bastian is that our attempts to study races have focused on physical characteristics that are deemed immediately inferior with little to no understanding of what these characteristics mean morally or spiritually for the mind of the races. Here Royce follows Bastian's critique of the physical sciences as creating an artificial division between science and philosophy under ethnology. As Bastian says, "when the so-called natural sciences arrived one after the other, from chemistry through physiology, they stood next to the realm of the mind, but, unable to find a mediating link between the particular scientific pursuit and the unknown operation of the mind, they tried to leapfrog the mind, to pretend its contents were of no importance."[69] Bastian then became intent on centering the study of the mind as the basis of ethnology. The sciences have failed accurately and objectively to study racial differences, so "if psychology follows the methods of natural science, these can then be transferred to philosophy, which should become more anthropologically oriented: the marriage of anthropology and philosophy must find its basis in scientific psychology."[70] Bastian believed that "this new psychology based on the principles of the natural sciences will, through the further development of psycho-physics, eventually unravel the unseen universe of the mind."[71] It becomes easier to see now why Royce criticizes the ethnological focus on skull, hair, and skin color without advancing toward a study of race psychology:

> . . . we ask ourselves just how these physical varieties of the human stock, just how these shades of color, these types of hair, these forms of skull, or these contours of body, are related to the mental powers and to the moral characteristics of the men in question, then, if only we set prejudice wholly aside, and appeal to science to help us, we find ourselves in the present state of knowledge almost hopelessly at sea. We know too little as yet about the natural history of the human mind, our psychology is far too infantile a science, to give us any precise information as to the way in which the inherited, the

native, the constitutional aspects of the minds of men really vary with their complexions or with their hair.[72]

Throughout "Race Questions and Prejudices," Royce repeatedly tells the reader that we must focus on the minds of men,[73] arguing quite adamantly at one point that "it is a man's mind, rather than his skull, or his hair, or his skin that we most need to estimate."[74] This is the direct influence of Bastian's insights and criticisms of racial physicalist accounts of psychological science.

There has been a tendency to suggest that such statements by Royce are antecedents of his liberalism and the humanism undergirding his views on race. This humanist ethos is interpreted as a concern with the character of individuals rather than their skin color. In reality, however, Royce's insistence is highly racialized and extends to the burgeoning questions of his day concerning the interaction of races in the projects of imperialism and colonial expansion. Royce says:

> We are now interested in the minds of men. We want to know what the races of men are socially good for. And not in the study of skulls or of hair, or of skin color, and not in the survey of all these bewildering complications with which physical anthropology deal, shall we easily find an answer to our more practical questions, viz.: to our questions regarding the way in which these various races of men are related to the interests of civilization, and regarding the spirit in which we ought to estimate and practically to deal with these racial traits of mankind.[75]

The mental states of races, their racial psychology and spiritual capacities, mediated the relationship that whites, or more accurately various European peoples had with alien races. The mind of these races is what creates the different strategies of colonization, say, the difference between how Royce deals with the Japanese versus the Negro in the South.

Royce has simply applied Bastian psycho-physics to the problem of colonialism and Western imperialism. Such an application is not out of the question in Bastian's own work. In "The Folk Idea as Paradigm of Ethnology" (1893), Bastian argues that the "goal of modern ethnology is to find an adequate methodology for scientific psychology."[76] To create reliable measures, ethnology must come to understand what Bastian calls *elementary ideas* as a comparative theory that seeks to unite both the physical and psychical realms of the races. If looked at in relation to a group's development, elementary ideas would appear to be "the individual cells or atoms which evolve, according to organic laws of growth into different streams of ideas,"[77] while folk ideas are the actual manifestations of these ideas with the physical world and specific geography of the people. Bastian argues that the folk idea could be substituted by words like "milieu, surrounding, or even survivals" and still keep its meaning.[78] The elementary ideas of races, tribes, and nations are central to the strategies of race contact. As Bastian says, "The practical value of the notion of elementary ideas lies in the contribution it can make to solving the urgent problems of the time, be they social problems, or questions of colonial policy."[79] Bastian then makes an argument against the use of violence under colonialism that parallels Royce's argument against lynching in the South. Bastian argues:

> In the latter [referring to colonial policy], the thunder of cannons has all too often unfortunately drowned more subtle forms of persuasion, persuasion which would have put the savage into the shackles of his own thinking and thus kept him dependent. This would only have required a careful uncovering of the logic and function of his thought processes, which could then have been applied to mutual advantage.[80]

Efficiency in the colonial project and a smoother path for the trotting toward civilization was at the forefront of most scientific inquiries of the time. Bastian, like Royce after him, sees racial psychology as helpful to the colonial endeavor. It means you can colonize without violence or death, but through psychology. As we will see later in chapter 2, this same type of reasoning, where the native or in the case of the South, the Negro, remains dependent and psychologically weak from repressive colonial structures, is of central concern to Royce. Royce takes from Bastian the excitement found in the new philosophical possibilities and psychological advances gained from race contact. Bastian sees the imperial conquests of the West as placing other races within the "historical horizon of awareness," a position in which "the 'observation of otherness' can clarify much and in a more objective way than any subjective navel-gazing could ever achieve."[81] Stated differently, the imperial reach of America and Europe brings the race theorist more subjects to study, which thereby helps develop the techniques and strategies of colonization, to their mutual advantage in Bastian's opinion.

What Royce learns from Frazer is more directly pointed toward the role that imperialism plays in moving humanity forward. In James Frazer's *The Golden Bough* (1890) the outright support for imperial domination and conquest is even more pronounced. Like Bastian, Frazer maintains that even civilized peoples had the legends, ideas, and myths of magic that he observed in primitive cultures at one point in their historical evolution.[82] Unlike the romantic notions of primitivism that emerged later in the twentieth century, at the turn of the century the "savage" was thought to need motivation toward civilization from the condition of savagery. Frazer was one of the most popular advocates of this view. He once remarked:

> No human being is so hide-bound by custom and tradition as your democratic savage; in no state of society consequently is progress so slow and difficult. The old notion that the savage is the freest of mankind is the reverse of the truth. He is a slave, not indeed to a visible master, but to the past, to the spirits of his dead forefathers, who haunt his steps from birth to death, and rule him with a rod of iron.[83]

Left within their own milieu, these primitive peoples would remain stagnate and backward. They are trapped, according to Frazer, in their own legends that resist science and account for reality mystically. This temperament hinders their move to civilization and places a unique duty upon imperial peoples who take civilization with them to their conquests. It is colonization, says Frazer, which brings intellectual progress and development of the human mind suppressed by savage thinking.

> Intellectual progress, which reveals itself in the growth of art and science and the spread of more liberal views, cannot be dissociated from industrial or economic progress, and that in its turn receives an immense impulse from conquest and empire. It is no mere accident that the most vehement outbursts of activity of the human mind have followed close on the heels

of victory, and that the great conquering races of the world have commonly done most to advance and spread civilisation, thus healing in peace the wounds they inflicted in war.[84]

Frazer insists that imperial conquests, much like those described in the opening sentences of "Race Questions and Prejudices," bring civilization to the world. These race contacts between white Westerners and alien races act as catalysts for primitives in their transition toward modernity. As explained in more detail in chapter 2 regarding the Japanese, whites used to associate themselves with *the conquerors* throughout history and adopt any inferior race that defeated a European peoples in battle as their own, or having some Anglo-Saxon blood flowing through their veins. Much like Royce's valorizations at the beginning of *California* (1886) discussed earlier in this chapter, Frazer too sees the imperial motivation to be a trait of the dominant and racially superior races. Royce sees this as a primarily Anglo-American trait, whereas Frazer includes more Asiatic peoples, but Frazer is clear that his inquiry is primarily concerned with the persistence of the Aryan race from antiquity to the present.[85] Such thinking is the anthropological basis for Royce's support of the white man's burden in essays like "Some Characteristic Tendencies of American Civilization" (1900) and "Provincialism" (1902).

The ideas Royce gathers from the work of Adolf Bastian and James Frazer are of central importance to how scholars frame Royce's challenges to biological determinism, and racial heredity, as well as the language of humanity, scholars have found appealing throughout Royce's commentaries on race. Royce does make pointed challenges to the mistaken ethnological doctrines that maintain a fixed racial heredity, but as I have shown, he was certainly not alone in such criticisms and not a pathfinder himself. Rather than being an exception, Royce is more a parrot of the times, repeating the research of others he judges congenial to his philosophical ideas. His commentaries reflect the findings and theories of more prominent white scholars in anthropology and the emergence of racial psychology to speak accurately about racial variation. There is no denying that Royce did say that he is a "member of the human race, and this is a race which is, as a whole, considerably lower than the angels, so that the whole of it very badly needs race elevation,"[86] but this elevation, this lifting up of "the whole," is the product of imperial conquest and colonial policy. The whole of humanity is not a commentary on the lessening of the white race to equality with the lowest rung of humanity; rather, it is a call for all of humanity to rise up to the apex of civilization. In short, this elevation is intimately tied to the advance of white civilization and the use of imperialism as the instrument to spread the spiritual ideal of Anglo-Saxonism.

Besides the direct influence Royce credits Bastian and Frazer for having on his thought, the reality is that there were no progressive sciences that could be called "anti-racist," during his lifetime or the several decades afterward. In other words, there are simply no historical resources to support the current arguments that Royce either embraced or invented an anti-racist idealist anthropology that challenges white supremacy and American imperialism. For example, in Franz Boas's essay "Human Faculty as Determined by Race" (1894)—one of the primary texts that announced the environmentalist stance on race in cultural anthropology at the turn of the century—Boas maintained that the defective ancestry of Blacks, which resulted in smaller brain sizes and cranial cavities, was the cause of their lower intelligence and general inferiority when compared to whites.[87] Mired in what Vernon Williams has called the Boasian paradox, Boas's work was constantly torn between his adamant stance against racial determinism and his reifications of racial inferiority. In sociology, the situation was no different. Spawned by the immense immigration of European peoples to America, the problem of "ethnicity" led sociologists like William I. Thomas and Robert E. Park to embrace the findings of Boas.[88] Unfortunately, this synthesis was not without dangers, as the descriptive findings of Boas's anthropological investigations became prescriptive formulas in the hands of Thomas and Park. Both Thomas and Park were convinced that races had different temperaments and uncritically reified the historical distinction between European logic and Black emotivism. This "romantic racialism," as George Fredrickson calls it, left the idea of white supremacy unfettered, as the Anglo-Saxon maintained his position as a pioneer and frontiersman, while the Black was described as "an artist, loving life for its own sake."[89] The Black's personality was expressive rather than actional, or in Park's words the Negro was "the lady among races."[90]

While many Royceans committed to Royce's seemingly progressive stances will be disturbed by the historical fact that all of the dominant institutions and practices were fundamentally racist, and those whites who questioned them were seldom to be found were fundamentally racist well into the mid-1900s, it is absolutely crucial for our encounter with Royce's work to understand that the contemporary sensibilities of racial equality and multiculturalism simply did not exist in the social, academic, or scientific milieu of these earlier times. Admitting this does bring about a certain clarity, because it forces the Roycean community to recognize that "white racialism, considered as an intellectual and ideological phenomenon, was not a monolithic and unchanging creed . . . , but a fluid pattern of belief, affected in significant and diverse ways by the same social, intellectual, and political currents influencing other basic aspects of American thought and experience,"[91] and that the sharp binaries assumed between racist biological determinists and environmentalists are false. According to George Fredrickson, around the turn of the century, "there was practically a universal agreement on these basic white supremacist propositions: (1) Blacks are physically, intellectually, and temperamentally different than whites, (2) Blacks are also inferior to whites in at least some of the fundamental qualities wherein the races differ, especially in intelligence and in the temperamental basis of enterprise or initiative, (3) Such differences and differentials are either permanent or subject to change only by a very slow process of development or evolution . . ."[92]

While some philosophers would find Frederickson's claim relevant only as a historical comment, it is important to note that such historical commentaries are relevant to how one reads and understands the meanings of authors. It is absolutely necessary in how one determines whether a historical figure is in fact talking about, perpetuating, or addressing racism in his or her own time. The apartheid ideology that runs throughout philosophy as a discipline and selects the content and tools utilized in "how one thinks philosophically" about history (usually excluding those Black, Indigenous, and Asian peoples, among others, their works and concerns) affects the answers offered by philosophers and their undisclosed loyalties to certain ideas. As we will see in Royce's earliest commentary on American racism, there is nothing in his philosophy that challenges these dominate views about Blacks, or aimed to resist the coerced assimilation of foreign races. To the contrary, Royce's theories support Anglo-American imperialism and the forced assimilation of alien races.

The Aberdeen Speech: Royce's Disclosure of Colonial Assimilationism in "Some Characteristic Tendencies of American Civilization"

While there are vast amounts of scholarship that revolve around the contributions of Royce's thought to American philosophy, to date, in the

four years since I announced and have written about Royce's Aberdeen
speech, there has yet to be an exploration of the colonial logic at the
heart of Royce's thinking about America. In a lesser known, indeed,
almost *un*known, work published in 1900, entitled "Some Characteristic
Tendencies of American Civilization," Royce comes clean, so to speak,
about America's indebtedness to British imperialism. Praising the symbiotic
relationship between Britain and America, Royce says "nations as near
to each other, not only in blood, but in their whole spiritual kinship
as are America and Great Britain, can never view each other's fortunes
and issues considerately and justly without learning from each other."[93]
Royce's lecture to the Philosophical Society at Aberdeen College is an
unapologetic testament to his belief that the destiny of America resides
in its burgeoning future within empire. He says at the beginning of his
lecture, "at a moment when the thoughts of serious people in this country
are fixed, not only upon the exciting events of the day, but upon the
future problems and the new responsibilities which, for you and for the
whole British Empire, must grow out of the present situation, I know
of no more appropriate topic upon which I can venture to address this
Philosophical Society than . . . [the] very crisis through which your Empire
is passing."[94] Royce does not proceed to give a talk from the perspective of a disinterested Westerner, rather he argues that the characteristic
tendency of American civilization, its regional organization, what Royce
will later generally identify as America's assimilationism, is a better model
for Britain's empire and could possibly arrest if not completely stave off
the decline of Britain's influence over its colonial lands.

Royce sees the decline and difficulties encountered by the British
Empire as an opportunity to observe and reassess the intertwined destinies
of America and England in doing the work of civilization. Royce in fact
goes to great lengths to articulate why America, including its philosophers,
must dedicate themselves to this emergent decline in empire. He says:

> Our destinies, despite very strong contrasts, are of necessity
> closely akin. Our hopes and interests, despite all that might
> tend to keep us apart, are intimately bound together. A
> moment when either of our two peoples is forced to face a
> serious crisis, to decide a great issue, to pass through grave
> trials, and to look forward to new duties, is a moment when
> we can most profitably learn from each other, and can at the

same time, through mutual and sympathetic observation, attain a clearer consciousness as to the meaning of our own history and of our task as servants of human civilization.[95]

Surprisingly, Royce will also use similar language and the idea of America's kinship to Britain to frame his later essay on "Provincialism" (see chapter 3). Whereas many philosophers and various scholars from new emerging fields were concerned and intrigued by the effects of imperialism on foreign peoples, Royce makes a different argument here that reaches far beyond the aforementioned debates about racial contact. Royce believes there is a biological and spiritual bond between America and Great Britain that makes their shared colonial destiny, their service to human civilization, inextricably bound. Ironically, Royce became somewhat of a prophet, given the joint ventures between Britain and the United States throughout the twentieth century ranging from World War I to the second Gulf War.

This adulation of Britain is not unexpected or surprising at the turn of the century; however, what Royce admires about Britain is not simply her modernization, but rather her imperial conquest of people of color the world over. Royce calls the method by which Britain expands its empire to different lands "direct" colonization, and he likens its spiritual reproduction—the propagation of it constitutionalism, its political ideals, its social order—to the process of budding.[96] This rule of different distant regions is decidedly British and does not describe the colonial tendency of America, who has learned to control alien populations within its own borders. Rather than attacking colonization, Royce views British imperialism as the paternal embrace of her "colonial children."[97] In sharp contrast to the common descriptions of Royce as an anti-imperialist, Royce describes British colonialism through various flirtations as "the government and protection of alien races . . . [is] an essential part of Britain's imperial duty—an art that never had been seriously undertaken,"[98] but one that Britain had made its own. Unfortunately, no masterpiece is created without imperfections, and no success without failure. Royce, recognizing this, assessed that the cost of British colonialism was its inevitable instability, as the various regions under British control still maintained autonomous cultural identities.

Though America had not yet mastered the colonial arts of its imperial parent, Royce believed America's gift of assimilation would allow Britain's colonialism to continue undisturbed. Royce writes:

> While your imperial arts have been largely those of benevolent government of your subject races, our social arts have been far more those of linguistic, political and moral assimilation. This word, *assimilation*, then, names our peculiar and most characteristic tendency. . . . The word applies not only to the assimilation of races, but to the organization into one close-knit nationality of the diverse types and regions of our country.[99]

Royce makes clear to the reader that assimilation means two very specific processes: one that brings races into the fold of the dominant Anglo-Saxon worldview, and the other that describes the organization of the society such that diverse races and communities are nationally tied together. Royce gestures here toward his current thinking about provincialism and its role in furthering the goal of racial assimilation and national stability, which would be published soon thereafter. Alien races are required to adopt the language, political agendas, moral sentiments of the dominant race, but such projects have failed with all groups outside of European stocks. Royce's idea of assimilation is asymmetrical; it simply does not allow for the contributions of alien races to fundamentally change the character and community they assimilate into. This is why assimilation contributes to the imperial cause—it divests the weaker race of the cultural practice and language that could disrupt the community and risk instability.

By describing assimilation as a social art, Royce elevated assimilation beyond a process of Americanization to an ideal in itself; this ideal, we will see, does much work for him as he describes the difference between sectionalism and wise provincialism, but it also gives the notion actual force when enacted in American society. Assimilationism was a way for whites to remain themselves and retain their pride in Anglo-Saxon (or at least European) heritage, while bringing the "foreigners to our own type of customs."[100] It is not only the process of bringing foreigners into a local community or region, but also the organization of a region to deal with this plurality. In fact, it is this ideal that motivates civilization for Royce, and more specifically the American national consciousness. For Royce, America's national consciousness has and always will have an English stamp. It is reflective of America as a white republic expressing the imperial aspirations of Britain. To successfully maintain this trajectory, America must extinguish cultural difference while maintaining its Anglo-Saxon character. Said differently, America must limit the reach of those who maintain their foreignness because it conflicts with the national (imperial) endeavor. This propensity is explained by Royce in his childhood memories of how *his community* dealt with the various racial and ethnic groups California. He says:

> . . . in general, even in a community composed, as my own native town was, of the most various nationalities, there was present the same tendency to an assimilation from the very outset. The foreigners determined no important part of our life. We, in turn, were moulding to our own ways their life. Our real interests lay in the country as a whole, in the exciting fortunes of the Civil War, in the history of our glorious past as represented by Washington. They, the foreigners, had no such interests and ideals to hold them together. In the end their systems of ideas must yield to ours,—and did so. Thus, as you see, we who were Americans early learned the necessity of tolerating that we might assimilate, while the foreigners, from the first, tended to accept the situation and to become assimilated.[101]

The *moulding* of foreigners to the ideals of white American communities is absolutely crucial to Royce's thought. It was imprinted onto his viewing of various racial and ethnic people since his childhood. The foreigner is not a person or self of reciprocal worth for Royce. Foreigners are a problem, until they become assimilated and, as such, their lives, cultures, symbols, histories, and the languages that define or rather demarcate their racial/ethnic difference must be made to disappear into the past. This interaction is unidirectional in the sense that the foreigner makes no imprint upon the life and culture of the dominant white racial group. What California shows, says Royce, is that "Anglo-Saxon civilization establishes itself,"[102] and that distinct racial and cultural groups like Native Americans, Chinese, or Negroes that "[give] us still our most pressing social problem"[103] will continue to remain foreigners—outside our communities and in need of repression. As unassimilable strangers, these races exist outside the Anglo-Saxon trajectory and inevitably become victims of the larger colonial ideal. The foreigners, or in this case the Chinese, had no cultural or historical standing next to the American ideal; rather, they are crushed and culturally destroyed by it. California is not the land of diversity and democracy, the typical world of diversity that many Americans romanticize when we think of the West; more accurately, it was one of the earliest experiments of America's domestic colonization, where Americans tolerated the differences of foreigners, but only so that the foreigners would grow to accept the American ways of life and give in to the call of assimilation.

I want to be clear: this interpretation is not to suggest that nationalism, or some narrow idea of the nation, is driving Royce's philosophy. Royce is pursuing this line of thinking based on ethnological accounts of race, specifically, the racial instincts he believes belong to the Anglo-Saxon. He is emphasizing a ground up approach to empire so to speak. The American nation or empire was an abstraction filled in substantively by the temperament and character of the local, the communities Royce attends to so carefully. Royce is dedicated to the development of local consciousness in communities that align with the imperial instincts of the Anglo-Saxon, not the idea of the nation or empire in and of itself. This is why Royce begins with the characteristic tendencies of America's communities—how they deal with the foreigner—as an example of how the nation can remain stable. Unlike the British, whose empire fell apart because the colonies, the communities of the conquered nation, were allowed to maintain their cultures, traditions, and ethnic practices, Royce suggests that America's empire will succeed by the extent to which immigrant peoples and alien races are divested of their own practices. The Pax Britannica fell because its colonies remained to culturally diverse and fractured. Royce sees the communities' ability to assimilate foreigners, specifically their ability to taken in, and deculturalize the alien, as the basis of stability and national flourishing. Royce is proposing a notion of empire that is reflective of the tendency—the cultural/provincial work—demonstrated by the American communities that come to compose the national.

Royce theorizes communities as wombs of white (Anglo) national consciousness. These local communities are beautiful and decorated with symbols that are meant to lure foreigners to the ideas of America. Like his warning to Southerners who boasted of their racial superiority to the Negro, Royce expects that local communities should be peaceful and inviting. They are to pull alien races into the places where irritations are kept to a minimum. Blacks and foreigners however represent threats to this harmony. Following Bastian, Royce understands that communities are to persuade the alien races toward Americanism. Remember, assimilation for Royce is not only about the pulling of foreigners into American culture, but also the organization of American communities into a closely knit nationality. Foreigners are not allowed to form the rules of these communities; they must yield to Anglo-Americans' ideals. In fact, provincial community itself is an ideal. As Royce himself writes, "our province, like our own individuality, ought to be to all of us rather an ideal than a mere boast."[104] Because these communities are an *ought*, "rather than as something that is already in our hands,"[105] there is an aspirational nature to the question of what communities aim to become. The community must aim to improve itself—it must strive toward the ideal that grounds its material existence temporally. The communities Royce describes are self-conscious—aware of themselves. They are not amalgamations striving to find meaning. Royce suggests that racial and national lines circumscribe this orientation, so it is necessary for these local communities to formulate pride, and loyalties that center the ideals of the occupant over those of the visitor. After all, these are the ideals that that foreigner must assimilate into to be part of the already existing province.

Royce offers no other competing account of how he sees racial and ethnic peoples or racial and ethnic difference generally. His texts mirror the imperial sentiment of his day without exception, despite the ongoing attempts by philosophers to free him of the meanings and associations of imperialism by rewriting history and changing the meanings of the words in his texts. Assimilation was the name he gave to his interaction with these nonwhite peoples in California and it remains the guiding practical concern of his mature philosophical reflections. Royce offers assimilation as proof of the colonial ideal shared between America and Britain that not only frames American provincialism but is aimed at teaching Britain this new art and ameliorating the ongoing crisis in British colonies. Royce even applies his ideas of assimilation to the British occupation of South Africa, and what would eventually become apartheid. With no hesitation, Royce remarks,

> I am sure that I but express what is in all your hearts when I put in words the wish and the confident hope that when, forty years from now, the wanderer visits the South African battlefields now so stubbornly and painfully contested, he may be able to say, without reserve, that your heroes there offered up their lives for the common cause of humanity, of organized civilization, of fraternal peace, and offered them not in vain—that race hatreds might be made to cease and not be perpetuated, and that your Empire might become, not only the protector of alien subjects, but the assimilator of men of

kindred blood, and the object of a common loyalty, even to
those who now, perhaps, fail to comprehend their true share
in your destiny.[106]

More than simply pointing out Royce's endorsement of what would
become the horrible system of apartheid, this quote shows that Royce
was a careful follower and advocate of Empire. Royce is well aware of
who can be considered a kindred spirit and who will remain a pressing
social problem. Like his proposal for British administration in the South,
there is a reoccurring theme in Royce's work as to how one should
deal with Blacks—the Negro problem. Royce urges Britain to establish
loyalty within the borders of its colonies and assimilate men of kindred
blood. This is an anticipation of the larger role Royce will develop in
his work on provincialism that uses order and loyalty to organize and
maintain national consciousness and allegiance to the ideal. Royce offers
a glimpse of the social systems that emerge under his ethics of loyalty.
In fact, Royce goes so far as to say that it is empire that assimilates men
of kindred blood and establishes loyalty. Royce's social program certainly
follows from his endorsement of Frazer's civilizational logic from *The
Golden Bough*, but it also suggests that the conquest that accompanied
such endeavors, and the "lives of imperial heroes," are memorials and
necessary to further drive the destiny of this colonial power. Both South
Africa and California offer a warning to the alien races who are forced to
assimilate into these local communities dedicated to the larger American
ideal of national unity and the cultivation of loyalty.

The American ideal is not without real, practical, consequences
for Royce's thought. It is dangerous, so dangerous, in fact, that it allows
Royce to conclude that America should take up with Britain the duty
of imperial conquest the world over. Royce sees America's art—their
technique—of assimilation as part of the drive of white supremacy and
useful in the crisis that has now befallen the British Empire. Assimilation—the social organization of the localities as well as the provincialism
that takes culture away from the foreigner—complements the administration of Britain leading to a shared imperial duty of American and British
conquest. Royce continues,

> *In taking up what is now inevitably known, in popular speech,
> as the white man's burden,* [Britain has a] "dear-bought wis-
> dom" . . . but on the other hand, in dealing with our less

alien and more plastic foreign populations, our civilization has indeed developed powers which you have nowhere had occasion, as yet, to display. . . . For our foreigners have not been, on the whole, alien races . . . they have been strangers upon our shores who were to be and who in large measure, already have been assimilated, so that they were not to retain their own civilization but acquire ours. Accordingly, while your Imperial arts have been largely those of a benevolent government of your subject races, our social arts have been far more those of linguistic, political, and moral assimilation.[107] (Emphasis added.)

The assimilationist program is not meant to preserve the culture of the alien race. Royce delineates between the colonial policy of the British, which focuses on government and the social art of assimilation that the Americans have developed. It is important to recognize that Royce sees some mutual benefit to an Anglo-American union—both nations pursuing the white man's burden. The British have not yet learned to assimilate foreign peoples. The lack of such skills means that those ruled could always revolt against the established colonial rule. Rather than simply being the protector of alien races, the British would do well to also learn to assimilate them. Again, this is Royce's attempt to improve upon the methods of colonization, since he recognizes that America needs British administration to some extent and Britain needs assimilation. This is Royce's improvement of the white man's burden as currently conceptualized.

The white man's burden, most famously introduced by Rudyard Kipling's 1899 poem, extended white superiority internationally and was a call for the unification of Europe and America's imperial destinies around whiteness. Calling forth the white man's yearning for domination and imperial conquest toward nations like the Philippines, Cuba, and Puerto Rico, uncharted territories filled with Black, Brown, and Asian bodies for labor and sexual conquest, allowed America to situate itself as the heir to civilization. Kipling urged the white race to "send forth ye best breed, go send your sons to exile" in an effort to ensure the victory of the colonial project.[108] The white man's burden conveyed the racial demands of white superiority and the reward of this racial sacrifice. As literary theorist Patrick Brantlinger writes, Kipling "clearly believed that the white race was charged with the responsibility of civilizing—or trying to civilize—all of the dark, supposedly backward races of the world."[109]

In 1898, Kipling wrote to George Cram Cook, a professor of English literature at the University of Iowa, a letter explaining what the white man's burden entailed. Kipling writes:

> For you see, you are on the threshold of your work which, thank God, is the white man's work, the business of introducing a sane and orderly administration into the dark places of the earth that lie to your hand. . . . The enthusiasm of your first conquest will die away: you will find yourselves brought horribly face to face with a vast amount of hard work; you will blunder horribly; you will fail, succeed, fail and succeed again. But in the long run you will come out all right and then you will be a nation indeed.[110]

English theorist Gretchen Murphy considers another question in her book *Shadowing the white Man's Burden: U.S. Imperialism and the Problem of the Color Line*, namely, what is the fate of the colonized? Kipling's letter to Cook "only promises that 'you will come out all right' in the end, a qualification that leaves unspecified the destiny of the colonized. . . . The poem is quite pessimistic about getting the colonized to embrace civilization."[111] Kipling's poem urges whites to take up their burden despite the blame and hate they will garner from those they colonize. Kipling writes: "Take up the White Man's burden—And reap his old reward: The blame of those ye better, The hate of those ye guard."[112] The white man's burden does not result in the presumed multicultural exchange many philosophers have asserted to be the case.[113] It is an imposition of the will of white (civilized) nations upon dark (uncivilized) peoples. Kipling was unapologetically calling for the conquest of racialized peoples.

Royce admits that assimilation is not always successful and as such requires the force of (British) administration. The white man's burden described by Kipling parallels both Royce's description of the aforementioned art of assimilation as peculiar to America's absorption of alien races within America's borders and the need to use administration to deal with the lingering problems of the unassimilable races (the problems) like the Negro. Is it coincidental then that we see Royce appealing to administration to civilize the Negro in the South after designating the Black race a lingering social problem? It seems far too coincidental that the same terminology and ideas are shared by Royce and Kipling as Royce lays claim to America's participating alongside Britain in the imperial race known as the white man's burden.

Conclusion: Thoughts on the Colonial Policy of Royce and Mistaking Turn-of-the-Century Racism for Twenty-First Century Anti-Racism

Because the recent adulation of Josiah Royce's theories of race demand that philosophers and social political thinkers alike uphold the ideological perspectives that defend and further Royce's usefulness on the American race problem, the various historical debates that have pointed out Royce's failure adequately to grasp racism in America and abroad have been ignored or dismissed as insufficient impediments to Royce's rediscovery in American philosophy. These international colonial pursuits are of central importance to how one both defines and defends Royce's conceptualization of the perils in his 1906 essay "Race Questions and Prejudices," and his theorization of provincialism. Royce has articulated a vision of his practical philosophy that only sees and deals with races as subjects of colonial power. Empire is in the background of his social program of assimilation and will be the driving force in his engagement with races. Races are represented to the white world as a consequence of the contact caused by the imperial endeavors of America and Britain (and other European powers) throughout the world. They were discoveries in a very real sense and classified as such in both popular and academic discourse.

In an effort to rescue Royce, some contemporary scholars have attempted to change the meanings of these terms while completely ignoring the actual meanings of others. To maintain the narrative, some Royce scholars have gone as far as to suggest that assimilation in its original formulation at the dawn of the twentieth century was really a multicultural process that aimed to respect the heritage of races still thought to be savage and uncivilized. For example, Jacquelyn Kegley has argued that "Royce's emphasis on assimilation again is about building community and about linking people to common American ideals, but it does not suggest that one has to reject the customs and mores of one's inheritance. It does not necessarily equate to racism."[114] Following the analysis of Scott Pratt, Kegley continues, "I see this in the context of Royce's own California experience and how in this new place people were able to form a provincial consciousness."[115] As previously shown, Royce understood Californians as conquerors of the land and peoples of the West. He admits to not honoring the rights and humanity of foreigners, regretfully, but argues that the perfection of the techniques of provincialism and the demonstration of their national traits (assimilation) far outweigh their offenses against foreign peoples. Kegley's interpretation has consistently avoided the specific passages and historical references in Royce's work to maintain that Royce is not involved either with racism or imperialism, despite Royce actually suggesting his broad support for programs that further the collaboration with Britain in the white man's burden and the colonial administration of Blacks in the South.

If Kegley does not believe that assimilation in America necessarily leads to racism, why is she not readily moved to provide the examples of such practices in America? Where are the examples of dominant white groups welcoming cultural and racial diversity into their local communities in the late nineteenth century, changing who they are by consequence? It would be of great interest to historians and sociologists alike to unearth evidence of a late-nineteenth-century theory of multiculturalism by an American thinker like Royce. The reality however is that Royce was simply not interested in building communities with darker races. He was interested in assuring that the Anglo-Saxon ideal of civilization persisted and was active in the local communities throughout America. If Kegley is correct, it would be astounding how much Royce intuitively grasped beyond the racialist sciences of his day. While Black scholars were adamantly debating against white theorists who maintained that they were inferior to whites well into the twentieth century, Kegley's version of Royce had already surpassed them and figured out as early as 1886 from his history of California that nonwhite (European) populations could not only learn from whites but maintain their own cultures while doing so as equals. If such a contention is true, it would mean that Royce had discovered multiculturalism almost a full century before commonly thought. Kegley simply asserts (with no textual evidence or historical contextualization) that Royce had developed a system of assimilation that did not require subjugated alien races to take on the ideas of the dominant race. Royce's emphasis on assimilation is about building communities by having foreigners accept the rules of white Americans, ensuring white Americans take on none of the foreigners. Assimilation as explained by Royce and formulated by Adolf Bastian is soft colonization. Kegley simply cannot claim that there are nonracist forms of assimilation in the late nineteenth century without doing the historical and philosophical work to explain how Royce's thinking differs from the orientations toward non-European peoples being explored within his own time.

What happens to unassimilable races, or those races outside of European stock who resist complete assimilation within the nation? How does Royce suggest we deal with races who do not conform to the American ideal? As we will see in chapter 2, Royce proposed British administration in the American South as a solution to the Negro problem. He urges Southern leaders to import the strategy that Britain employed in Jamaica to control Blacks in the Southern United States and protect white womanhood, even if it meant recreating Jamaica's apartheid regime upon America's soil.

Race Questions and the Black Problem

Royce's Call for British Administration as a Solution to the Black Peril

No colony can be made by a theory of Imperialism, it can only be made by people who want to colonize and are capable of maintaining themselves as colonists.

—Sir Sydney Olivier

Continuing the themes established in his 1900 essay, Royce's 1906 work entitled "Race Questions and Prejudices" emphasized the growing importance of race theory's applicability to the actual contact between races. In a tone quite different from the social consciousness usually attributed to Royce's work, Royce confesses that he tackles the race question because immigration and imperialism have increased the white man's contact with alien races to such an extent that they are of practical concern, or as Royce himself says, "such increased importance of race questions and prejudices, if it comes to pass, will be due not to any change in human nature, and especially not to any increase in the diversity or in the contrasting traits of the races of men themselves, but simply to the greater extent and complexity of the work of civilization."[1]

Contrary to the popular conceptualization of Royce seeking to challenge the racial science of the day, Royce aims to reflect on the emerging racial contact between European nations and alien races caused by imperialism. It is this direct contact with non-European peoples that places the race problem at the forefront of his mind. Royce writes: "Physically speaking, great masses of men are to-day brought into more frequent and closer contact than was formerly possible, because of the ease with

81

which at present the numerous means of communication can be used, because of the increase of peaceful migrations, and because of the *imperial ambitions* of several of the world's great peoples."[2] The race question is of central concern to Royce because the imperial ventures of the white races have made necessary their further understanding of race psychology. Royce believes these racial contacts demand a certain practicality in the work for civilization, since "we find to-day more ways and places in which men find themselves in the presence of alien races, with whom they have to learn to live in the same social order."[3] Royce is trying to figure out how the "great" races maintain a social order alongside alien peoples, which will remain conducive to the imperial goals of the West.

Royce's reflections on race contact are based on his accounts of the imperial conquests and events of his day. He is reflecting upon: the East Indian coolies laboring side by side with Negroes, the white men in the British West Indies dealing with the Negro population, South African conflicts with Zulus and Kaffirs (Kaffir is an Arabic term popularized by the English as a derogatory racist slur, equivalent to the word Nigger, used to refer to various African nations; it was not utilized by the Xhosa or other groups to describe themselves),[4] and the Russo-Japanese War. Reflecting upon the conflicts the white race is having all over the world in their contact with different races frames how Royce thinks about race and racism in the United States. Royce is very explicit about his approach toward the study of race. He writes:

> and when, with a few only of such typical instances in mind, we turn back to our own country, and think how many different race-problems confront us, we then see that the earliest social problem of humanity is also the most recent problem. This is the problem of dealing with the men who seem to us somehow very widely different from ourselves, in physical constitution, in temperament, in all their deeper nature, so that we are tempted to think of them as natural strangers to our souls, while nevertheless we find that they are stubbornly there in our world, and that they are men as much determined to live as we are, and are men who, in turn, find us as incomprehensible as we find them.[5]

Looking at this picture of the world, the contact whites have with Black and Yellow peoples raises questions and some concern as to the future of the imperial endeavor endorsed by multiple European nations. In this contact, Royce asks which races are the superior ones and which are the inferior ones? "What race or races ought to rule? What ones ought to yield to their natural masters? To which one of these races has God, or nature, or destiny, ordained the rightful and final sovereignty of the earth? Which of these types of men is really the human type?"[6] These questions do not arise from a moral curiosity or from some protest against the racial order of the day. These questions are formulated from the vantage point of empire. Royce asks race questions intimately bound with his romance with Anglo-Saxon civilization, and his answers to those questions necessarily debase those cultural/ancestral identities that fail to live up to the ideal of "American civilization," as he envisioned it in his lecture of 1900. This makes racial and cultural groups like the Chinese, Indigenous peoples, or Blacks remain outsiders and foreigners in America. Royce frames these aforementioned queries about race contact with a simple question: "Are races by their presence and their rivalry, essentially perilous to one another's interests? And if so, what one amongst them is there whose spread, or whose increase in power or in number is most perilous to the true cause of civilization?"[7] Here we arrive at the concern driving Royce's engagement with anthropology, sociology, and philosophy, and it is in this vein—the continuing preservation of Anglo-Saxon civilization—that Royce asks further "is it a 'yellow peril,' a 'black peril,' or perhaps, after all is it not rather some form of 'white peril' which most threatens the future humanity in this day of great struggles and of complex issues."[8]

This chapter is a historicization of Royce's seemingly progressive stance on race at the turn of the century. I begin with a discussion of the perils. I aim to clarify what is actually described by William Garrott Brown's idea of white peril and how Brown conceptualizes the racial tensions between Blacks and whites as the effect of the exodus and immigration of racial groups in the United States. I then turn to the Yellow peril, specifically analyzing Royce's statements on Japan. I analyze his views as part of the general reaction whites had during the early 1900s to Russia's defeat by the Japanese, and I show that Royce's attitude was in fact a popular disposition that signaled the inevitable shift of race science away from biological determinism toward more environmentalist explanations, as I described in detail in the last chapter. I then engage what I take to be the misinterpretation of Royce's actual position on Black Americans in the South. More importantly, I argue that contemporary Royce scholars have continued to revise Royce's disposition toward Blacks, to deemphasize Royce's commitments to anti-Blackness and his endorsement of using of British strategies of colonial policy in the American South to address the myth of the Black rapist, or what was referred to as the Black peril. Ultimately, I conclude that Royce's reflections on American race relations were firmly rooted in a colonial and assimilationist logic that ultimately sought the cultural destruction of African and other nonwhite peoples.

The white Peril: Understanding Racial Conflicts Expressed by the Term

Contrary to the arguments raised in Jacquelyn Kegley's "Josiah Royce on Race: Issues in Context" (2009)[9] and Shannon Sullivan's "Whiteness as Wise Provincialism: Royce and the Rehabilitation of a Racial Category" (2008), Royce's questions are not meant as critical interventions against white imperialism. He aims to look at race questions "fairly and humanely,"[10] but his perception of what is fair and humane differs a great deal from the assertions of racial equality or the problematizations of "whiteness" that many scholars credit Royce for in their current writings. By attending to the moral and political threats of the white peril, Royce is in fact framing this essay around race problems as they currently exist in "our own country,"[11] not the critical possibilities of whiteness being problematic as an oppressive historical category in itself. In fact, the very structure of Royce's essay supports this interpretation of his text, as he, respectively, deals with the yellow peril (the economic and military rise of Japan as an Asian power), the Black peril (the assumed danger of Negroes to whites, especially in regard to the rape of white women), and the white peril—a term popularized in the early 1900s by Harvard professor William Garrott Brown—that spoke to the impending moral and political degradation of Southern whites who increasingly turned to violence and lynching to address their economic competition with Blacks.[12]

Recently, Shannon Sullivan replied to my use of William G. Brown and the historical understanding of "the white peril" in an essay entitled "Transforming [w]hiteness with Roycean Loyalty."[13] In that article, Sullivan argues that William Garrott Brown's definition of "white peril" is not the definition understood by Royce himself. In fact, Sullivan goes on to argue:

On his part, Royce briefly discusses lynching in his essay, but nowhere does he mention race-based patterns in industrial employment or the moral damage to white people that white suppression of black labor might produce. In short, I don't see any evidence in these two essays that Royce interpreted white peril as white people suffering from rather than producing peril for other races.[14]

Sullivan then concludes that since my previous work is probably correct and Royce was an *anti-Black racist*, he probably did not read the work of William Garrott Brown (whom she mistakenly assumes is Black), because Royce did not read or engage Black authors.[15] I am sure the reader can appreciate the irony here that suggests Royce is too racist to be familiar with the racism analyzed by Black authors in his own lifetime. To be clear: the argument presented by Sullivan concedes that Josiah Royce is in fact an anti-Black racist that would not read Black thinkers or have his thinking influenced by Blacks during his lifetime, while simultaneously arguing his thought is useful today for Black people because he was among the first American philosophers to speak to and understand the problem of race. Despite Royce's reticence toward Black thinkers and their work, there is a praise bestowed on Royce's writings on race that is said to parallel the perspectives of the Black thinkers in his own time. Sullivan explains that "it seems unlikely that Royce was reading African American thinkers, such as Brown, and thus more likely that his use of white peril echoed by Lynch, who is white."[16] Sullivan is specifically referring to George Lynch's "The [w]hite Peril" published in *The Nineteenth Century and Beyond: A Monthly Review* in 1905.[17]

There are a few very serious issues with Sullivan's framing of what the "white peril" is and how it is being deployed in her work. First, Sullivan is factually incorrect in her assertion that William Garrott Brown was Black. There was a William G. Brown who was the first Black superintendent of Louisiana during Reconstruction. He was born August 12, 1832, and died May 14, 1883.[18] So I am quite secure in saying that it is unlikely that William G. Brown was publishing anything in 1904. William Garrott Brown (1868–1913), however, was at Harvard as early as 1894 with Josiah Royce and both *Harvard Graduates' Magazine* and *The Quinquennial Catalogue of the Officers and Graduates of Harvard 1636–1910* list Josiah Royce as an assistant professor from 1885 to 1892 and a lecturer thereafter.[19] The same catalogue lists William Garrott Brown as an assistant in the library at Harvard from 1893 to 1896, when he was thereafter promoted to the deputy keeper of university records in 1896 until 1901. In 1901 he became a lecturer.[20]

In fact, a review of Brown's article, "The [w]hite Peril: The Immediate Danger of the Negro" (1904), that appeared in *The American Monthly Review of Reviews* in 1905 has a lovely picture of Mr. William Garrott Brown who is undoubtedly white.[21]

Second, Sullivan misunderstands the scope of concerns considered by the term *white peril*. William Garrott Brown's "The [w]hite Peril: The Immediate Danger of the Negro" is not simply about labor conflicts between racial groups; it speaks to the economic consequences of racial contact between Blacks and whites. Brown's article more so concerns the problem of proximity and proportion to Black bodies in cities that he observes in his travels from Virginia to Texas. With the more open economic opportunities available to Blacks in Southern cities, these localities present a ripe area of study and theorization as to the race problem. These realities are merely instigated by class dynamics. Brown, reflection upon his observations of the South, writes "I was convinced that a very important and a very deep change, a change in the basis of the entire industrial system of the South, is quietly in progress."[22] Brown understands much of the ongoing awareness of racial tensions in the United States was ignited from the movements of populations. He explains: "Two movements of population are, perhaps, the most important: an exodus and an immigration. There is a steady and widespread movement of [N]egroes from the countrysides into the towns, and out of the State into the North; and there is a moderate but fairly steady, and apparently increasing, inflow of whites."[23] The inflow of whites is not only from movement of various white populations in the United States but also, says Brown, a consequence of immigration, since "some portion of our immense immigration from Europe is at last being diverted, be it only in driblets and wavelets, from the great Eastern cities and the growing States of the West and Northwest to the oldest of all the Southern States."[24]

Even in cities where there has not been a decrease of Blacks, the economic shifts post-Reconstruction are seeing "more white men are turning to kinds of work which used to be done by [N]egroes only."[25] The growing white male workforce displaced Black male workers in industry. Stereotypes concerning the unfitness of the Black male laborer and his inability to perform as well as an increasingly skilled white male workforce in mills confined many Black men to poverty and unemployment in an already rigid racist regime. The industrialization of the South and the increase of poor whites in areas traditionally occupied by Black workers worsened the racial dynamics these areas. Brown observed,

> the rapid emergence of the native poor whites, the South's great unutilized industrial reserves, from the narrow limitations which slavery set them, and which nearly three hundred years of ignorance, inertia, and prejudice had strengthened into a Chinese wall of hopeless conservatism. They have come at once into competition with the [N]egroes, either direct, and on fairly equal terms, as in the tobacco factories, or indirect, and far more fatal to the Negroes, as in the cotton-mills. What at present appears is that they no sooner entered into this great industry than the [N]egroes were excluded from it altogether. The victory is signal. The effect of the exclusion on the [N]egro's future can scarcely be overestimated. But this is only one of many advantages which in the townward movement, strong in both races, the poor white is winning in the search for town employments.[26]

This meant that Blacks (specifically, Black male laborers, since domestic employment was not threatened by the shift as severely) who traditionally occupied certain occupations were not only being displaced, but confined to the lower rungs of Southern society. This confinement was not only enforced by distinctions between the employed and unemployed, it was also supported by violence.

> The [N]egroes have never ventured into any serious rivalry with the white unions. They do, it is true, form unions among themselves, which are, as it is said, "affiliated" with those of the whites. But what this means in practice is that both unions are controlled by white men. Even when the whites in a particular trade or a particular establishment are only a minority, they have their way. [N]egroes rarely or never offer to take the place of white men who strike or are locked out. The explanation doubtless is that, with good reason, they fear white men of the working class worse than they fear employers and capitalists, who frequently belong to the class

so often described as the natural protectors of the blacks. It seems to be a fact that white workingmen from the North are more bitterly opposed to sharing any occupation with [N]egroes than the native whites are. However, the situation in the Southwest may indicate that when the whites have sufficient numbers to monopolize the city trades they will incline to exclude [N]egroes altogether.[27]

Immigration of whites from the North and from Europe worsened the race problem in the South. These individuals coalesced against Black workers to preserve the racial order of the Southern states and made segregation not merely a spatial arrangement, but also part of the economic order of industry. In short, the industrial modernization of the American South had the effect of increasing the social mobility and class position of whites—enhancing white freedom—while increasing white control over Black labor. The supposed freedom from slavery that many philosophers believe to be ushered in by the twentieth century was merely a reconstitution of Black serfdom by allowing poor whites to coerce Black labor classes into submission and agrarian dependency given their exclusion from industry. As Brown writes, "The white man whom the [N]egro has to fear is no longer the man who would force him to work. It is the man who would take his work away from him. The danger, the immediate menace, is from rivalry rather than oppression."[28]

Not to be mistaken as overly sympathetic to the plight of the Negro, Brown suggests that this seemingly disadvantageous exclusion of the Negro from society and politics produced by Southern economic arrangements has the unintended benefit of creating a permanent labor class. "There is sense in saying that to exclude the [N]egro from politics was a good way to get him to work. He, like other human beings, probably works at times for the mere reason that there is nothing else in particular to do. It is also quite probably true that in his present stage he works best, as he fights best, under the eyes of those he looks to as superiors."[29] There is no point however for the Negro to dwell on these handicaps, as they will not change. He is placed in an inferior social position and caste as a laborer; he must learn to accept this inferior status and simply work more—work harder—to win the competition with poor whites.[30] However, this is to admit, says Brown of the reality of America, he is not really meant to overcome the racial barriers erected by the dominance of whites in the South. "The misery of all our debating about him is that we cannot honestly pretend to be glad that he is here, or to desire that his seed shall increase,"[31] says Brown. The only way to address his inferior station is through "money in his purse"; the ballot, constitutional amendments, congressional legislation, are for naut.[32]

As shown by Brown, racial peril was framed as the movement of populations, be it exodus or immigration, and the contact these races had with each other that resulted from these dynamics. Similarly, Royce addresses perils in these terms in the beginning of "Race Questions and Prejudices." Showing his consistency with my interpretation of the times and his work, Royce explains that race contact with alien races is due to migration and the imperial ambitions of the world's great (i.e., white) peoples. This is to say that there are various aspects of these imperial ambitions; some are rooted in foreign colonization like that of South Africa, and others are domestic like that of the American South. The white peril, like the Black peril or Yellow peril, describes the various problems that arise from these types of race contact. Sullivan is again historically incorrect in arguing that the white peril had different meanings. In reality, the white peril, the Black peril, and the Yellow peril are terms of the day used to express various political, economic, and social problems that arise between whites and other races. Roderick Jones's "The Black Peril in South Africa," which was written in 1904, makes this very point and shows that white thinkers are focused on various aspects of race contact in different lands. Jones observes:

> The process of evolution has begun. When it is completed, the relative position of the black and white populations in South Africa will be—what? Look to the United States and you shall find some hint of the answer. There the two races are at each other's throat. The Negro has become a power in the land, socially, politically, and economically, and his power is a constant source of embarrassment and irritation to the white. Yet half a century ago the American Negro was bound hand and foot in the fetters of slavery, and plunged in ignorance as dense as that of the most benighted Kafir. Who shall say that the Kafir half a century hence will not exercise a similar power, socially, politically, and economically, if not a greater, in South Africa? Personally I have no doubts whatever on the subject. The impulse which came to the Negroes of North America with the Civil War, to strive

after something beyond that to which they had been born, has now come to the South African Negro, less obtrusively perhaps, but no less decisively.[33]

This is why Royce was specific in speaking about South Africa and the presence of Kaffirs in the opening paragraphs of "Race Questions and Prejudices." He, unlike the philosophers of today, understood the role that history and race played in setting the boundaries and challenges of race contact and social organization. Economic conflict, racial instincts, and racial coexistence (or races sharing the same space) were of primary concerns to Americans at the dawn of the twentieth century. For example, the Black Peril also referred to the rape of white women by Black men that colonialists feared was the inevitable consequence of Black/white race contact. The moral panic created around the white woman was used to justify the killing of Black South Africans much like the myth of the Black rapist was used for lynching in America.[34] Royce was observing race contact with imperial forces around the world and thinking about the problems that arose in all these contexts.

Finally, Sullivan misunderstands George Lynch's "The [w]hite Peril," which asks for Westerners to think of the past and present moment after the Russo-Japanese War from the perspective of the Orient. Lynch concludes that the white peril created the Yellow peril.[35] In the summary review of George Lynch's "The [w]hite Peril" written in the *Review of Reviews* the authors claim that Lynch argues that the white peril is passing away in Asia.[36] A similar case is made by Sidney Lewis Gulick's *The [w]hite Peril in the Far East: An Interpretation of the Significance of the Russo-Japanese War*, where he argues in a chapter entitled "Yellow Peril vs. [w]hite Peril" that the white man's presence in Asia is the cause of the racial conflicts between and the political repression of Japanese and Chinese peoples.[37] While the Lynch article is specific to China and Japan, Sullivan is now asking the reader to believe that the white peril solely refers to US-Sino-Japanese relations; yet, when confronted with the far-ranging implications of the white peril as it relates to the American South and Royce's unfavorable statements toward Blacks, she wants the reader to isolate the term to white imperialism and domination so that it gives the appearance that Royce was questioning white supremacy. Sullivan is trying to manipulate the term to fit her own narrative despite the overwhelming historical evidence that shows the white peril to be intimately connected to the Black and Yellow perils and involved with the contact of whites with other races the world over, even in the American South. Remember, Sullivan published several pieces on Royce without ever mentioning the Russo-Japanese War's impact on the science of white supremacy, or her now-current theory of the white peril referring to American imperialism. It is only after my research and challenge that she now claims Royce is trying to question America's imperial ambitions.[38] This recent shift actually contradicts her previous writings, which argued in favor of viewing Royce as naïve of the global reach of white supremacy. In her introduction to *Race Questions, Provincialism and Other American Problems*, entitled "Royce's 'Race Questions and Prejudices,'" Sullivan argues that Royce's "obliviousness to the racist domination of imperialist colonialism also can be instructive by alerting us to the dangerous deceptiveness of 'peaceful violence,' many forms of which exist today."[39] How can Sullivan maintain both claims simultaneously? How is it that Royce is both "oblivious to the racist domination of imperialist colonialism" and challenging white imperialism against the East as understood by George Lynch's definition of the white peril? This is a complete shift in her previous stance in an effort to defend her narrative of Royce rather than a robust historical understanding of the debates and texts involved. In short, there is simply no evidence that supports the standard interpretation, namely, that Royce aimed or aims to challenge white imperialism and the concomitant rise of whiteness amid it. Quite to the contrary, we will see that his imperial sensibilities drive both his newly found appreciation of the Japanese as well as his admiration for colonial administration in Jamaica. For Royce, maintaining America's imperial legacy, its national projection, should be the foremost concern of true Americans.

The Yellow Peril: How Japan Dealt with the white Peril of the West

Despite Royce's admission of what the "recent war between Japan and Russia has already meant for the future races of men in the far East,"[40] he takes great care to make sure the reader understands that he is in no way sympathetic to the argument raised by some tender souls that "it is they [the Japanese] who are our racial superiors."[41] Royce's announcement that he is "no worshipper of any new fancy or distant civilization, merely because of its temporary prominence,"[42] is purposely directed against the myth that the recent emergence of an Eastern power refutes the legacy of Western domination. Whereas Black thinkers (as I will detail later) saw the defeat of Russia as the end of Anglo-Saxon domination, Royce's reaction was much more tempered. For Royce, "the recent war has shown us what Japan meant by imitating our Western ways, and also what ancestral ideals have led her sons to death in battle, and still hold the nation so closely knit to their Emperor."[43] Thus, what Royce learned to admire in the Japanese was not novel at all, since he (along with many white intellectuals) saw in Japan the ideal of progress and civilization that up to that point was exclusive to the (white) West.

As a simple matter of historical fact, the Yellow peril referred to the anxieties the West had with the growing economic and military presence and power of Japan and China. In the 1880s with the rise of Chinese immigration to the United States and the growing influence of China in the East, American novelists and journalists lent to an ever-expanding paranoia of an Asian imperial power.[44] By 1882, however, with the increasing demonstration of Japanese military power and the influx of Japanese immigrants into America, Japan became the icon of the horror increasingly known as the Yellow peril.[45] From the mid-1880s to the turn of the century, most of the Japanese immigrants were males.[46] Like Black men, Asian men were referred to as boys, and Asians generally were derogatorily described as yellow monkeys, yellowbellies, and yellow bastards.[47] The Yellow peril was not solely isolated to the fears Western powers had of Japan's military might or white American's racism toward Asians. Like the Black peril, it was associated with a hypersexualization of Asian men and their lust for white women. As literary scholar Gina Marchetti argues, "Within the context of America's consistently ambivalent attitudes toward Native Americans, Hispanics, African Americans, and other peoples of color, the yellow peril has contributed to the notion that all nonwhite people are by nature physically and intellectually inferior, morally suspect, heathen, licentious, disease-ridden, feral, violent, uncivilized, infantile, and in need of the guidance of white, Anglo-Saxon Protestants."[48] Similar to the stereotypes surrounding Blackness, "one of the most potent aspects of these yellow peril discourses is the sexual danger of contact between the races. Although the power of the lascivious Asian woman to seduce the white male has long been part of this fantasy, a far more common scenario involves the threat posed by the Asian male to white women."[49] These paranoias concerning Japanese immigrants was especially acute in California and of central concern to many intellectuals writing on the Yellow peril at the turn of the century.[50]

Japan's victory over Russia in 1905 marked a transformation in the presumed character of the Japanese people recognized the world over. Intellectuals on both sides of the Pacific now dedicated great time and effort to understand the Japanese race and its emerging imperial program. Sidney L. Gulick, a noted professor of Japanese culture and the [w]hite peril, argued in *The American Japanese Problem: A Study of the Race Relations of the East and the West* that "Japan's amazing victory over Russia has raised doubts among white nations. The despised Asiatic, armed and drilled with Western weapons, is a power that must be reckoned with. In the not distant future Asia, armed, drilled, and united, will surpass in power, they aver, any single white people, and it is accordingly a peril to the rest of the world."[51] The defeat of Russia signaled a break in the white supremacist mythology of the West. Until Japan defeated Russia, explains Gulick, the West's "world-wide conquest has gone on without serious check. In 1904, however, for the first time since modern history began has a colored race successfully defended its homeland from white invaders for that was the significance of the Russo-Japanese War."[52] Japan had convincingly shown that the notion of white superiority was little more than a myth. As historian John Dower explains, the "immensely gratifying win over a white power . . . completed Japan's new perception of itself as the genuinely male force in world affairs—opposed to, and intrinsically superior to, not only a female China, but also a feminine United States and Russia."[53] The United States and its unchecked imperial ambitions were no longer assured. Gulick believed Japan's victory was a model for other Asian countries and established a means of resisting the white peril across the continent. "To all Asia she points the way of national independence and the way in which to meet the White Peril, [but] does she also point for Western nations the way in which to meet the Yellow Peril?"[54]

The questions asked by Royce were not so different than the questions being asked by thinkers across the world at the turn of the century. Unlike H. A. Millis's *The Japanese American Problem*, which focused primarily on the influx of Japanese immigrants into the United States and the peculiar anti-Japanese sentiment in California, Gulick's work considers the historical trajectory of race contact(s) globally. According to Gulick, "All past civilizations have been provincial, narrow minded, puffed up with race pride, scornful, able to see but little good outside themselves. Their local character and provincial spirit, however, were inevitable consequences of isolation. They were, nevertheless, necessary steps in human history, as inevitable as the crudity of a boy in his teens."[55] The increased mobility of persons and technology now allowed different races to know and learn of each other's existence. This expansion, the increased contact of races, drove humanity to evolve. As Gulick explains, "new civilization is coming with the New Humanity and the New International Mind. It is to be truly cosmopolitan and correspondingly rich, for it will include and preserve all that is good and true and beautiful in each of the local civilizations."[56] Gulick hoped that the civilizations of the twentieth century would not be as provincial as they were in the past. He believed they could take in the ideas of other groups and become more cosmopolitan as a result. The problem with this vision however was white people, or more accurately the white peril. With the founding of America came the white race's lust for land and profit. "Exploration and conquest went hand in hand. Little bands of armed white men found themselves superior to countless hosts of colored foes,"[57] and whites soon became convinced that "the world and all that is therein were made for their special benefit; that all the peoples and wealth of pagan lands were legitimate objects of plunder and spoliation; that it was their divinely given right to own, rule, and exploit every land and people they discovered."[58] This mindset made race conflicts or perils inevitable and prevented the cosmopolitan vision Gulick had so hoped would triumph over the obstinate fury of white superiority.

Much less hopeful in the possibility of white transformation, the darker races of the world celebrated the Russo-Japanese War as the beginning of a new racial epoch in which the "backward races would no longer be thwarted by the Euro-American imperialists."[59] And while unexpected, Japan's victory "convincingly demonstrated for all the world to see that white hegemony over non-whites was merely situational, not genetic, a matter of strategy and tactics, not race."[60] This undeniable blow to the doctrine of white supremacy gained the attention of both Blacks and whites and urged white thinkers to reformulate race in such a way that the defeat of Russia did not refute Anglo-Saxon superiority. The result was an effort, which could be seen as early as 1910, to describe Japan's modernization as the result of its imitation of Anglo-Saxonism. As is usually the case, Black scholars were at the forefront of this newly emergent "racial draft." Throughout the early 1900s Black scholars like Booker T. Washington, Archibald Grimke, and W. E. B. Du Bois flooded Black newspapers like the *Washington Bee* and the *Colored American*, criticizing whites' attempts to reinvigorate white supremacy by claiming Japan as one of their own.[61] Kelly Miller, for instance, attacking the fickleness of white supremacy argued:

> Fifty years ago you doubtless would have ranked Japan among the benighted nations and hurled at their heathen heads some derogatory query as to their contribution to civilization. But since the happenings at Mukden and Port Arthur and Portsmouth, I suppose that you are ready to change your mind on the subject. Or maybe, since the Jap has proved himself a "first-class fighting man," able to cope on equal terms with the best breeds of Europe, you will claim him as belonging to the white race, notwithstanding his pig eye and yellow pigment.[62]

It is important to understand the hypocrisy of white supremacy exposed by Miller's analysis. The idea of Anglo-Saxon superiority was not simply an a priori racial claim about the white race generally; it was also a claim concerning the superiority of the white male body—the fighting man. When Japan beat Russia, it effectively refuted the racial mythos projected by Europe. The Yellow man proved he was superior and could in fact beat the white man in actual conflict. He was now a fighting man, a racial trait that was supposed to belong only to the white race. Because Europe would never allow for such a reconfiguring of racial hierarchies, or one that would place the Yellow man on equal footing with the white races, Europe began to claim Japan as one of its own—a Yellow race with some traces of Anglo-Saxon blood. Not surprisingly, this contradiction was even noted by Japanese thinkers themselves who sought to set the record straight. As renowned Japanese author Okakura Kakuzo said of the West's arrogance, "the average westerner . . . was wont to regard Japan as barbarous while she indulged in the gentle arts of peace: he calls her civilized since she began to commit wholesale slaughter on Manchurian battlefields."[63] Insofar as both African American and Japanese perspectives recognized the contradiction of affording Japan a cultural status based on their imitation of Western imperialism to build an Eastern imperial power, this lends credence to the claim that Royce's praise of Japan remains intertwined in his 1900 colonial logic.

Words like race, people, and nation had very peculiar and different meanings in the ethnological age. As A. H. Keane explains in *Ethnology*:

> The nation comprises all the inhabitants of a given region
> subject long enough to one political system to have acquired
> a certain outward uniformity, a common standard of social
> usages, interests, aspirations, generally also language, literature
> and religion. But although not involving common origin, it
> tends towards ethnical uniformity or unity, by the gradual
> fusion of diverse elements in a uniform type. Some nations,
> such as the Swedes, have in great measure acquired such
> uniformity, and with them race and nation become practically
> convertible terms.[64]

The nation is thereby an expression of the process by which a people
becomes unified and reflective of the character of the people who occupy
it. This idea is of central importance to Royce's conceptualization of
provincialism and adds some needed clarity to how Royce thought about
the imitative and independent aspects of races. To be an imitative race
is to be without national, and hence racial, uniqueness and dependent
on other races for civilization.

Royce's analysis is similar to this ethnological account generally,
but even more so in his description of Japan in "Provincialism." Royce
explains a "generation ago the Japanese seemed to most European observers to be entering upon a career of total self-surrender. They seemed to
be adopting without stint European customs and ideals. They seemed to
be abandoning their own national independence of spirit. They appeared
to be purely imitative."[65] There was no national resistance to the lessons
of Europe. It was thought that the Japanese were completely defined
by ideals and values of the dominant racial group.[66] After the war with
Russia, however, Europe saw a different Japan. Royce suggests such an
event was a monumental shift in how the world perceived the Japanese.
Royce remarks, "Yet those of us who have watched them since, or who
have become acquainted with representative Japanese students, know how
utterly superficial and illusory that old impression of ours was regarding
the dependence, or the extreme imitativeness, or the helpless docility, of
the modern Japanese."[67] A closer look however showed that the Japanese
were a rather plastic race. They took the gifts of the European but utilized
them within and for the purpose of their own nationality. This plasticity, the gathering of ideas from beyond for a purpose of one's own, is
the mark of provincialism. This is the lesson the Japanese show to the
American provincialist. Royce understood now that the Japanese were

not an imitative race. They did not simply absorb the ideas of other civilized races and lose their national independence. Rather, says Royce,

> we now begin to see that the feature of the Japanese nation-
> ality as a member of the civilized company of nations is to
> be something quite unique and independent. Well, let the
> Japanese give us a lesson in the spirit of true provincialism.
> Provincialism does not mean a lack of plasticity, an unteachable
> spirit; it means a determination to use the spiritual gifts that
> come to us from abroad in our own way and with reference
> to the ideals of our own social order.[68]

Royce is fascinated by Japan because they took in foreign ideas and made them serve toward demonstrating the force of their national inde-pendence. It is important to understand what Royce is celebrating. He admits that Japanese people are a model of wise provincialism, because of their plasticity. The Japanese learned new ideas from the outside, just like he believes America can learn from the British. They can take in new ideas from beyond themselves and use them to enhance their national traits, which is exactly what Royce is arguing should happen between the United States and Britain. It just so happens that America needs to learn from Britain the practice of administration, while Britain needs to learn the art of assimilation. Wise provincialism is the idea that national and local entities can maintain their provincial racial core while develop-ing new ideals by learning new ideas even when they come from abroad to guide the community toward its communal identity and nationally unifying characteristic. Japan simply showed they were a dominant race and could not be assimilated; thus, they have a strong national trait like Americans and the English.

As applied to Japan, the Yellow peril was the racialized fear America had of an Asian menace challenging the imperial destiny of America and flooding American shores with waves of Japanese immigrants to further their conquest of the West. Recently, Jacquelyn Kegley has responded that she "cannot find any evidence in the text that this is such a refer-ence—there is absolutely no discussion of that idea in the passage [that Royce is addressing the rise of an Eastern imperial power]; it concerns rather our 'false images' of the Japanese."[69] Here again Kegley's retort is based more on a selective reading that pieces various unrelated phrases together—the product of her misunderstanding of the terms deployed by Royce and the historical moment in which he writes—than an actual analysis of the problems and perils he concerns himself with in the essay. The false images of the Japanese Royce addresses are concerned with whether or not the Japanese were in fact a warrior race after their victory over Russia. This is why he begins his essay with a mention of Russia's defeat. At the very heart of this question is whether the Japanese are imitative or provincial. Royce himself however is very clear that his analysis of the Japanese in *Race Questions, Provincialism, and Other American Problems* is about his "characterization of their national spirit," especially in essays like "Provincialism."[70] If national ideals unify nations to causes for which the communities of the nation live out and sacrifice their lives, then the Russo-Japanese War would satisfy the same criteria of thinking that Royce offers for the American Civil War, the Boer War, and the imperial aspirations he wishes for the United States. These are wars to unify disparate lands under one ideal. In other words, Royce was clear that he did not believe Japan would or could derail the imperial duty of America and Britain given the strength of Anglo-Saxon ideals; he was nonetheless adamant that they had shown evidence of wise provincialism, because they were not so dependent on Western ideas that they lost their own self-determinacy. As we will see in chapter 3, Royce understands that provincialism allows the nation to take in foreign ideals and use them toward the imperial goal and "good" of the whole. This is what he sees in Japan and why he casts aside the old idea that the Japanese are in fact a dependent and imitative race.

Perils in Black and white: Understanding the Debate between Thomas Nelson Page and Josiah Royce over the Administration of the Negro

Royce always maintained a particular racial aversion to Blacks, or *Niggers* as he called them at least once.[71] At the outset of his section on the "Negro problem," Royce announces that "the Negro has so far shown none of the great power of the Japanese. Let us, then, provisionally admit at this stage of our discussion that the Negro is in his present backward state as a race, for reasons which are not due merely to circumstances, but which are quite innate in his mental constitution."[72] Here again Royce contradicts the anti-racist sentiment many white scholars attribute to his work. Instead of challenging the Southerner's knowledge of Blacks, which served to justify the historical construction of the Black as a criminal and rapist of white women, Royce acquiesces to the Southerner's racist beliefs, claiming that he "speaks with no lack of sympathy for the genuine and bitter trials of our Southern brethren."[73] Quite explicitly, Royce concerns himself with the experience of the white Southerner over and against the brutality toward Blacks at the hands of whites. While Elizabeth Duquette's "Embodying Community, Disembodying Race: Josiah Royce on 'Race Questions and Prejudices' "[74] tries to frame Royce's essay as a project of social revolt against lynching, there is very little in Royce's actual work that supports this contention.[75] Royce is interested in the national character of America, not the safety of Blacks. This is why he advocates efficient colonial administration over lynching as the means to better control Blacks. Royce believes that the social control of Blacks should be efficient rather than violent, a system that allows whites to live out their racial superiority peacefully without having to appeal to mob violence to instill fear in the Negro population. Royce believes the social control of Blacks should be a system that teaches them to learn their places beneath whites and accept their inferiority through an admiration of whites' moral superiority.

Royce's attention to race contact in the South, the Black/white perils, is dedicated to answering one question—"How can the white man and the Negro, once forced, as they are in our South, to live side by side, best learn to live with a minimum of friction, with a maximum of cooperation?"[76] In trying to solve this "race problem," Royce does disagree with the Southern methods of educating the Negro about his proper place (lynching), but in no way does this disagreement change or improve the social status of or refute the dominant thinking about the "Negro" in the South. Royce is concerned with the moral consequences of lynching and the barbarism of the Southern strategy for making Blacks submit to white superiority. In fact, the first thing Royce notices about Jamaica is that there is no race problem, or in other words, "there is no public controversy about social race equality or superiority. Neither a white man nor a white woman feels insecure in moving about freely among the black population anywhere on the island."[77] By defining the race problem as the threat that Blacks pose to whites' freedom of movement within colonized spaces, free of fear, Royce clearly announces his racial allegiance. Just as in the 1900 essay delivered at Aberdeen University, Royce commits himself to the English model of race relations that emphasizes the efficient colonization of the Negro. By modeling the administration and reticence of the English colony, Royce believed that the South would "gain the confidence of Blacks."[78] Because of his segregationist beliefs, Royce would never suggest that Negroes be allowed to occupy civil service positions in which they governed whites, but he does suggest that Negroes be allowed to oversee their own people in limited capacities. Royce reasoned that this system, unlike the threat of lynching, would make the Negro "accustomed to the law; he sees its ministers often . . . as men of his own race; and in the main, he is fond of order, and respectful towards the established ways of society."[79]

Whereas the South maintains a racial pedagogy rooted in the social irritation of racial differences, administration is "truly an English social pedagogy. It works in the direction of making the Negro a conscious helper towards good social order."[80] By socializing the "backward races" to accept the natural authority of whites, Royce contends that the race problem will be eliminated. He says:

> For the Englishman, in his official and governmental dealings with backward peoples, has a great way of being superior without very often publicly saying that he is superior. You well know that in dealing, as an individual, with other individuals, trouble is seldom made by the fact that you are actually the superior of another man in any respect. The trouble comes when you tell the other man, too stridently that you are his superior. Be my superior, quietly, simply showing your superiority in your deeds, and very likely I shall love you for the very fact of your superiority. For we all love our leaders. But tell me that I am your inferior, and then perhaps I may grow boyish, and may throw stones. Well, it is so with races. Grant then that yours is the superior race. Then you can afford to say little about that subject in your public dealings with the backward race. Superiority is best shown by good deeds and by few boasts.[81]

What Royce proposes is not the type of moral revelation that challenges or uproots whiteness. He begins his support of English administration by delineating the English from backward peoples. The English maintain superiority through demonstration. This is simply how they rule. By not publicly decrying their superiority, the English organize societies such that in dealing with backward races, they are thought to be enlightened and gain the obedience of lesser people through their benevolence. To the contrary of many Royce scholars who insist that this aforementioned quote is evidence of Royce's racial progressivism, Royce's proposal is an appeal to strengthen white authority by making it the apotheosis of America's racial strategy when dealing with Blacks. He is explaining to Southerners the tenets of domestic colonialism and reiterating that his assimilationist strategy would also require an administrative program for Blacks that was introduced in "Some Characteristic Tendencies of American Civilization" two years prior. Royce claims that inferior races would be drawn toward and "love" the virtue demonstrated by white rule. The superiority of whites could come to be accepted as natural without the constant irritation of lynching and various race frictions. Like Bastian, Royce urges the South to think of the moral psychology of the Negro, which allows whites to rule without violence.

The moral elevation of whites over Blacks is part of Royce's argument for supporting colonial administration over the mob violence associated with lynching. In fact, Royce believes that Jamaica empirically proves that English administration is superior to the Southern strategy of lynching, because administration solved Jamaica's race problem and "it has done this without any such result as our Southern friends nowadays conceive when they think of what is called 'Negro domination.' Administration has allayed ancient irritations."[82] As J. W. Garner writes in his review of Josiah Royce's *Race Questions, Provincialism, and Other American Problems* published in *The Dial,*

> The maintenance of an efficient country constabulary into which Negroes are admitted is one of the many policies which, in the opinion of Professor Royce, have been adopted to secure the loyalty and respect of the Negro population. Moreover, the English habit of ruling the inferior race without publicly claiming the virtues of superiority tends very greatly, he thinks, to remove a source of irritation which lies at the bottom of much of the trouble in North America.[83]

Royce was well understood by those in his own time as advocating for a more efficient program of white rule, not its abolition. A strategy inspired by Britain's administration program would satisfy the white Southerner's need to be the moral superior of the Negro, while correcting the barbarous behavior of the Southerner toward the Negro more generally. Royce thinks the Negro problem threatens social instability and risks sectionalism, so a more efficient administration of the Negro is necessary to protect the South's post–Civil War commitment to provincialism. Royce was understood by the thinkers of his day to be refining the methods of racial managerialism in the South. By not boasting and taunting inferior races, the white race could naturally live as superiors without social irritation.

While it seems that Royce's work is more progressive than that of Southern lynchers, a closer reading of "Race Questions and Prejudices" suggests that his thinking was rather solidly in line with the sentiments supporting the South's political and economic repression of Blacks. It is certainly true and readily apparent that Royce's work differs from the work of Thomas Nelson Page's *The Negro: The Southerner's Problem* (1904),[84] since Page advocates the use of lynching as a means to punish and enforce a sense of (lawless) order against the Negro man for his ravishing (rape) of the white woman. Royce does not advocate lynching as a response, but a closer examination of Royce's work shows this to be a disagreement about the means or method of oppressing Blacks rather than the discontinuation of Southern racism. Page argues that lynching is created by necessity as a means to arrest Negroes' abuse of freedom, and their growing ideal of equality during Reconstruction. Royce's response to Page, which has been previously read as a stance against lynching in favor of equality and democracy for Blacks, is in fact nothing more than a disagreement between Royce and Page as to how best to control the Negroes and keep them in their "proper place." According to Page lynching is politically justified and necessary to the defense of Southern whites.

> Then came the period and process of Reconstruction, with its teachings. Among these was the teaching that the Negro was the equal of the white, that the white was his enemy, and that he must assert his equality. The growth of the idea was a gradual one in the Negro's mind. This was followed by a number of cases where members of the Negro militia ravished white women; in some instances in the presence of their families. The result of the hostility between the Southern whites and Government at that time was to throw the former upon reliance on their own acts for their defence or revenge, with a consequent training in lawless punishment of acts which should have been punished by law. And here lynching, in its post-bellum stage, had its evil origin.[85]

Lynching by Page's own admission is a response not only to the alleged threat Black men pose to white women, but to the teachings of Reconstruction, whose lessons of equality with that of whites, and that whites are the enemy of the Negro, placed Blacks in direct conflict with whites. Page argues for understanding the Southern problem (the trials and tribulations of dealing with the Negro) as a problem of the Black peril, or the threat Black men pose to white Southerners' way of life, the virtue of their women, and the purity of their race, created within the Negro's insistence for equality.

This racist Southern doctrine which insists that the Black man is a ravenous beast is not challenged by Josiah Royce; quite to the contrary, Royce says that he speaks "with no lack of sympathy for the genuine and bitter trials of our Southern brethren when I say that I suppose the mistake which I now point out."[86] The mistake Royce brings to the attention of the South is not about the threat of the Black male rapist the Southerner invents to justify lynching, only that lynching provokes anger and resistance to the social order among Blacks. There is a remarkable contrast in Royce's statements on lynching and those of Frederick Douglass in *Why Is the Negro Lynched* (1895)[87] or Ida B. Wells-Barnett's *Southern Horrors* (1892),[88] both of which argued that lynching is the virulent response whites had to the threat Black men posed economically and politically during Reconstruction. As Wells-Barnett writes, lynching is merely "an excuse to get rid of Negroes who were acquiring wealth and property and thus keep the race terrorized and 'keep the nigger down.' "[89] The "mistake" Royce speaks to is not the accidental characteristic of skin color that is emphasized and taken to be an indication of the inferior, animal-like nature of the Negro, nor is it how the Southerner continues to mistakenly frame the race problem around the racist mythology of the Black rapist, despite this being exposed by both Douglass and Wells-Barnett. Despite his knowledge of the new anthropological findings concerning races, Royce still maintains the cultural, social, and political legitimacy of white racism in the South—their perceived fear of the Negro—and only asks Southerners to modernize their colonial methods in dealing with this problem. Royce offers a plea to white Southerners dedicated to the effective protection of their women's womanhood—alluding to the Black Peril—to embrace a repressive policy that teaches the Negro to respect the law of the South and avoids miscegenation. Royce is specifically challenging Thomas Nelson Page on the issue of lynching, but not as a moral advocate for the Negro. Royce is arguing for colonial efficiency. He thinks controlling the Negro population can be done more efficiently through administration than lynching. Thomas Nelson Page considered Royce's alternative in *The Negro*, but he ultimately concluded that British administration was utopian and not as practically effective as lynching.

Having read Page's *The Negro*, Royce specifically engages Page over whether the administrative alternative is superior (more practical and effective) to the more aggressive lynching strategy, which breeds irritation and prevents Blacks from learning their place. In *The Negro*, Page acknowledges Royce's point and concedes that there are colonial models outside of America where Blacks have acted as their own enforcers of (white) law and punished criminals themselves. Page admits, "It is possible that in every community Negroes might be appointed officers of the law, to look exclusively after lawbreakers of their own race. The English in the East manage such matters well, under equally complicated and delicate conditions."[90] He continues, saying that such a policy might be applicable to the Negro problem in the South, that "somewhat in the same way, the Negroes might be given within their province powers sufficiently full to enable them to keep order among their people, and they might on the other hand be held to certain accountability for such good order."[91] However, such a policy was controversial and unlikely to work in Page's view, because the advocates of such a position must understand that relying on Blacks to prevent Blacks from raping white women was against the race traits that made Blacks rapists. Page simply did not believe that policy could control the biological and racial urges of Black men toward white women. This is why he concludes that such administrative alternatives are utopian. The Negro could not act differently, or more accurate to Page's view, the Negro could not *be* any different. Page is both adamant and clear in his opinion of administration working in the South when he says, "these suggestions may be as Utopian as others which have been made; but if they cannot be carried out, it is because the ravishings by Negroes and the murders by mobs have their roots so deep in racial instincts that nothing can eradicate them."[92]

Royce takes a different view of the race problem and lynching, which revolves around these two questions: "Is, however, the irritation which seems to be the accompaniment of some of the recent Southern methods of teaching the Negro his place an inevitable evil, a wholly necessary accompaniment of the present transition period in the South? [And] must such increase if race-hatred first come, in order that later, whenever the Negro has fully learned his lesson, and aspires no more beyond his station, peace may later come?"[93] Royce is of the view that lynching increases racial irritation and outright racial conflicts between whites and Blacks in the South. These conflicts prevent Blacks from learning their proper (inferior) place, beneath whites. In other words, lynching destroys the social pedagogy needed in effective colonies that allow Blacks to naturally and peacefully accept their oppression. "Now irritation, viewed merely in itself, is not an enlightening state of mind. It is, therefore, according to our modern views, not a very pedagogical state of mind," says Royce.[94] Irritation, then, presents itself as a very real obstacle to socializing the Negro to accept the moral superiority of whites and their social inferiority as Blacks. After a comparative study of the South's situation and its closeness to other English colonies, Royce advances a strategy that he believes will allow Blacks to accept the indoctrination (it is hard to call this "pedagogy" anything else) of white supremacy, allowing their socialization to occur without the reoccurring racial conflicts in the South that make Blacks hate rather than admire white civilization and colonialism. So while it is true that Royce has some disagreement with Thomas Nelson Page, this disagreement in no way challenges Page's racist views about Blacks, but specifically concedes the threat Blacks pose to white women, only offering an administrative solution:

> Mr. Thomas Nelson Page in his recent book on the "Southern-
> ers' Problem" speaks, in one notable passage of the possibility
> which he calls Utopian, that perhaps someday the Negro in the
> South may be made to cooperate in the keeping of order by
> the organization under State control of a police of their own
> race, who shall deal with blacks. He even mentions that the
> English in the East Indies, use native constabulary. But this
> possibility is not Utopian. When now I hear the complaint of
> the Southerner, that the race-problem is such as constantly to
> endanger the safety of his home, I now feel disposed to say:
> "The problem that endangers the sanctity of your homes and
> that is said sometimes to make lynching a necessity, is not a
> race-problem. It is an administrative problem."[95]

Admittedly, Royce understands that such a proposal offering any control to the Negro is radical in the South, but Royce is adamant that if you want to protect your women, Jamaica has shown you how. Royce believes miscegenation is due to racial inequality, not social equality as thought in the South. Addressing Southerners' fear of administration leading to race mixing, Royce states: "Here, as elsewhere, however, it has been rather the social inequality of the races, than any approach to equality, which has been responsible for the mixture, in so far as such has occurred."[96] Slavery created shame, a visible disadvantage, to be associated with dark skin. As such, maintains Royce, the enslaved sought to mix with whites to gain the advantages of lighter skin. If there was administration that sought to give Blacks pride in ruling themselves, then Blacks would not seek out white women. This is why Royce says, "If race-amalgamation is indeed to be viewed as always an evil, the best way to counteract the growth of that evil must everywhere be the cultivation of racial self-respect and not of racial degradation."[97] Royce believes that the racial degradation of Blacks excites their desire to intermix to escape the public stain of their own color. If one aims to counteract miscegenation, one must address the stigmas and shame associated with Blackness. This is not a race problem, meaning it is not a problem of race traits or inevitable racial frictions between whites and Blacks; rather, it is a problem of administration.

At this point it is necessary to address a common retort to Royce's anti-miscegenation. Throughout Royce literature, Royceans have often attempted to lessen the impact of this statement by claiming it was merely hypothetical, or that Royce himself is not in fact asserting the inferiority of Blacks, but only allowing the Southern audience to think so, so that he can follow the hypothesis to its natural conclusion, which in this case would be the colonization of Blacks in the American South. While it is certainly true that "if-then" statements can express hypothetical statements, they are also able to describe the material implications of propositions as well. Consequently, Royce could believe that the implication of the race amalgamation being an evil is the cultivation of racial self-respect. Even if one grants that Royce is in fact addressing the problem hypothetically, this fact in and of itself does not mean that he rejects the antecedent. For Royce to say that a proposition is hypothetical simply means that he is leaving empirical grounds of actual truth or falsity to follow a conditional course of reasoning. The evidence presented throughout the first chapter seems to indicate that Royce was somewhat sympathetic to the antecedent given his views of Blacks in the United States and, as we will soon see, in Jamaica.

If indeed it is to be believed that Royce was proposing a mere hypothetical, why does he not come to disown the premise at its conclusion. Royce certainly does not reject the idea that race amalgamation is evil and, absent some clear indication of doubt or disbelief in the premise, it is certainly not adequate to formulate an apologia based in one interpretation of a conditional statement. Some might suggest that Royce is in fact formulating race amalgamation as a hypothetical because he disagrees with it, but as noted Royce scholar Randall Auxier explains in *Time, Will, and Purpose: Living Ideas from the Philosophy of Josiah Royce*, Royce did not subscribe to the unholy trinity, or "the tradition of associating logical (mathematical), psychological (or cognitive), and ontological necessity with one another."[98] To some extent, Royce accepts the racial inferiority of Blacks to the Anglo and American, and the danger of Blacks to whites. Since he accepts some formulation of these ideas and proposes a philosophy of ethics rooted in the colonization of Blacks in the American South, there is some degree of buy-in to these racist characterizations. As a colleague of mine remarked regarding the evidence of Royce's racism: "well, if it looks like a duck, quacks like a duck, waddles like a duck, it's a duck."[99]

Royce is adamant in defending his proposal of British administration in the American South. Confronted with the aversion Southern Americans had for civility toward the Negro, he explained that Jamaica had solved the problem of racial friction and efficiently manages its Blacks.

> If you say all this speech of mine is professorial, unpracti-cal, Utopian, and if you still cry out bitterly for the effec-tive protection of your womankind, I reply merely, look at Jamaica. Look at other English colonies . . . the Southern race problem will never be relieved by speech or by practices such as increase irritation. It will be relieved when administration grows sufficiently effective, and when the [N]egroes themselves get an increasingly responsible part in this administration in so far as it relates to their own race. That may seem a wild scheme. But I insist: It is the English way. Look at Jamaica, and learn how to protect your own homes.[100]

Protect your own homes, Royce urges. Let the Negroes rule themselves. Let them enforce the good against their own. This is the English way. The readings of Royce that place him at complete odds with Thomas Nelson Page miss the specificity of the debate that Royce is having with Southern proponents of lynching. Royce's disagreement with Thomas Nelson Page confirms that he disagreed with lynching but preferred the strategies already utilized in British colonies to control the Negro. Royce believed that once employed in the South, administration would make the Negro subservient and acquiescent to the repressive social dynamics of Southern living. Administration is simply a better way to keep the "Negro in his place," peacefully, and without the brutish instrument of lynching.[101] Why does Royce appeal to the fear the South has of the Negro and his threat to white womanhood throughout his speech, if he was truly on the side of Black leaders like Du Bois, Douglass, or Wells-Barnett as many contemporary Royce scholars claim? If Royce is truly of the mind that the Negro is biologically equal to whites, why does he offer administration as a strategy to maintain social inequality? The answer: Royce accepted Negrophobia and racism as the basis of his thinking about Blacks, and as shown by his relationship with Sydney Olivier, it is this racist disposition that clouded his understanding of what really brought stability to Jamaica.

Olivier's Twist: Negrophobia and the Jamaica Model of Colonization

What is perhaps most troubling about Royce's allegiance to British colonialism is that he chose to pursue this course of imperial logics, despite his correspondence with noted Fabian scholar Sir Sydney Olivier (intermittent governor of Jamaica), with whom Royce, by his own admission, variously discussed "Race Questions and Prejudices" at the time of its 1906 publication in the *International Journal of Ethics*.[102] While Royce was adamantly championing the administrative efficiency of British colonialism and American assimilationism, Olivier was challenging the ideological basis of the "white man's burden" as nothing more than a concocted myth that attempted to justify the legitimacy of the color line through ethical appeals to civilize African people in the West Indies and South Africa.[103] This discovery is of the utmost importance to Royce scholars who continue to argue that Royce's racial progressivism and his place as a "race thinker" in American philosophy is well deserved, because it shows beyond a doubt that besides the dozens of Black thinkers at the turn of the century insisting on the equality of races and criticizing European colonialism, there was also a British scholar—with whom Royce had contact—who challenged the superiority complex of Anglo-Saxonism and the ethical (civilizing) basis of British colonialism. Because of this relationship, it is no longer accurate for white scholars to claim that Royce did not know of the detrimental consequences of Western colonialism.

Before a new wave of philosophers begins to tout Olivier's work as anti-racist and cutting edge as well, it is important to recognize that Olivier was not a total heretic in his own time. He still believed in European expansionism and African barbarism.[104] However, unlike many of his contemporaries, Olivier argued that the European's quest for wealth only existed as an "undeniable right to go and *peacefully* seek his fortune in any part of the world *without molestation.*"[105] This insistence on "peaceful seeking without molestation" is absolutely crucial to understanding the force of Olivier's stance in contrast to Royce's imperial position. Olivier recognized a tyrannical disposition in the white man's encounter with people of color that "becomes distasteful when he begins to condemn and coerce uncivilized peoples into the mould of his personal interests under the pretext of doing them good."[106] Olivier saw that the moral crusade of British colonialism was in fact an ideological justification for whites to exploit African peoples' labor under the banner of spreading Anglo-Saxon ideals and civilization. "In hardly any nation except England and the United States," says Olivier, "is it possible, or thought necessary, that there should be a public pretence of international philanthropy in connection with Imperial expansion."[107] Unlike Royce, who claims that British colonization and American assimilation is the duty of great nations molded by the spirit of Anglo-Saxonism, Olivier believes that there is "no reason at all for taking moral credit for colonization,"[108] because it always represents an unjustifiable evil, since it necessarily separates the Africans from the fruits of their labor and their particular racial legacy.

Unlike Royce's thinking on the race question, Olivier does not pretend to look at race questions "fairly and humanely"; he recognizes that whites are always blinded by their rationalizations that attempt to justify the oppression of Blacks under the myth of civilizing them. His message to whites invested in thinking about Blackness was clear, "we [whites] must disenchant the facts and eliminate all the glamour which our assurance as to own moral standards and our desire to think the best of ourselves hang about them, before we can hope to form any judgment of the aspect in which those facts appear to the African."[109] What makes Olivier's perspective so different from Royce's is that Olivier spent over twenty years in the administration of the British West Indian colonies and was both the colonial secretary and governor of Jamaica for quite some time.[110] Because Olivier lived on West Indian islands where whites were actually the minority, his perspectives are quite different from Royce's Americanist outlook. Rather than present the reader with abstractions about Blacks, Oliver bases his arguments about race contact with Africans on actual observations.

As previously argued, whereas Royce seems to indicate an aversion to race amalgamation, Olivier argues that it is, in fact, race amalgamation—what he later calls race fusion—that has defused the race problem in Jamaica. As early as 1905, in an essay entitled "The White Man's Burden at Home," Olivier thought it necessary to address the recommendation of Rudyard Kipling that "America should take up the white man's burden"[111] and continue the ill-conceived notion of the color line. According to Olivier, a person of mixed race is "potentially a more competent vehicle of humanity."[112] "Whereas the pure race in its prime knows one Man only, itself, and one God, its own Will, the hybrid is incapable of the exclusive racial pride, and inevitably becomes aware that there is something. . . . Human, which is greater than the one race or the other, and something in the nature of spiritual power that is stronger than national God or Will."[113] Because Negrophobia—the unreasoning racial prejudice—is not the primary anxiety of the British in Jamaica as it is for Americans who fear the danger of Black men to white women and the inferiority (both genetically and socially) of Africans, Olivier does not believe race mixing is necessarily an evil or avoided in the imperial project.[114] "Because the "circumstances of Jamaica are different from those of Southern States, in that [it has] practically no poor white class, or only a very small white class,"[115] or stated differently, because Jamaica does not suffer under the weight of the "white peril," Olivier observes that there is less economic competition between whites and Blacks and therefore less need to perpetuate racial differentiation and claims of white superiority.

In the United States, Olivier observed that the Negro is raised under the excesses of whites' Negrophobia and disciplined with strategies of lynching, violence, and terrorism that are spread by the contagiousness of America's racist paranoia. But, in Jamaica, the Negro "has thus far been raised, and a freedom of civic mixture has been made tolerable, by the continuous application of the theory of humanity and equality: equality in the essential sense of an endowment in the Infinite: a share, however obscure and undeveloped it may appear, in the inheritance of what we call Soul."[116] Because Royce's Negrophobia demands his maintenance of America's anti-miscegenation, he ignores this aspect of racial mixture in

Jamaica and prefers to maintain that British administration can succeed under the strict Southern color line. Olivier, however, understood that a

> class of mixed race is a valuable and indispensable part of any West Indian community, and that a colony of black, colored, and white has far more organic efficiency and far more promise in it than a colony of black and white alone. A community of white and black alone will remain, so far as the unofficial classes are concerned, a community of employers and serfs, concessionaires and tributaries, with at best, a bureaucracy to keep peace between them and attend to the nice adjustment of this Burden. The graded class in Jamaica helps to make an organic whole of the community and saves it from this distinct cleavage.[117]

What is most poignantly shown by Olivier's work is not only the inadequacy of Royce's thinking about race, but also the white supremacism inherent in his American perspective on race. At one level, Royce is simply incorrect in his evaluation of Jamaica's race relations. The tripartite racial system with the mulatto as the managerial class is vastly different from the Black and white segregation of the American South and complicates what Royce believes to be pacifying to the Negro problem in the British system. On a much more revealing level, we see that Royce interprets the British presence in Jamaica with the intent of philosophically justifying Black subjugation, since it is the management of Blacks in the public by others that creates what Royce perceives as social stability. Since Blacks are not demanding a change in their condition in Jamaica, Royce sees this as optimal for stability regardless of the conditions in which the Jamaican people actually live. In what may be Olivier's most convincing assault on Royce's theory of colonization, he states:

> The essence of civilization is to disguise the self-seeking and violence by organizing social injustice and corporate class interests, a process which frees the individual from the appearance and consciousness of personal responsibility. . . . His personal interests transfigured to him as that of his profession, his class or his country, presents itself in the gratifying aspect of altruism; his class interest as an essential social order, his

national conquests as God's purpose for the governance of the world . . . and so quickly imposes [itself] on any community . . . that develops any sort of corporate consciousness—as for instance in the recently prevalent absurdity of the myth of the Anglo-Saxon race.[118]

This however did not mean that the mulatto class of Black-white sexual relations was in any way an answer for America's race problem. One the one hand, Olivier shows us what Royce himself misunderstands about Jamaica's race relations, but on the other Olivier is still a colonizer and offers a racial system in which Blacks are ruled by their mixed-raced progeny. The importance of Jamaica to American race relations was not lost on Black civil rights leaders or thinkers. For example, Walter White, president of the NAACP from 1931 to 1955, understood that Jamaica had fundamentally different racial stratifications in their society that made them quite distinct to the segregationist logic of the United States. In the United States, there were strict separations between Blacks and whites. There was no legal intermingling allowed and by effect a less socially recognizable mulatto or mixed population in the United States. Whereas the English sought to utilize the mulatto to aid their administration of the Black population, the United States enforces racial distance through racial distance. Mr. White explains:

In contrast to the division between white and colored peoples in the United States, there is in the West Indies and others, a tri-partite problem of race relations with whites, blacks and mulattoes. The latter mingle freely with whites in business and other relations and even socially. But neither white nor mulatto has any extensive contact on an equal plane with the blacks. It is this system which has enabled the English whites in the islands to rule and exploit though they as rulers are vastly inferior numerically to blacks and mulattoes.[119]

Again historical context matters in how we think about race and the models being deployed by Royce to justify his approach to America's race problem. Walter White, like Olivier, recognizes that the model of racial subordination coming from Jamaica depends of social contact and a mulatto race. Jamaica has a different system of colonial rule than that of the United States, especially the South whose segregationist policies and violent racial proxemics forbid Black male to female miscegenation.

The Southerner's Rejection of Royce's Colonial Strategy: The Racial Condition He Sought to Import

What does the failure to ask a basic question, "What was life for Blacks under British colonial rule in Jamaica like?" mean for the seemingly earnest and reflective scholarly works aiming to maintain that Royce was racially progressive? How can one make any actual determination of Royce's philosophy regarding race and Blacks in the South without knowing, or at least investigating, the conditions, the degradation he sought to import/impose upon Black Americans in the South? Not one scholarly work to date has attempted understand, much less describe, the actual conditions and lives of Black people living in Jamaica under the system Royce believed could be created in the United States as a solution to the South's race problem.

The early twentieth-century Jamaica Royce would have seen would have been anything but a free society for Blacks. As historian Patrick Bryan remarks in *The Jamaican People, 1880–1902: Race, Class, and Social Control*, "The strategy of the white ruling class in Jamaica had always been to maintain their dominion over the black and coloured population."[120] In late-nineteenth-century Jamaica, Blacks took on a new definition more indicative of Britain's colonial benevolence. No longer slave, but certainly not free, Blacks became a "subject people to be systematically civilized, their environment had become the mission frontier."[121] The racism cemented within the Jamaican society during slavery flourished alongside the centralization of white social authority and class division. For whites in Jamaica, "the challenge of emancipation consisted in organising production around free labour while keeping alive the spirit of inequality that had marked the plantation system."[122] By the 1890s Jamaica was thought to be the exemplar of modern colonial theory. As evidenced by W. P. Livingstone's *Black Jamaica*, it was clear that the island had become the test case of social Darwinism and informed how the elite engaged the Black population. As Bryan explains,

> General attitudes of the elite of Jamaica to blacks and coloureds were conditioned to a considerable extent by the persistence of the social structure of the island which left whites in a superordinate and blacks in a subordinate social position. Economic change, even where it adversely affected whites, did not diminish their cultural authority. The emergence of social Darwinism as the new prism through which to view

the evolution of human societies reinforced white social
authority and confirmed the subordination of blacks within
the racial and class structure. Quasi-scientific racism and its
growing association with imperialism solidified the traditional
socio-racial structure of Jamaica.[123]

Jamaica's society was divided along racial and class lines. The economic
and political power of the island was concentrated in the hands of the
white minority. Despite class differences, whites found comfort and solidarity in their unique position in the Caribbean as being not-Black. This
fleeing from Blackness not only solidified white racial unity, but marked
the borders of the mulatto population's distance from Blackness as well.
Because Jamaica was built around a tripartite racial schema, Blackness
was relegated to the bottom of the racial and economic hierarchy of the
island. The Black population was the least educated and aspirational, and
the mulatto class was taught they were the Black's superiors.

As Brian L. Moore and Michele A. Johnson explain in *Neither Led
nor Driven: Contesting British Cultural Imperialism in Jamaica, 1865–1920*,
"As a vital part of the civilizing mission, the schooling of the children
of Jamaica had very clearly defined objectives. . . . Primary education
was designed essentially for lower-class children in order to create good,
Christian, British colonial subjects, functionally literate but not so well
educated that they would be attracted away from the agricultural sector
that was believed to be the cornerstone of the economy and society."[124]
Jamaican children were economic assets to the colony. They were future
workers. "Jamaica's children, like their parents, were integrated into the
colonial economy. The lifestyle of Jamaica's working-class children was
dictated both by the belief systems of parents and community and by
the position of their parents at the bottom of a racially structured class
society.[125] Impoverished and kept systematically poor and dependent on
work, Black families were sustained through the exploitation of children.
In the late nineteenth century, Jamaican children no older than six or
seven were expected to work. When these children matured to their early
teens, around fourteen to sixteen years of age, they would be organized
in juvenile labor gangs that work ten-hour days for weeks on various
estates.[126] Despite doing the same work as their adult counterparts, Black
children were paid a smaller wage than other workers.[127] At the age of six,
Black boys were taught to work the grounds. Agricultural labor became
part of their education; it prepared them for their adult occupations.[128]

This is not to suggest that there was not a Black middle class, but this class was marked by education and occupation, not land ownership and wealth. Those of the Black middle class were in service occupations as teachers, artisans, or nurses. They did not run institutions on the island or government.[129] The foundation of Jamaica's society was the poverty and disposability of the Black labor class. The Black labor class suffered from disease, illness, lack of medical services, and deliberate societal neglect. To suggest that Black Americans could be enhanced through the reproduction of this condition in America only demonstrates the racist disregard Royce had to the conditions and suffering he saw Black people endure in Jamaica. Royce accepted the inferior social organization of the island as not only natural, but optimal.

Royce's support of British colonial administration was not only well known, but publicly endorsed and debated as a strategy for dealing with the South's Negro problem. Royce's position on Jamaica fit so nicely within the purview of American and British imperialism that it gained the attention of world-renowned journalist William Thomas Stead. Stead was the creator and editor of the *Review of Reviews*, a publication that spanned across the empires of America, Europe, and Australia by the mid-1890s. W. T. Stead was a loyal supporter of the Anglo-American union and imperialism. He was a close friend and executor of the infamous imperialist Cecil Rhodes and a well-known editor of imperialist propaganda.[130] Stead saw an imperial resonance in Royce's work that mirrored his own and that of Cecil Rhodes.[131] Stead offers Royce's "Race Problems and Prejudices" a favorable review because it stands apart from the popular criticisms of British colonization. As Stead explains, "We have so often heard nothing but doleful and despairing criticisms of the English way in the West Indies, that this American tribute is all the more grateful."[132] Royce's citation within the literature of his time in support of the imperial control of native races is key to how the philosopher of today should accurately situate and utilize Royce's race theory.[133]

In the May 1906 edition of the *Review of Reviews*, Stead penned a celebratory review of Royce's support for the use of British administration on American Negroes titled "How to Deal with Negroes: An Object Lesson from Jamaica." Stead wrote:

> Mr. Josiah Royce, of Harvard, pays the British a very handsome compliment in his paper on "Race Problems and Prejudices" in the *International Journal of Ethics* for April. The

paper itself is one which will delight the heart of M. Finot, the chivalrous champion of the equality of all races; but for us its most interesting feature is the high tribute which Mr. Royce pays to the British Administration of the West Indian Islands, notably of Jamaica. He holds up our West Indian colonies as examples to his countrymen who are perpetually complaining of their Negro problem in the South.[134]

Stead's review highlights several previously commented upon distinctions of the time in Royce's thought. On the one hand, Royce is utilizing environmentalist theories that see the biological inferiority of Blacks to be mistaken. On the other, Royce does not believe that darker races should be self-determined; they were meant to be ruled and assimilated into, or managed within—as in the case of Blacks—empire. Stead places him in the company of Mr. Finot in this regard.

As discussed in the introduction, Black thinkers utilized arguments by any number of white authors that could be used against the idea that the Negro race was innately inferior. While many progressives in the early decades of the twentieth century became somewhat skeptical of the biological basis of racial inferiority, this idea was often in tension with the idea that native or backward peoples needed to be led to civilization. Often white thinkers would assert that the backward races were not doomed but could be led toward civilization if properly guided. For example, Edward Blyden quotes Finot in *African Life and Customs* in favor of the idea that milieu or environment is more responsible than biology for a race's cultivation, but he rejects Finot's belief that Blacks are civilized by their imitation of Europe's culture. To African authors like Blyden, the much-touted culture of Europe was barbaric. The imperial ventures and cruelties of Europe often cast as civilization were in fact Europe's failings to many of the darker races. This presumption of Anglo-Saxon (white) superiority over darker races is why imperialists and those who support the inequality of the races are celebrating Royce's admiration for how the British control the Negro population. Despite Royce's scientific disagreements with ethnologists, his political idealism still endorsed white superiority and was understood as such by his contemporaries.

Royce's theorizations about race and the social organization of racial groups within America were actually engaged much more seriously by other white professors and historians than Blacks. Many of Royce's white commentators adamantly disagreed with Royce's endorsement of the Jamaican model. They saw it as racially regressive, a malicious racial strategy designed to completely subjugate and repress Blacks in the South. John M. Mecklin, for instance, insisted that Royce's proposal was committed to the complete subjugation of the Black race in the United States. He was adamant that Royce intended a strategy that confined the Black American to peasantry and poverty. Whereas Jamaican Negroes only knew themselves as laborers and servants to the whites of the island, the Black American had developed aspirations fitting their condition of political freedom and economic possibility. In *Democracy and Race Friction: A Study in Social Ethics*, Mecklin explicitly criticized Royce's paternalistic strategy as little more than a reflection of his racist disposition toward the Negro. Mecklin explains, "The 'orderly, law abiding, and contented' character of the Jamaican Negro which Professor Royce found so charming is the outcome of the benevolent paternalism of the English regime, the fundamental idea of which is the complete subordination of the Negro to the will of the white."[135] In fact, in a 1917 commentary on Royce's contribution to American philosophy, Mecklin attacked Charles M. Bakewell's claim that Royce's interpretation of the race question was indeed useful.[136] Mecklin was adamant that Royce's contentions, that "race prejudices and antipathies are human illusion, [and that the] conditions in Jamaica are for all practical purposes so closely akin to those in Southern states that we may safely draw parallels between them,"[137] were actually the rants of a man who was "more of a preacher of righteousness than a careful student of the facts, a champion of higher spiritual loyalties as he understood them rather than the accurate interpreter of life."[138] Mecklin explains that Royce's administrative strategy returns the Negro to the repression of the Southern plantation. It is a position that is dedicated to maintaining the Negro as a laborer and ultimately a peasantry class to whites.

> The [N]egro, who has never known any other conditions, accepts this as part of the eternal order of things with the result that the status of the ruling white and that of the masses of the peasant Negro labourers are entirely separated, and occasion for friction is reduced to a minimum. The sections of the South where there is the least friction between the races are found on the plantations of the "black belt," where, as in Jamaica, the Negroes outnumber the whites, and

where, the war amendments and the "Bill of Rights" to the contrary notwithstanding, a paternalistic regime is in force similar in many ways to that in Jamaica. Again, any parallel between Jamaican conditions and the status of the Negro in this country must recognise a difference of the very greatest importance between the two countries, namely, that from the emancipation of the Negro to the present in the United States he has had dinned into his ears the democratic doctrine of his inherent equality with the white, and hence his inalienable right as a class to all the privileges and emoluments of the community on an equal footing with the white.[139]

Mecklin criticizes Royce for his romanticization of the British administrative strategy. He insists that that such repressive policy is not the basis of England's relations with backward races, but Royce's desire for the return of antiquated conditions previously endured by the Negro.[140] Whereas the American Negro condition has been cultivated by a yearning for democratic freedom and equality to whites, Mecklin points out that the Jamaican has only been confined to the position of a laborer and ruled by whites. Royce's strategy is merely an attempt to realize his own intentionality toward Blacks and his desire for the race to remain socially subordinate and serve as workers for whites in the South. As recognized even among his contemporaries, Royce is not aiming for the liberation of Blacks but their efficient subjugation.

Surprisingly, it was another Southern segregationist who identified the contradiction of Royce's British strategy, which insisted there was no racial character Negroes were committed to preserving, while insisting upon the racial (Anglo-Saxon) character and superiority of the white races. In *The Basis of Ascendency: A Discussion of Certain Principles of Public Policy Involved in the Development of the Southern States*, Rev. Edgar Murphy made a charge against Royce's Jamaican strategy similar to Mecklin's. In the first decade of the twentieth century, Murphy concerned himself with the future of the Southern states and their policy toward the Negro. This concern revolved around one central question, "Shall the principles of its policy, in relation to its weaker racial or social groups, be repressive or constructive?"[141] Regardless of the ethnological debates that were prevalent in his time, Murphy believed the Negro problem to be a concrete social dilemma. Murphy contends:

> To prove that all men, ages ago, were much alike and that
> we may not declare dogmatically against the ultimate parity
> of racial groups, does not abolish the obvious consideration
> that we have now to deal with the stubborn realities of a
> world in which races are not upon a par—either in their
> social or industrial efficiency—and in which the respective
> families of men are alike no longer. The State cannot base a
> present policy upon prehistoric conditions.[142]

How one deals with race in the first decade of the twentieth-century South requires a certain practicality that he believed to be absent from the proposal of Josiah Royce. Murphy argued that Royce "seems to underestimate the meaning of race."[143] While Murphy believed that there was in fact a racial temperament that made the Negro a Negro and consequently was partially responsible for his condition, there was also an obvious dereliction by the state to enforce economic and political policies to benefit the condition of the Negro. Murphy writes:

> That the negro's powers are not the powers of the white man,
> and that his present capacities are at many points not equal
> to the economic competition presented by the stronger race,
> is due in part to the fact that the negro is a negro: but how
> far is it also due to the fact that that sense of "security as
> to his property and his person." . . . The fact that the negro
> is a negro, the State may not alter; but the fact that the
> Negro—quite as much at the North as at the South—has
> not been adequately accorded the economic support of the
> profounder social forces of security, opportunity, and hope,
> the State may largely alter if it will.[144]

Murphy took great offense at Royce's description of the South's race problem as "merely the problems caused by our antipathies"[145] and "the childish phenomena of our lives."[146] While Royce was willing simply to dismiss the South's race problem as mere illusions driven by animus, Murphy suggests that there is something in races that are worth preservation. While Murphy's sentiment runs counter to our twenty-first-century anti-essentialism, which holds that race has no biological or culture determination within the racial group, he is expressing a fundamental challenge to assimilationists, namely: Is the inferior race truly so inferior that there is nothing in the race that can be a gift to the world? This thinking about race is not unusual to those committed to the findings of ethnology. Even Du Bois's ethnological treatise, *The Conservation of Races*, held that the non-European "race groups are striving, each in its own way, to develop for civilization its particular message, its particular ideal, which shall help to guide the world nearer and nearer that perfection of human life for which we all long."[147] Murphy simply reiterates this significance of race in his response to Royce, saying that "a sane and righteous and wholesome adjustment of race relations is not advanced by a spurious 'catholicity of race' which would ignore the very existence of the factors which give to our problem its reality."[148] Any strategy attempting to deal with race that does not value the historical significance of race to the weaker group would simultaneously invalidate the claim of the stronger group to civilization. Murphy explains that such an argument

> is but a subtle way of saying to the weaker group that it has nothing individual, nothing peculiar to itself, which it must sacredly conserve in the interest of all; it is also but a subtle way of making it impossible to say to the stronger group that its individuality is, in all its finer and happier achievement, a thing too sacred, too indispensable to the service of the world, to be delivered upon the one hand to the dragging pressure of lower groups, or to be surrendered, upon the other hand, to those self-corrupting antipathies to which it is forever tempted.[149]

Murphy deliberately points out the contradiction of Royce's claim, which maintains that inferior races allegedly have no sacred gift to share with the world because race is irrelevant, while simultaneously maintaining it is because of the gift of civilization the white race possesses that it has the (white man's) burden to advance the lower races. Murphy insists if race has no historical significance, then that claim must apply to the supposed duty the white race has for imperial conquest. Murphy tells his readers that he intends to give a more thorough and in-depth critique of Royce's Jamaican strategy in a chapter he was writing titled "Lessons from Jamaica?" in his book *Issues, Southern and National*.[150] Unfortunately, Murphy completed all the chapters for the book except his critique of Royce before he died.

The writings by American philosophers dealing with "Race Questions and Prejudices" have not benefited from a comparative philosophical analysis of Royce's critics or the historical backdrop from which Southerners might have responded to his proposal to import British administration into the United States. The limitation of philosophy, its lack of concern for the actual condition of people in society, has deleterious consequences for how we think of the lives and material conditions (poverty, work, daily activity) of Black Americans in the early 1900s. If our approach to racism concerns itself only with how the historical idols appear in the analysis, then it is easy to lose sight of the conditions Royce himself found acceptable for Black Americans, citizens of the United States. Up to our present date, Royceans have unapologetically engaged in a philosophical project more interested in protecting the emerging legacy of Josiah Royce from the demonstrable attacks he waged against the darker races (Black Americans and non-Anglo-Saxon peoples the world over) than turning their attention, even for a moment, to the suffering Blacks endured in Jamaica under the British system Royce seems to admire so dearly.

The debates in ethnology and the recently emerging field of anthropology were nuanced and complex. The resistance of philosophers to combing through archives and historically situating the thought of their figures only makes understanding these debates extremely difficult, since the picture many philosophers have of America in the late 1800s is impressionistic. Royce's thinking about race and civilization is part of a complex story of evolution, ethnology, and idealism. It does not benefit American philosophers to oversimplify these debates in our present discourse or scholarship to get to a more amenable picture of Royce's philosophical project. If we fail to understand what American thinkers, some of whom are highly regarded philosophers, were engaged in, we fail to grasp what might be learned from these literatures. In the late 1960s, Lymon Moody Simms Jr.'s "Josiah Royce and the Southern Race Question" understood that Royce argued for a strategy whereby "Negroes in the South were spiritually homeless, [and] called upon white Southerners to inculcate among Negroes a feeling of oneness with the Southern community. This could be accomplished by encouraging [N]egro self-respect and instituting measures designed to make the Negro 'a conscious helper toward good social order.' "[151] The idea that Josiah Royce's thinking about race could be insightful in the twenty-first century, when it was acknowledged to be "dated and a little more than short-sighted" in the twentieth century, is somewhat ironic.[152]

Conclusion

Given the imperial legacy of Royce's work and his dispositions toward Blacks, it should be apparent even to the most casual observers that Royce's philosophy is fraught with racist colonialism. It is here that the opening quote by Sydney Olivier really demonstrates the problem of Royce's thought, because instead of merely being guided by colonial principles, Royce urges white Americans through provincialism to become better colonizers—an idea of such consequence that it shall remain an obstacle to future anti-racist readings of Josiah Royce's work. Some readers may still be unconvinced by the case made by this chapter. I ask the reader to endure a little longer and explore the parallels between Royce's 1900 speech at Aberdeen University and his 1902 publication entitled "Provincialism." I ask the reader to pause for a moment and consider the consequence of whites being the dominant racial class and benefactors of Anglo-Saxon civilization, upon the so-called strangers of America—the Blacks, Indigenous, Asians, among others. What power is gifted to the white population under such an arrangement? What would it mean to be Black (a stranger), or an "alien race," as Royce phrases it, in this America? Because Royce's thought is so dedicated to the assimilation and the eradication of all cultural and racial differences, would life as an African American, Asian American, or Native American, even be possible? In chapter 3, I conclude that these lived realities are not only impossible but condemnable, from Royce's point of view, because their self-determined activity would in fact threaten the stability of the country and risk sectionalism much like the great war of the nineteenth century.

3

No Revisions Needed

Historicizing Royce's Provincialism, His Appeal to the white Man's Burden, and Contemporary Claims of His Anti-Racism

R oyce mentions that one of the earliest articulations of his arguments for "Provincialism" was delivered at Iowa State University in 1902 as the Phi Beta Kappa Address.[1] Provincialism has been the focus of many social political and ethnic visions of Royce's contemporary relevance. Some may find it strange that "Provincialism" is therefore not the focus of a book about race, such as this one, but rather is only considered as a stage or accumulation of Royce's thinking about America's racial problems, despite the essay's being written after "Some Characteristic Tendencies of American Civilization" (1900), but before "Race Questions and Prejudices" (1905). "Provincialism" is the most practically situated articulation of Royce's idealism within American society. It expresses how the ideal of loyalty is taken up by communities of people in America. As Royce himself writes in the introduction to *Race Questions, Provincialism, and Other American Problems*, "The first essay printed here—'Race Questions' . . . is an effort to express and justify, in the special case of the race-problems, the spirit of which I have elsewhere defined as that of Loyalty to Loyalty,"[2] while the second, entitled "Provincialism," discusses "the need and uses of that spirit in American life."[3] Rather than seeing these ideas in stark contrast or contradiction, Royce imagines provincialism to be the means through which the ideal (loyalty to loyalty) is communally manifested in American life and necessary to his administrative strategy toward the Negro, as discussed in chapter 2. As such, there is no distance between Royce's conceptualization of loyalty to loyalty and its societal manifestation as provincialism. Unlike his previous and subsequent engagements with race, which attempt to justify his beliefs about races within the debates between anthropologists and sociologists, "Provincialism" appeals to the American citizenry to adopt provincial values that preserve, cultivate, and stabilize post–Civil War America.

Whereas Royce's Aberdeen speech leaves the reader with an understanding of how "the most potent institutions of our life in extending our civilization have been the churches, the law courts, and the schools . . . and newspapers,"[4] "Provincialism" describes the processes and ideas he hopes will continue to perpetuate the imperial legacy of the British in, or rather, through America. Speaking to the learning of federal ideals and the spiritual guidance of older civilizations, Royce writes, "not only have these things been so in the past, but similar needs will, of course, be felt in the future. We shall always be required to take counsel of the other nations with whom we are at work upon the tasks of civilization."[5] As announced in 1900, Britain is the closest kinship America has in its task of civilization. (Higher) provincialism then becomes a means by which America maintains and nourishes this national ideal. Provincialism is thereby central to maintaining the assimilative power of America and acts as the bridge between the ideal and the practical creation of loyalty in communities and among individuals. Remember, Royce argues that "the chief cause of the vast assimilative power of the American civilization has been . . . the fact that the strong national consciousness, the pride in being one great and independent people, has joined itself in every case with local pride, and then with that large heritage of ideas which we have from you."[6] Royce was far from a democratic thinker regarding nonwhite peoples. Those peoples were to be ruled, repressed, or assimilated in the service of civilization. Every social institution from the university to the elementary school was to be used for the inculcation and assimilation of foreigners to the American ideal—the Anglo-Saxon ideal.

Recognizing the aforementioned problem in Royce's work, some contemporary philosophers have attempted to correct Royce's racism and imperial program through an appeal to his ethics—or what is generally referred to as loyalty to loyalty. This gesture makes two irreparable mistakes. First, the idea that ethics can address racism is not a historically proven philosophical method or approach; it is merely an ideological assertion emerging from the integrationist discourses of the 1960s,[7] which assumes that racism is about attitudes and not power.[8] Second, and this is a matter of Royce's philosophical corpus, loyalty to loyalty *is* his program of racism and colonization. Royce's ethics is not separate from the ideal it attempts to concretize in the world. "Loyalty is the practical aspect and expression of an idealistic philosophy," says Royce.[9] Loyalty manifests itself to the world as set of relations the community has to others, and in the case of race questions, it is the obligation white communities in America have to the colonial ideal that makes the Negro problem and the presence of alien races appear as a threat. In other words, the identification of this community and *that other*, who is outside this community and must be assimilated, is only possible because one grasps the ideal. Under false forms of provincialism, or what Royce calls sectionalism, differences remain between groups within America and threaten national unity.[10] Under wise provincialism, however, racialized others are recognized and seen as alien or foreign but made to conform to the communities to preserve national unity and stability. This is not to simply indict Royce for a decadent ethnonationalism. Rather it is an attempt to show the dialectic at work in the relation between the local and the national, the community and the nation, the people and the ideal in Royce's thought. Race as we have seen in previous chapters risks instability and risks obstructing the Anglo-Saxon ideal that is placing America in contact with Britain.

"Provincialism" has the same language and sentiment of Royce's earlier essay, "Some Characteristic Tendencies of American Civilization," regarding Britain and the Civil War, as well as some very important comments on the nature of the Negro problem. To date however there has been no attempt to explore the connection these texts have to the social ethics Royce offers in his thinking about America's assimilation of alien races and those races Royce describes as unassimilable. This chapter is an exploration of the relationship between his aspiration for wise community and the place of alien (nonwhite) races. Throughout "Provincialism" Royce reminds the reader that there is a need to assimilate foreigners into the dominant race's ideas to create and sustain regional and national stability in America. The resemblance this argument has to Royce's Aberdeen address shows Royce to be a scholar who concerns himself with *foreignness*, and *racial otherness*, as part of his thinking about the practicality of loyalty to loyalty and the manifestation of American provincialism.

The effect of this exploration in Royce's philosophy is not simply descriptive. Provincialism utilizes the spirit of loyalty to condemn cultural difference, since the aim of loyalty is local stability. In order to establish national unity, local difference is extinguished to prevent factions from emerging. The presumed inferiority of savage races in comparison to the white Anglo-Saxon predicts the direction of this conformity. In the communities envisioned by Royce there is no cultural pluralism, there is only conformity to the ideals, symbols, and religion of the dominant white/Anglo-Saxon ethnic group. This is an English and American trait for Royce. A skill undemonstrated by other European groups like the French, "who are not a colonizing people, [and] seem to possess much less of this tendency [to assimilate.]"[11] Royce's particular substantiation of white supremacy is somewhat nuanced. While he does orient himself racially, as in the case of the Kaffir or recent rise of Japan against Russia, he makes very specific distinctions in the capacities of different ethnic groups to utilize assimilation and the provincial. Stated differently, Royce's imperial and racial endeavors are Anglophilic. They are founded on this idea that the Anglo-Saxon ideals, most readily manifested by the British and its children in America are destined to rule over others through assimilation. This assimilating tendency is what impressed Royce during his time in Australia and New Zealand. He observed that in Australasian colonies they had already acquired as sense of their "glorious past history . . . their romance of the heroic days, and in consequence, their provincial loyalty and their power to assimilate new comers."[12]

The languages, religions, and customs of nonwhite races are confined to the first generation of these groups, and eradicated by the second. Children of immigrants are educated away from their original culture, and unassimilable groups are subject to colonial policy and "administration" as shown in chapter 2. Royce believes it is America's destiny to be a republic defined by the values of the Anglo-Saxon: a white republic. He is not arguing for or imagining a heterogeneous America at the turn of the century in the way many liberal academicians think of America more generally in the present. As such, alien races or foreigners were pressured on pain of having no future at all to take on the cultural signs and ideas of a white population. This chapter aims to address this asymmetry between white American groups and racialized populations who were by definition outsiders.

Provincialism as the Instrument of Colonial Assimilation: Understanding the Relationship between the Colonial Ideal and the Colonizing Community

Royce describes assimilation as having two components. The first is how scholars and laypersons alike traditionally think of the term with regard to inferior races taking on the dominant culture, but the second component is what most concerns us here. Royce maintains that assimilation also refers to "the organization into one close-knit nationality of the diverse types and regions of our country."[13] Articulated at the end of the first section in his 1900 Aberdeen address, Royce begins his reflections on provincialism with a testimony to power of imperial thought and the saving grace of European civilization. In section 2 of "Characteristic Tendencies," Royce observes that the imperial aspirations of the United States place them closer to the colonial legacy of Britain than ever before. Whereas in the past, the United States could simply content itself with the assimilation of foreigners, now, says Royce, "We, too, are henceforth to undertake the business of accomplishing, in distant regions, the protection and the government of alien populations, who will never become assimilated to our own."[14] Royce believes that America and Britain complement each other's colonial yearnings, since Britain is now confronted with "knitting closer the social, if not also the political constitution of your Empire, and of assimilating peoples with whom it is your destiny to live,"[15] while America must learn the skill of foreign administration.

The greatest test of national unity for Royce was the American Civil War. Throughout the second section of "Some Characteristic Tendencies," he reminds the reader that this war over slavery was the "great crisis of our national history."[16] The North and South had to relearn national cooperation and unity, but the South especially had to learn to cope with this defeat. Royce explains, "In the South, the story of the Civil War—a war so earnestly fought out to the point of an absolutely honourable, because inevitable defeat—this story, I say, now survives, in the ideals of the new generation of Southerners as a very precious memory of heroism and of endurance. It survives in sentiments of pride, and of affection for their dead."[17] Royce makes a peculiar comment in this paragraph that leads the reader to believe that the conflict over slavery was necessary and honorable to the future of the United States. He writes:

> We begin to see now that both the Confederate and his conqueror worked together, in the mysterious way that history so often exemplifies, to escape from the bondage of a destiny which the past had transmitted to that generation, to solve a problem which, alas, we fallible mortals in that land could only solve by fighting, and to prepare the way for a truer union that could only come into existence when the old issue had been thoroughly and honourably fought out.[18]

Why does Royce choose the phrasing of "the Confederate and his conqueror"? Royce suggests, as will be explained more in chapter 4, that
there is a true unification that occurred over the issue of race in the
history of America. Because America is a young empire, Royce articulates a history and program that attempts to move America beyond its
antiquated institution of slavery toward institutions and ideas that enable
imperialism. The Civil War is presented by Royce as a necessary step to
American's maturation toward empire, a war that grew from the brute
institution of American slavery toward a modern system of colonialism.
The Civil War matured America. It developed past disunion to empire
while maintaining its allegiance to racial hierarchy. It enabled the nation
to become self-conscious and committed to the importance of loyalty—the
importance and shared union between the once divided North and South.
Royce says, "the memory of the Civil War always helps us to look deeper,
to know that the most formidable appearances of weakness of character
which we can observe are but superficial symptoms, and that at bottom
our people are the inheritors of the blood and of the traditions of the
men of '61."[19] Rather than simply being a memory inspiring national
unity, the Civil War spirit accumulates around racial unity and destiny
as well. Royce is surprisingly clear in this regard. He says:

> . . . our war, just because it had to be fought out to a
> finality, resulted in attainments which our civilization could
> never have won without it. No desire for a renewal of any
> of its most essential issues survive amongst us in the minds
> of people whose feelings are of any serious social or national
> significance. The future of the American [N]egro is still a
> great problem; but nobody desires to see him again a slave,
> or seriously wishes the old slavery days back again.[20]

The Negro remains a great problem for the country, but he need not
return America into the conflicts over slavery. The nation must move on,
unified, beyond slavery. The strategies after the war must both attend to
the lingering Negro problem and the historic division between the North
and South concerning this racial problem. This section of "Characteristic
Tendencies" foreshadows the conditions by which provincialism and loyalty
are nurtured. The nation is not meant to be merely a description of the
entity and people that comprise it; it is also a description of the ideal,
the racial and imperialist destiny of the republic now unified.

After the Civil War, Royce realized that the Negro was not the only threat to America's national unity. Around the turn of the century, America found itself home to multiple foreigners through immigration. Hailing from countries throughout Europe, "the newcomers have brought to our shores languages, customs, traditions, and religious interests, which were not ours. In many cases, they have naturally tended to group themselves into little communities, such as you find in many of our cities, and such as, in some cases, have occupied considerable country districts,"[21] observed Royce. He is clear that in order to maintain *one* civilization, foreign ideas must give way to the one true American ideal. He writes, "Now a critical issue for our destiny was, of course, from the first, the question whether these various types of people should retain, for a series of generations, their own national or social characteristics and prejudices, their own speech, their own mutual antipathies; or whether they should become one with us."[22] Royce concluded that the alien race must become one with America so that they do not risk social instability and disunity.

By 1902, with the initial writing of Royce's essay "Provincialism,"[23] Royce was convinced that the end of the Civil War was the triumph of national unity over the dangers of sectionalism and America's recommitment to "learning common federal ideals and looking to foreign lands for the spiritual guidance of older civilizations."[24] Invoking the spiritual kinship America shares with Britain, Royce continues that "we shall always be required to take counsel of the other nations in company with whom we are at work upon the tasks of civilization. Nor have we outgrown our spiritual dependence upon older forms of civilization. In fact we shall never outgrow a certain inevitable degree of such dependence."[25] Because America's success as a nation is dependent on its ability to learn from Britain's historical success as a "world civilizer," Royce commits himself to developing a philosophy of America that reflects the "spiritual" embodiment of the colonizing idea. "Provincialism," says Royce, "like monogamy, is an essential basis of true civilization. And it is with this presupposition that I undertake to suggest something toward a definition and defence of the higher provincialism and of its office in civilization."[26]

Royce thought of provincialism and colonialism as a synergy of two ideals. They were simultaneously the means and ends of the other. Provincialism, insofar as it is understood as a social philosophy, is the process through which America's teleology—as a national unity—is achieved. The ideals and pride one has in his or her local community is not a source of multicultural inclusion or "tolerant white communities";

rather, provincialism—that pride in local customs and traditions—is the most effective means of assimilating strangers and foreigners into American society.[27] Royce created a system through which the national idea(l) is preserved within local communities, and these local communities are wise as measured by the extent to which they reflect the ideal to which the nation aspires. This dialectical relationship between the national and local is what makes communities the foundation of his ethics of loyalty to loyalty. Royce is surprisingly clear about provincialism's role in this regard.

> Now you, who know well your own local history, will be amongst you of this tendency to idealize your past, to glorify the bounties that nature has showered upon you, all in such wise as to give the present life of your community more dignity, more honor, more value in the eyes of yourselves and of strangers. In fact, that we all do thus glorify our various provinces, we well know; and with what feelings we accompany the process, we can all observe for ourselves. But it is well to remember that the special office, the principal use, the social justification, of such mental tendencies in ourselves lies in the aid that they give us in becoming loyal to our community, and in assimilating to our own social order the strangers that are within our gates. *It is the especial art of the colonizing peoples such as we are, and such as the English are, to be able by devices of this sort rapidly to build up in their own minds a provincial loyalty in a new environment.*[28]

To truly understand Royce's philosophy of provincialism, we must understand what it is that Royce aims to avoid. Remember while highly enamored by British colonialism, Royce is disturbed by the sectionalism that various cultural groups still maintain under British rule. Diversity, be it racial, historical, or linguistic, was a threat to this national coherence and inspired in Royce a fear of lack of national unity that would ignite in America the same type of crisis he saw in British imperialism during the early 1900s. Royce's emphasis on "assimilating to our own social order the strangers that are within our gates," is particularly troublesome to Roycean scholars who are claiming their work is driven by concerns of plurality and racial/ethnic diversity. Royce's civilizational account of history makes Britain's colonialism the predecessor to American colonization. Royce is not making a theoretical argument about the possibilities of American colonialism, he is arguing that America *does colonize*, and *should colonize* the racial/ethnic other, and *assimilation* is the means by which this happens. Royce is deliberately exact in the aforementioned quote: "*It is the especial art of the colonizing peoples such as we are, and such as the English are, to be able by devices of this sort rapidly to build up in their own minds a provincial loyalty in a new environment.*" Provincial loyalty is built through the especial art of colonization, and carried out by colonizing peoples such as we (white Americans) and the English (British). However one might seek to sanitize through revisionism the implications of this colonizing tendency, there is a very real consequence to how one thinks about the cultural/racial/ethnic existence of the peoples historically victimized by such totalizing ideals as community, order, and nation. Royce is continuing an American tradition of oppression and Anglo-Saxon domination, not challenging it. Royce's work is proof that he reads himself and the Anglo-Saxon temperament of America as an active cultural ideal striving toward civilization.

Royce deliberately draws the reader back to his previous thinking about American assimilation and British administration. Provincialism emphasizes the process by which others are taken in by the existing communities and transformed into Americans aspiring to the Anglo-Saxon ideals. The existing community does not change in the process of assimilation. It is the foreigner, the alien, the racialized, who bears the burden of conformity. It is this process that makes history, the symbols of the past, and the past itself, an instrument of assimilation. The civilizational/colonizing personality of the Anglo-Saxon is meant to be dominant. Unlike Britain, who reached out to conquer alien races, America has dealt more with strangers "upon our shores," or within the country, than with racial peoples outside of it, and this new colonial situation, where people came into the colonizing nation, instead of remaining outside of the nation as a colony, requires that these strangers "not retain their own civilization, but acquire ours," as a matter of successfully carrying out the white man's burden. Royce continually warns the reader that the racialized character of what we now call whiteness, by its very nature, cannot exist among cultural/racial diversity in a nation dedicated to *higher provincialism* and unity. Since the purpose of whiteness, that historical category forged upon the castings of Western superiority, is the subordination of nonwhiteness, it becomes very difficult to understand how a philosopher like Royce, who is averse to cultural difference and insistent on Anglo supremacy, can supposedly transform whiteness into a culturally sensitive and liberatory category. Regardless of the varying opinions over whether whiteness can be changed (despite the sociological and historical evidence to the contrary), at the end of the day, theorists interested in pursuing the *provincial revision* are left with Royce's own words, which compel whites to

> learn to view your new community [so] that every stranger who enters it shall at once feel the dignity of its past, and the unique privilege that is offered to him when he is permitted to belong to its company of citizens,—this is the first rule of every colonizing nation . . . thus, then, I have pointed out the first evil with which our provincialism has to deal—the evil due to the presence of a considerable number of not yet assimilated newcomers in most of our communities.[29]

Royce's provincialism is a medium through which the white (Anglo-Saxon) citizen was charged with propagating the wedlock of British and American colonial destinies. The citizen learns both the colonial heritage and imperial aspirations of America to indoctrinate the foreigner to this cause. This process of assimilation that arose to deal with the white citizen's intermingling of foreigners—alien races and strangers—is so absolute that Royce refers to it within the emerging crises of empire, of which American civilization cannot understand without reference to the imperial legacy of Britain.[30] In the case of race relations, Royce's thinking is unequivocal—if they are not white, and able to claim Anglo-Saxon heritage, their culture must be destroyed by assimilation for the continuance and stability of the nation.

Is Wise Provincialism a Colonial Ideal?

Royce has articulated the goals of the local community, but how does the assimilation of alien races occur within these communities? Royce argues that America's "power of assimilating a large number of new comers to our own language and ways, [belongs to] two classes of causes, the material and the ideal."[31] The material cause is quite obvious from Royce's point of view. It is the contact with alien races made possible by America's imperial expansion within the United States and abroad. Royce speaks to the growth of America almost from a position of efficacy, how efficient it is in bringing alien populations under its auspices. He writes:

> The physical continuity of the country, the gradual extension of settlement from place to place, the large developments of modern industry which have led to a constantly increasing connection of the life of one part of the country with the life of another—all these are features which necessarily have had a great influence in helping our people to a unity of consciousness, and in making it plain to the new comers that they must adapt themselves to an already existing situation if they were to find their way under our conditions.[32]

Referring to his series of lectures in 1899 published subsequently as *The World and the Individual* (1900), Royce remarks, "In my discussion to this society a year ago, I had occasion to mention the fact that, to my mind, our nation, which had been so much accused of materialism, is really under the influence of very ideal motives."[33] Contrary to the dominant move among American philosophers to separate Royce's idealist metaphysics from his social ethics, Royce sees the two integrally connected. He in fact argues that the origins of the idealism that grounds both his metaphysics and assimilationism are of colonial origin, belonging to that of the British. "I had hardly then so much occasion as I may now have to point out to what a great extent these ideal motives are of English origin," writes Royce.[34] As pointed out in previous chapters, Royce's theories rely quite heavily on the science and scholarship of German and English universities as well as the thinking of continental European countries of the late nineteenth century.[35] His preoccupation with social stability are based on the problem of racial contact which is increasingly driven by the domination of Western powers and the emerging problem of racial (linguistic and religious) difference within various geographies. Empire, and the peculiar rise of America within this traditionally English ethos, is foundational to how Royce directs his idealist project toward the real world. The social and political vision of America, and consequently the managing of populations with America's society, rely on the colonial foundation—the ideal motives—of England and Germany. While there may be some disagreement over the extent to which Royce's idealist metaphysics are in themselves colonial in nature, my position simply argues that the constitution of his metaphysics and his (social philosophy) ethics reify each other regarding the problem of racial difference and America's relation to raced peoples as "others" and "non-American." The problem repeated over and over again by Royce's reflections on race and empire is how one proceeds with the racial and ethnic differences in such a way that it does not divide the nation or corrupt the white Anglo-American ideas that form the basis of America's (cultural) communities. Strong communities require these strong white ideals to form the basis of community and stave off the effects of the racial and ethnic diversity threatened by foreigners and Blacks. The expansion of territory by the United States makes this a philosophical as well as a political problem.

The ideals that define America belong to the heritage of Britain. The ideas that serve as the basis of the union between America and Britain are not merely descriptive. Royce believes the history of ideas between these two nations is both heritage and destiny. The idea triumphs over the material world, because Britain has shown the power of the idea to establish itself the world over. Royce writes, "The American has been dependent for his social successes upon the retention of a very large body of ideas that the whole history of these United Kingdoms has brought into existence. And ours is a world where, after all, ideas in the long run conquer. To such ideas, material conditions are on the whole secondary."[36] Ideas motivate nations into empire and it is for this sake that knowledge is produced and accumulated within the nation. Britain has shown which ideas can project themselves into the world as incontrovertible. It's the colonial legacy of Britain that Royce believes substantiates the ideas of the Anglo-Saxon.

Royce speaks of British civilization with an earnest homage. The legacy of the English serves as the building block of America's civilization and the evidence that the idealism proposed by Royce has material consequences in the world. Royce writes, "It is a wonderful thing to begin a national life with the possession, in great measure, of the social, political, and the ideal fruits of an older civilization."[37] Royce continues,

> If one must mention in particular the masses of older ideas
> that have been of the most importance to us, one first thinks
> of the English system of common law. This system with us,
> as in your Colonies, has extended the range of its application,
> and has received a new life under the special conditions of
> our Commonwealths. Then, in the second place, the Eng-

lish language itself, with its greatest literary treasures, has
been ours. And with a language and a literature, there goes,
of course, a vast treasury of ideas. And, in the third place,
we are the inheritors of your ideals about human freedom,
about individuality, and about tolerance towards strangers
and towards all strange conditions. These are ideals which
have characterized the whole life of the Anglo-Saxon people.[38]

These ideas are not mere abstractions. They serve as the basis of relationships the Anglo-Saxon has with the world. There is an empirical basis to
the language and literatures, the ideas, which come to define the height
of European civilization. The ideas of Britain represent the most effective basis of civilization the world over—these ideas are the pinnacle of
civilization for Royce. Royce goes so far as to say that it is the colonial
heritage of Britain that has taught America the basic principles by which
to both improve itself and the tolerance to assimilate others.[39]

Royce then offers his experience as a Californian as a "more concrete suggestion"[40] of how "these fundamental ideas of our civilization
come to be applied in our life."[41] As explained in chapter 1, Royce saw
California as an example of the provincialism he sought ideally. Royce
tells of California from his perspective as a young child. In sharp contrast
to the contemporary readings of Royce as a multiculturalist, Royce does
not describe California as a geography of multicultural exchange and
mutual respect for cultures. In fact, he is quite adamant that it was the
complete opposite—a place dedicated to the assimilation of foreigners
and resistant to the culture of alien races through and through. Royce
recalls that as a child he was surrounded by various nationalities: French,
Spanish, German, Irish, English, and the unassimilable Chinese,[42] but he
insists that these cultures were of no significance to the national ideals
that actually united the multiple regions of the United States. Royce tells
his audience that "even in a community composed, as my own native
town was, of the most various nationalities, there was present the same
tendency to an assimilation from the very outset."[43] Royce explains this
example of assimilation quite explicitly. "The foreigners determined no
important part of our life. We, in turn, were moulding to our own
ways their life."[44] California is a concrete example of how provincialism is the local expression of a national ideal—an ideal Royce believes
centers around the national unity of America as an emergent imperial
power. Royce in fact writes, "Our real interests lay in the country as a

whole, in the exciting fortunes of the Civil War, in the history of our glorious past as represented by Washington. They, the foreigners, had no such interests and ideals to hold them together. In the end their systems of ideas must yield to ours, and did so."[45] It is no mistake that Royce continues to insist that America is a child of Britain—who possesses its ideas, literatures, and history—and thereby inherits its legacy of imperial conquest and colonial administration regarding nonwhite peoples.

Provincialism is merely one aspect of America's peculiarity that emerges as a means to assimilate various groups locally toward the national ideal. Royce writes, "The chief cause of the vast assimilative power of the American civilisation has been . . . the fact that the strong national consciousness, the pride in being one great and independent people, has joined itself in every case with local pride, and then with that large heritage of ideas which we have from you."[46] This is not a world of cultural exchange; rather it is the philosophy of an empire dedicated to avoiding sectionalism and preserving national unity despite the cultural, racial, and linguistic differences that are increasing within its borders. By allowing local communities to socialize strangers into the national idea, Royce believes America has improved upon British colonial methods. By involving local communities, America has been able to "extend our realm very widely, without having the portions of that realm grow as far apart as the mother country and her Colonies."[47] This insistence that local pride mirrors national consciousness allowed America to "meet the foreigner without great concern regarding his new type, if only he would respect our essential customs. It has, meanwhile, shown us that in the conflict of ideas not his but ours would be the determining features of the further development of our civilization."[48] Provincialism is an idea that attempts to eliminate the instability that can potentially arise from the presence of multiple races, languages, and religions within America. It is an idea that protects the consciousness of the nation at the local level. Local pride grasps onto foreigners and deprives them of their racial and cultural identifiers. It is important to remember that some groups are unassimilable and therefore require administration, but provincialism aims to divest alien races, in principle, of their differences.

Wise provincialism functions as the ideological stiches that both join and maintain the association various geographies share. Royce thinks of provincialism as a philosophical idea that mediates the extremity of thought and preserves social stability and societal identity. Royce has great hope in this approach. He says, "To be sure, as I hope, there will also be, in absolute measure, more and not less patriotism, closer and not looser national ties, less and not more mutual sectional misunderstanding. But the two tendencies, the tendency toward national unity and that toward local independence of spirit, must henceforth grow together. They cannot prosper apart."[49] The unity of the national and the local are necessary for the growth of empire. It is the synergy of both that drive civilization forward, and it is education that makes this synthesis possible. Royce ends "Characteristic Tendencies," with a reflection on the role that education and academic knowledge has in the reproduction of Anglo-Saxon values and an organized social consciousness in America. Alongside the Catholic Church and religion more generally, Royce observed that schools are among the "institutions that have helped us toward the power to assimilate our foreign population."[50] Royce comments that there has always been an almost instinctive feeling that "without organized learning our national ideal could not prosper. Organized learning means organized and well-knit social consciousness."[51] Much like Royce's reflections on the pedagogy of the Catholic Church, which discourages in the children of immigrants the ability to cultivate their ethnic language or practices, organized social consciousness uses education to inculcate the ethnic populations of American society into the ideas of Anglo-Saxon civilization. Royce believes quite strongly that philosophy itself—the liberal arts—are central to this program. Royce explains:

> The system of ideas of which I have spoken, ideas whose origin is so truly English and whose special development on our soil are so truly due to our peculiar national genius—this system of ideas, I say, can only be preserved, understood, improved, and in the best way applied and kept assimilative, in case it becomes understood through learning, and interpreted by wise teachers, and kept in close touch with the consciousness of humanity through the prospering of all forms of science and of the liberal arts amongst us. This we have felt. Hence our enthusiasm for educational reform and advancement.[52]

The national genius America has inherited from the English can only remain assimilative if it is expressed as a form of propaganda—articulated by teachers as universal forms of knowledge both scientific and philosophical. This is how the provincial loyalties are maintained without contradiction and disconnection to the larger national consciousness.

Royce is describing a social order founded on the idealist principles of a young American empire. He understands that the failure to enhance the national consciousness of America alongside that of the local province threatens sectionalism and by effect the unifying (national) ideal. He is attempting to learn from the Civil War where national consciousness projected by the North came into conflict with the provincial loyalties of the South. Royce has outlined how communities function such that they can control the possible sources of conflict and instability from the outside, but what of the individual? Controlling this excess of the local, of the individual man's loyalties and causes, is the charge of Royce's ethics of loyalty.

Loyalty to Loyalty as a Post–Civil War Doctrine

If "Race Questions and Prejudices" and "Provincialism" are indeed the practical manifestations of Royce's philosophy of loyalty to loyalty, what can we now say about Royce's loyalty to loyalty as a system, an ethics? Does it now become possible to see Royce's loyalty to loyalty as philosophy committed to the same end as provincialism and British administration, which is national stability? Josiah Royce publishes *The Philosophy of Loyalty* as a collection of the lectures he gave between 1906 and 1907 at Harvard and other universities across the United States.[53] Royce is usually read as offering a system of ethics to mediate the general passions and senti-mentality of human behavior. However, his terminology of loyalty often depends on an obviousness of human understanding, an intuitiveness and popular or shared belief in the value of loyalty over other dispositions like disloyalty or betrayal, which is not precisely captured philosophically. I am not the first to observe this aspect of Royce's ethics. Randall Auxier's *Time, Will, and Purpose: Living Ideas from the Philosophy of Josiah Royce* in fact steers away from Royce's terminology of loyalty because of its impreciseness. Auxier admits, "It is not clear to me that Royce made the best terminological choice when he settled upon it."[54] Dwayne Tunstall, on the other hand, explains in *Yes, but Not Quite: Encountering Royce's Ethico-Religious Insight* that "Royce is a poet-philosopher in the sense of being a philosopher who carefully hones words to communicate truths about the world, some of which transcend the boundaries of discursive thought."[55] Remarking upon Royce's *Philosophy of Loyalty*, Tunstall writes, "like poetry, Royce's philosophy, at its best, dances on the fringes of ineffability."[56] This question of imprecision may seem to be simply a semantic argument, an all too common feature of academic philosophical discussion. However, I would suggest there is something more at stake in Royce's choice of terms. Loyalty presents itself as of metaphysical origin rather than owing its existence to Royce's societal observations.

Previous work on Royce's philosophy of loyalty often suggests that it is an extension of Royce's *Conception of God* (1897) and *The World and the Individual* (1900),[57] but is this the only genealogical origin of Royce's insistence upon a loyalty to loyalty ethics? Having established Royce's genealogy of race and his fear of social instability and ruin, I believe that Royce's loyalty to loyalty originates from the atephobic disposition Royce has toward races and foreigners. It is a philosophy undergirding the ability of individuals to rationalize their commitment to communities and the national ideal that defines those multiple and varied locales. Royce urges the reader to understand, "I shall try to give you some fragments of a moral philosophy; but I shall try to justify the philosophy through its application to life."[58]

Royce begins his thinking about loyalty by distancing himself from the idea that loyalty can be the valor shown through war. "War and loyalty have been, in the past, two very closely associated ideas. It will be part of the task of these lectures to break up, so far as I can, in your own minds, that ancient and disastrous association . . ."[59] The traditional view of loyalty endorsed by Steinmetz holds that it is the warrior who best embodies this value. Royce argues that Steinmetz believes "war gives an opportunity for loyal devotion so notable and important that, if war were altogether abolished, one of the greatest goods of civilization would thereby be hopelessly lost."[60] Royce admits that he agrees with Steinmetz concerning the importance of loyalty as a human value and aspiration, but he adamantly disagrees that war is the best means by which this value can be realized in the lives of those who seek it. Why does Royce center his discussion of loyalty on a disentangling of the ethical principle from the glory and horror of war? Like his previous discussions of the Civil War and the threat of war from colonization, I believe Royce is suggesting that loyalty is a rational principle that avoids confining the advance of civilization to warfare. Loyalty is not an exclusive value in Royce's thinking. Justice, charity, industry, and wisdom are all values that can be expressed as a kind of enlightened loyalty.[61] Loyalty is simply the end at which a value or constellation of values aims. Said differently, Royce is not after a constellation of values to be produced by his ethical system.

He is concerned with the end toward which distinct values aim. Royce argues that the "deliberate centralization of all the duties and of all the virtues about the one conception of rational loyalty—is of great service as a means of clarifying and simplifying the tangled moral problems of our lives and of our age."[62] These moral problems emerge as those involving the contact and understanding of racial others. I believe loyalty still attempts to address these conflicts.

Royce defines loyalty provisionally as "the willing and practical and thoroughgoing devotion of a person to a cause."[63] One is loyal when they first have a cause to which they are loyal, then when said person willingly and completely dedicates themselves to this cause, and finally expresses their devotion to this cause practically and acts consistently in service to this cause.[64] Royce has previously established the idea(s) that guides humanity in history and through empire. Now he is concerned with the means through which individuals themselves come to this realization, not through predeterminism, but rational choice. Royce achieves this by showing that loyalty must involve sociality. The loyal person is in fact a person who is not simply driven by an emotional relationship to a cause, but by service and devotion to it. His or her life is dedicated to the enhancement and realization of this cause.[65] The cause is embodied by the person and guides his or her reality completely. This cause however is not simply personal; it is not only one's dedication to their own achievement or end. Royce explains that "the cause to which a loyal man is devoted is never something wholly impersonal. It concerns other men. Loyalty is social."[66] What then does Royce intend this sociality and its relationship to the person to do as an ethics?

Royce believes that humans are social beings, who learn to participate and live in the social realm through imitation. We learn to speak and play through imitation. Imitation is, as Royce says, "itself due to our instincts as social beings."[67] Because we are born social, imitation leads us to our own will through our mimicking of the will of others. Social conformity and imitation do not repress the individual according to Royce, but offer the individual the tools to express their own particular renderings of their social world. "Teach men customs, and you equip them with weapons for expressing their own personalities," says Royce.[68] These customs are relayed to us through schools, churches, and our communities, the same conveyors of values Royce speaks of in "Some Characteristic Tendencies." Royce believes, despite this acculturation, that "social conformity gives us social power. Such power brings to us a consciousness of who and what we are."[69] By becoming conscious of the lessons taught to us by our society, those sacred (Anglo-Saxon) values that have shown themselves to stand above others in history become one's rational choices, the rational embrace of one's *own* endorsement of superior ideas. This self-consciousness of the individual's choice to embrace the cause shows the individual (and this is Royce's answer to the ethical individualists in "Individualism") that the cause is both personal and impersonal. In other words, the cause both concerns oneself and links other human beings, together in its activity. So like provincialism and Royce's thinking about post–Civil War America, "Loyalty, tends to unify life, to give it centre, fixity, stability."[70] Remember it is (all) stable social relations that give rise to causes to which one may be loyal.[71]

Loyalty then achieves the same effect as assimilation. It is a commitment in which the individual embodies and extends the idea that births community—the close knitting of others. Loyalty is the system of rationalization that marries the individual to the ideal—the cause of the nation. It is the expression of the provincial ideal within the individual, or how the individual rationalizes his or her desire for the wise provincial community and aspiration as a citizen, who is responsible for America emerging as an imperial nation. As Royce himself writes, "You cannot be loyal to a merely personal abstraction; and you also cannot be loyal simply to a collection of various separate persons, viewed merely as a collection. Where there is an object of loyalty, there is, then, a union of various selves into one life."[72] Loyalty to loyalty is thereby the safeguard to this sociality that emerges from the self-conscious individual. Royce writes:

> If loyalty is a supreme good, the mutually destructive conflict of loyalties is in general a supreme evil. If loyalty is a good for all sorts and conditions of men, the war of man against man has been especially mischievous, not so much because it has hurt, maimed, impoverished, or slain men, as because it has so often robbed the defeated of their causes, of their opportunities to be loyal, and sometimes of their very spirit of loyalty.[73]

The cause of the individual must then enhance the conditions and possibilities of others' loyalty, or as Royce explains, one pursues one's "individual cause as to secure thereby the greatest possible increase of loyalty amongst men."[74] Loyalty to loyalty exists then when the loyal individual's "choice may be so directed that loyalty to the universal loyalty of all mankind shall be furthered by the actual choices which each enlightened loyal person makes when he selects his cause."[75] Loyalty to loyalty is the individual preserving the social relationship, the stability and peace, necessary for individuals to become self-conscious of the sociality their loyalty entails. Too often causes tend toward war and death—they become lost causes—and lead one to violate the ethics of loyalty to loyalty that is social stability and the individual's rationalization of the provincial community.

The Problem with the "Provincial Revision" and Other Ahistorical Justifications for Using Royce as an Anti-Racist Thinker

A somewhat recent challenge to my interpretation of Royce laying claim to white America's legacy as a "colonizing peoples" was raised by Mathew A. Foust's *Loyalty to Loyalty: Josiah Royce and the Genuine Moral Life* (2012). According to Foust, my original 2009 article "Royce, Racism, and the Colonial Ideal" left out the words "of such mental tendencies in ourselves lies in the aid that they give us in becoming loyal to our community" in the block quote in footnote 26, and by effect ignores a central point in Royce's account of wise provincialism and Royce's understanding of community. Foust concedes that Royce *may have feared* plurality, to the extent that it could cause a national crisis similar to the Civil War, and the historical customs, consciousness, and culture carried by diverse peoples (i.e., the racial, ethnic, or linguistic differences that define them), but he believes that such fear "need not entail a fear of diversity or an endorsement of racist colonialism."[76] Foust argues that "Royce stipulates he is not advocating narrowness of spirit, distinguishing his provincialism from false sectionalism, dubbing it sometimes higher provincialism and at others wise provincialism."[77] In an apologetic tone, Foust maintains, "whatever Royce's various personal predilections may have been, he is clearly declaring the need for a shift from unwise provincialism—the kind that he sees as deeply divisive and as responsible for the Civil War (as well as the crisis in Britain)—and wise provincialism, the kind that sustains unity and therefore reduces the chance of conflict, especially on the scale of war."[78]

Here Foust tells the reader more about his understanding of racism beyond the words he simply writes. Foust makes a dreadful mistake
in characterizing the question of Royce's racism as a matter of "personal
predilections," which is perhaps why he simply does not grasp the historical nuances of the arguments waged or understand the philosophical
matters at hand. The question of racism around the turn of the twentieth
century is not about personal biases. It is and always has been a civilizational insistence that the world and the ideals in that world should
be white/European/Anglo-Saxon. This historical reality created by white
supremacy only left a few options regarding white/Anglo-Saxon contact
with Black/primitives: Anglo-Saxon dominance where the "lesser races"
were assimilated and made loyal to America; genocide, as was the case
of Indigenous peoples in America; or colonial segregation, or what we
commonly refer to as apartheid. Racism, especially at the turn of the
century, concerns questions of racial superiority or inferiority expressed
in science as well as the organization and policies of various "civilized"
natures toward "savage" peoples—specifically, how superior white groups
should rule those racialized groups.

A cursory reading of W. E. B. Du Bois's "The Souls of [w]hite
Folk" in *Darkwater* (1920) that frames whiteness as white supremacy,
colonialism, and imperialism explains the seriousness of situating what
is specifically meant by and encountered in the physical and political
manifestations of American racism. Racism and an individual's racial
identification with whiteness was not a matter of individual taste or
disposition. Du Bois describes whiteness as "this new religion . . . on the
shores of our times,"[79] with funny effects on "the strut of the Southerner,
the arrogance of the Englishman amuck, the whoop of the hoodlum who
vicariously leads your mob."[80] It is no coincidence that the chapter from
Darkwater entitled "The Souls of [w]hite Folk," which was originally
published as two separate essays "The Souls of [w]hite Folk" (1910) and
"Of the Culture of [w]hite Folk" (1917), takes up the same actors—the
Southerner, the British, the lynch mob—as Royce's racial trilogy, given
its closeness to the publication of Royce's monograph entitled *Race Questions, Provincialism, and Other American Problems* (1908). The reflections
offered by Josiah Royce's "Provincialism," which tied America's imperial
future to the colonial past of Britain and celebrated the violent heritage
shared between them, was also analyzed by Black thinkers of the time as
well, but unlike Royce, the cultural and historical union of America to
Europe through Britain was seen as a growing danger to the lives of the

darker races. Colonies are those places where "niggers are cheap and the earth is rich,"[81] and not without consequence to the historical framing of a thinker like Royce that sees himself both as a colonizer, like the great men of Britain, and an advocate of the modernization of colonial strategies in the American South. For members of the darker races, provincialism, as well as the debates in Royce's own time concerning the white peril, and the white man's burden following the Russo-Japanese War, was about the solidification of white domination over the darker races throughout the world. Du Bois remarks toward this looming threat:

> America, Land of Democracy, wanted to believe in the failure of democracy so far as darker people were concerned. Absolutely without excuse she established a caste system, rushed in preparation for war, and conquered tropical colonies. She stands today shoulder to shoulder with Europe in Europe's worst sin against civilization. She aspires to sit among the great nations who arbitrate the fate of "lesser breeds without the law" and she is at times heartily ashamed even of the large number of "new" white people whom her democracy has admitted to place and power. Against this surging forward of Irish and German, of Russian Jew, Slave and "dago" her social bars have not availed, but against Negroes she can and does take her unflinching and immovable stand, backed by this new public policy of Europe. She trains her immigrants to this despising of "niggers" from the day of their landing, and they carry and send the news back to the submerged classes in the fatherlands.[82]

Foust's misunderstanding of what is exactly under discussion when speaking about race, and/or racial contact at the turn of the century and in Royce's "Provincialism," is of grave consequence to his position as a defender of Royce in a debate about racism and America's colonial endeavors. Not only do such comments point to the need for textually and historically situating Royce in his historical milieu—by this I mean to say: having a rigorous intellectual history as the basis of philosophical interpretation rather than seemingly intuitive impressions of individuals invested in the figure written about, who then revise the figure's text and that figure's terminology to fit twenty-first-century inventions of race and racism—but this particular response demonstrates how Royce's defenders have revised his thought to fit their twenty-first-century interpretive agendas rather than reflect the debates and engagements to be found within his own time. Foust demands the reader to suspend history and reject the intellectual historical context of Royce's reflections about the world around him. Foust then asks the reader to imagine a world where Royce is freed from the theodicy of his texts, a world where we arrive at a predetermined conclusion without any investigation of the text before us, namely—Royce is not a racist, thus his work cannot be racist, regardless of what he actually writes, or admits himself to be within his own works. Under Foust's interpretation, Negrophobia, xenophobia, and colonialism need not be racist, or racially averse or hostile to racialized others, despite the historical reality in which all these ideologies have been used to justify the most heinous policies and crimes against Black, Indigenous, and Asian peoples throughout the history of America. For Foust, these concerns are dealt with secondarily, taking a backseat to the preservation and defense of Royce's larger provincial project.

Whereas Royce is very clear about his reliance on assimilation to maintain social order, Foust suggests we should not take Royce at his own words. Rather than offer a serious engagement with what Royce means by stating that Americans and the English are colonizing people who utilize loyalty to assimilate newcomers, Foust offers an apologetic. Foust begins by contending that Royce's argument for assimilation is ultimately friendly and welcoming to the stranger. According to Foust,

> Royce holds that provincial tendencies aid us both in becoming loyal to our community and in assimilating others to our community. At this juncture, all this seems to mean is that cultivating pride in customs, ideals, and the like of our community is conducive to becoming loyal to our community and that helping newcomers to such pride will be conducive as well to their becoming loyal to our community. Such a position could very well be put forth by a racist colonialist, but it could just as plausibly be put forth by a person wishing for the harmonious coexistence of diversity and unity.[83]

Foust wants to contend that what Royce really means, despite his self-identification as part of a colonizing people, is that the engagement with newcomers and strangers is gregarious, going so far as to argue that "even if Royce was a begrudging accepter of diversity, the wish to avoid crisis by means of harmonious coexistence of diversity and unity constitutes an embrace of national plurality, not an attempt at its obviation."[84] In support of this contention, Foust cites Royce stating "to make him welcome is one of the most gracious tasks in which our people have become expert. To give him fair chance is our rule of life."[85] Foust then moves to suggest to the reader that "we should not ignore his [Royce's] stated openness to widening the scope of the community to include members from outside its immediate ken. His worry is that the social tendencies of a community will undergo constant mutation in attempting to accommodate the social tendencies of newcomers, resulting in a diminution of community spirit."[86] In order to put a "friendly" face on colonization, the conformity and social control necessary to maintain social stability, Foust intentionally misrepresents Royce's text in "Provincialism" to the reader. Royce actually says:

> The stranger, the sojourner, the newcomer, is an inevitable factor in the life of most American communities. To make him welcome is one of the most gracious of the tasks in which our people have become expert. To give him his fair chance is the rule of our national life. But it is not on the whole well when the affairs of a community remain too largely under the influence of those who mainly feel either the wanderer's or the new resident's interest in the region where they are now dwelling. To offset the social tendencies due to such frequent changes of dwelling-place we need the further development and the intensification of the community spirit. *The sooner the new resident learns to share this spirit, the better for him and for his community.* A sound instinct, therefore, guides even our new communities, in the more fortunate cases, to *a rapid development of such a local sentiment as makes the stranger feel that he must in due measure conform if he would be permanently welcome, and must accept the local spirit if he is to enjoy the advantages of his community.*[87] (Emphasis added.)

Reading Foust's citations in the context of the paragraph they originate from shows that Royce is still trying to deal with the issue of (race) contact. In a white republic, who would be the stranger and newcomer to Royce? Contrary to Foust's view of the Roycean community as a "dynamic structure, taking on new forms with the inclusion of new members while at the same time striving to remain the same,"[88] the reality presented by Royce's text suggests that *conformity* is the necessary condition for one's permanent acceptance into the community. Royce is clear that being a welcomed stranger is a contingent relationship and only offered so that it "makes the stranger feel that he must in due measure conform, if he would be permanently welcome."[89] This is not rhetorical, some post-structural interpretive measures seeking to pull some obscure meaning from the text. This is simple. Royce articulates a position that is shown to be consistent through three separate texts over the span of a decade. Royce is very clear that wise provincialism maintains unity and offers strangers the advantages of a loyal community by the extent to which the stranger conforms to the local spirit of the already established spirit of the community. This is a repressive social ethos, not a community of inclusion that believes that other cultural ideals other than that of the Anglo-Saxon have a role in the history and civilization of America. Foust aims to convince the reader that his reimagining of Royce's benevolently assimilated community is in fact Royce's original idea without making any effort to situate how the victims of this assimilation, those people that "must in due measure conform," will react to this cultural imposition.

What Foust does not understand is that the issue at hand is not a charge against Royce's demand for "becoming loyal to our community," but that using assimilation to build community, the demand that others give up their culture, language, racial/ethnic ideals to be part of white communities, is in fact racism and rooted in colonialism. Ultimately, I am forced to wonder what is it about Royce, and his notions of community, that allows and encourages contemporary Royce scholars to claim without proof or text that these communities are in fact diverse and plural, when Royce is clear that these practices of diversity are destabilizing, evil, and a very real danger to the growth and imperial future of America, and then enforce such an interpretation by the communal consensus of Royceans against historical and archival evidence to the contrary.[90] Such loose expositions of Royce's text appear more reflective of ideology than careful textual exegesis.

Wise Provincialism as Wise whiteness: Sullivan's Interpretation of Royce's Race Thinking and Her Solidification of whiteness

These contestations over Royce's contribution to American race theory do not end at textual debates. For some scholars, Royce's provincialism has gained a decidedly novel role. The most recent popular use of this perspective is Shannon Sullivan's article entitled "Whiteness as Wise Provincialism: Royce and the Rehabilitation of a Racial Category,"[91] which argues that Royce's thinking on wise provincialism can serve as a model for an anti-racist conservationist theory of wise whiteness. According to Sullivan, this turn to Royce "is not as surprising as it might initially seem given that Royce wrote explicitly about race in 'Race Questions and Prejudices,' "[92] where he argued for "an anti-racist, anti-essentialist challenge to then current scientific studies of race."[93] Unfortunately, however, Sullivan's essay, like many works of white scholars before her, ignores the actual historical context of Royce's seeming resistance to the science of his times, and the actual concerns addressed by the phrase "white peril." Despite the historical evidence and the writings of Black thinkers to the contrary, Sullivan merely asserts, without textual support or consideration of Royce's 1900 speech at Aberdeen University, that Royce is in fact an anti-racist racial conservationist.

At this point in the book, it should be clear to the reader that Royce is simply not willing to abandon his belief in the superiority of Anglo-Saxon ideals or the historical legacy those ideals had in the rearing of British and American colonialism. Like many of the revisions to historic white philosophers over the race question, Sullivan's work merely reproduces the popular consensus (interests) the discipline has in maintaining the legitimacy of American philosophy, as proof of Royce's anti-racist stance, rather than evidentiary support for this interpretation, that can somewhat pale Royce's blatant appeals to the duty of the white man. Even if Sullivan could somehow deny the historical relevance of environmentalism and the actual context of the term "white peril," it remains a mystery as to how a self-identified "critical race theorist" interested in whiteness studies could so casually ignore both the theoretical and practical consequences of endorsing Royce's colonial project as liberatory praxis.

Sullivan can only retrieve a racist figure like Royce because of the disciplinary structure of philosophy—its Eurocentric bias—that invalidates the work and legacy of Black thinkers doing much more radical scientific and philosophical research than Royce. In other words, it is through the disciplinary structure of racism that excludes and invalidates the work of Black thinkers and theorists that Royce emerges as a source of race theory. Sullivan's engagement with Royce, her interpretations, which rely on a certain naïveté regarding history and Black people within history, have currency in philosophy, because Blacks (be they philosophers or at large thinkers) are not "an audience" in the discipline. Even when Black figures are included in discourses concerning racism, their inclusion is based on an appeal to the very structures (conference committees, journal editors, white philosophy organizations) responsible for the ongoing exclusion in the first place. The consequence of this underrepresentation of Black voices and bodies is that American philosophy allows the creative energies of white scholars to run rampant, so to speak, in their attempts to revive white historical figures in regard to race, without any attention to the very real dangers of white thinking and thought.

For example, before the intervention made by my work and that of Dwayne Tunstall, and the subsequent reflection by Marilyn Fischer's "Locating Royce's Reasoning on Race," there was no discussion of Royce's anti-Black racism. In fact, his call to colonize Black people in the American South was celebrated as a progressive alternative to lynching. Similar to the case of Addams, where we find the actual racist supposition of Black men as the natural rapists of white women, American philosophy embraces a peculiar revisionism whereby all white thinking that did not support the most atrocious acts of racism like slavery, lynching, segregation, or rape, become anti-racist. Here again, the consequence of ideo-racial apartheid in American philosophy is apparent. Independent of Royce, Sullivan's work makes an interesting claim that urges whites to become conscious of their unconscious racial identity—a claim that should be philosophically pursued—but in its current form, the case for wise whiteness reads as yet another attempt to save American philosophy from its unsightly racist past, and it is in this light that I would argue that Sullivan's account of Royce's provincialism, as a basis for wise whiteness, is more fictive than philosophical.

Like many other "white conservationists," Sullivan fails to specifically articulate the cultural elements and local traditions that would comprise whiteness. Besides defining wise whiteness as "an umbrella for the infinitely rich and complicated ways that white people embody their whiteness,"[94] and claiming based on this definition that the elimination of the term allows white supremacy to escape unnoticed under the particularity of varying white ethnicities, Sullivan altogether ignores the need to actually articulate the customs and traditions that she believes resonate so deeply within Royce's thought. Whether or not there are actual cultural artifacts worth preserving in whiteness—though doubtful—is debatable, but Sullivan's second claim that "in the case of white ethnicities, insisting that whiteness always be considered in connection with other axes of identity can collapse race into ethnicity and work to deflect attention away from white domination and oppression," seems to be a problematic reason to preserve whiteness as a racial category. Black scholars have always understood the ethnic and in some cases racial absorption of various historical peoples into whiteness. This was the debate Black Americans had in the early 1900s concerning the Russo-Japanese War, and it extends backward to the mid-1800s. As early as 1859, for instance, Frederick Douglass criticized the United States government for allowing white ethnic groups, who were not born in the United States, rights that it denied to Black and Brown Americans.[95] Richard Rees's *Shades of Difference: A History of Ethnicity in America*, goes through great lengths explaining this process with particular attention to the Irish. His project demystifies the idea that white ethnicities were in fact distinct and absolved in the construction, perpetuation, and enforcement of whiteness, in fact, he argues the construct of ethnicity itself was central to the growth and preservation of whiteness.[96] Unless one isolates oneself to the discussions of "white ethnicity" in the discipline of philosophy, Sullivan is hard pressed to show how the elimination of "whiteness" involves its concealment in particular "white ethnicities."

Instead of concrete demonstrations of "wise whiteness," Sullivan offers the imagery of John Brown's abolitionism as an example of whiteness's anti-racial potential. While Sullivan does admit that it is "difficult to pinpoint a nugget of 'wholesome' whiteness to use as a starting point for its transformation,"[97] it seems somewhat inaccurate to present John Brown's raid on Harper's Ferry in 1859 as the primary example of wise whiteness in the twenty-first century. Sullivan seems to ignore two crucial aspects of John Brown's abolitionism. First, as read in the twentieth century by Black thinkers like W. E. B. Du Bois, Brown was inspired by Caribbean, specifically Haitian revolutionary influences, so his actions were not based solely on a white self-consciousness.[98] Brown hoped his raid would inspire slave insurrections, which he would then arm with the weapons from the raid. His abolitionism was not simply born of his own reflections on whiteness; they were dedicated to violent revolt and the death of slave-holding whites. Second, and perhaps most important, John Brown's actions endangered the lives of many Black communities, who had to suffer the white backlash for his actions. Frederick Douglass, who commended Brown's courage and actions against slavery, had to flee to Canada, because he was thought to have an association with Brown's plot,[99] and Martin R. Delany, who rejected Brown's plan from its inception, fled to Liberia.[100] These historical points demonstrate not only the difficulty of implicating Royce's provincialism in a narrative of radical anti-racist whiteness that itself is not historically coherent, but the potential dangers such activism may pose to people of color.

In her most recent book, *Good [w]hite People: The Problem with Middle-Class [w]hite Anti-Racism* (2014), Sullivan develops her theory of wise provincialism as a unifying theme of the text.[101] In Sullivan's most recent text, she again attempts to situate whiteness, specifically poor whiteness, as a valuable reminder and insight into the function of white domination.[102] Unfortunately, her dedication to the inclusion of the poor white voice only solidifies the inferiority of Black life and experience within these publics. The reality is Black people, especially Black males, have often been the victims of poor whites. While the membership of the Ku Klux Klan has varied throughout the centuries, the economic and political competition enfranchised Black males posed to poor whites was often the catalyst behind KKK violence and lynchings.[103] Similarly, the threat enfranchised Black men posed to white women's emerging political power also prompted Women Ku Klux Klan organizations against Black economic and political activity.[104] Sullivan seems to be oblivious to the very real dangers and sexual mythology involved in the class dynamics between poor whites and Blacks.

Perhaps this lack of historical sensibility arises from a misconstruing of the present. Sullivan begins with the idea that "today white domination in the United States and many other Western countries operates by means of covert white privilege, rather than overt white supremacy."[105] While Sullivan is not a Black person, the material realities of Black death in America, the protests over the shooting of Black youth, specifically young Black males, the attention to the expanding prison industrial complex, and the rise of Black unemployment, the conversations surrounding the Latino population boom seem to indicate that many of the issues Blacks confronted in Jim Crow segregation and the failure of desegregation remain the same issues of the twenty-first century. Instead of addressing the systemic and cultural consequences of white supremacy, namely, Black poverty and death, Sullivan concentrates her efforts on the rehabilitation of whiteness, specifically the class division used by middle-class whites to elevate themselves above poor whites. In order to repair whiteness, Sullivan insists that the white middle class confront their racial class status by listening to white supremacists and including them into the public and political spaces of democratic deliberation. She writes, "In the name of expanding democracy to include people of color—as it well should—American society often attempts to render white supremacists and white trash speechless and minimize their participation in the public, shared sculpting of the world based on their particular desires and concerns. Even if enacted with good intentions, however, this exclusion is problematic."[106] Sullivan believes that "it is counterproductive to racial justice movements to say that differences between white allies and white supremacists such as disagreements over whether white people are superior to nonwhite people or whether people of color should be respected as full persons, are outside the realm of political deliberation."[107] If the inferiority of Blacks, Latinos, and Indigenous people is now debatable publicly and accepted as a legitimate democratic concern, how does one counter the endorsement of this position by whites persuaded by the argument of white supremacists?

Sullivan can offer no safeguards to nonwhites in such a public. In fact, Sullivan goes so far as to argue, "For people concerned about racial justice to unilaterally exclude white supremacists—and I'm thinking here of middle-class white people in particular—is for them to reenact the dehumanizing and destructive marginalization that white supremacists inflict upon people of color."[108] Is this a pragmatic strategy under the presidency of Trump that was ushered in by the rise of hate crimes, white ethnonationalists on university campuses, and a shared fear among Blacks, Muslims, and immigrant populations? Since Trump's election, the efforts to deport Mexican immigrants and surveil Latino citizens have increased. Black men are still disproportionately killed by the police, and their murders are rationalized by the state and multiple state-level courts as justified. Muslims are being terrorized and denied entry into the United States because their religion is constructed as terroristic. These are the racist ideals propagated as being synonymous to the cultural heritage and preservation of the white race. Our contemporary political moment repeats the crisis of the country at the turn of the century. The diversification of world and nation threatens the societal and cultural order of local white communities in the United States. Now, just as then, white Americans are fearful of cultural difference, terrified of race—Blackness—and are using the police, ICE, and other social mechanisms of discrimination to rally around and protect whiteness. Under such a wise provincialism dedicated to the cultivation of wise whiteness, white supremacists are given a public and an audience. Deliberation is now constitutive of community and a necessity, since the exclusion of the poor white or white supremacist's voice inevitably leads to their silence and dehumanization. The danger of whiteness is not simply theoretical, as in one centering its exploration above those of Black, Brown, or Indigenous peoples, but concrete in that the white audiences that are part of this democratic community can be convinced of their own racial superiority. These white people listening to the white supremacist can be lawyers, teachers, police, or judges. Their position in society can be utilized to the detriment of nonwhites just as they are today. Rather than remedying the worsening race relations of the United States, Sullivan's program, because it potentially educates a public in white supremacy, is actually quite dangerous. As in Royce's philosophy, when whiteness is maintained as the necessary racial and cultural center of knowledge and ideas, it is those races defined outside of whiteness that are actually dehumanized and threatened. Like Royce's wise provincialism, it is white racial identities (like the card-carrying white supremacist and the slaveholder) and the values these voices command in the world that determine what (civilized) communities reflect. In other words, the voice of the white supremacist emerges from Sullivan's system as more valuable than the lives of Black people, because they must be included in the public despite the threats of harm or fear they incite toward Blacks, Latinos, and Indigenous peoples.

Conclusion

Instead of being met with the typical reactions of mainstream philosophers, this exposure of Royce's racism and the dangers of his provincialism should challenge scholars in American philosophy to look to other Black, Indigenous, and Latino/a scholars that actually spoke about race and American racism, who dedicated their lives to writing books, pamphlets, and reflections on these injustices, rather than already canonized white scholars who encounter the race problem in passing, in one or two articles, without any actual insight into the reality of these anti-Black maladies. The sheer amount of revisionism needed to make these white thinkers appear even moderately reflective of racism should give the thoughtful scholar pause. The challenge set before American philosophy today is not simply one of historical accuracy, but philosophical integrity, in that it challenges scholars who are obsessed with saving white thinkers from their own racism to expand their horizons and abandon the ideo-racial apartheid that maintains the imperial scholarship of the discipline.

Royce has developed an intricate system of colonial domination. He has offered an idealist architecture, so to speak, which links national unity to provincial loyalties and, most importantly, to the individual's rational endorsement of the imperial cause. Royce imagines a world driven toward the realization of the colonial ideal whose gift is not only a participation in the magnificent legacy of Britain, but the stability of an empire who controls those races who threaten it from within by the sheer force of its ideology. In the next chapter (chapter 4), I situate Royce's idealism in relation to the ethnological racism of his mentor, Joseph Le Conte. It was Royce's striving for unity, his need for cultural homogeneity, that led him to make his idealistic metaphysics a repressive social ethics.

4

On the Dark Arts

The Ethnological Foundations of Royce's Idealism
as Derivative from Joseph Le Conte's
"Southern Problems"; or The Evolutionary Basis
of Royce's Assimilationist Program

For the last several years, Royce scholars have continued to speak of Royce's interest in race as if it has been a natural attribute of his ethical character and progressive foresight. This approach taken up by scholars in their reading of Royce's social ethics and race theory persists, despite the evidence showing that Royce's proposals to remedy the race problem was criticized in his own lifetime as white supremacism and harmful to Black Americans. John M. Mecklin was central in advancing these criticisms of Royce's work. Perhaps his most radical intervention into the debates concerning Josiah Royce's racial corpus is his view that Royce's racial program was dedicated to the elevation of the superior white race and the complete subjugation of the Black. Unlike the Le Contean framing of Black emancipation, which held that slavery was eliminated in part because the slave had evolved beyond the institution, Mecklin's research, specifically his two essays attending to "The Evolution of Slave Status in American Democracy," showed when the "demand for labor ceased because of the increase of white labor and when the diminished supply rendered it more difficult to get profitable slaves, the same economic laws [which necessitated slavery initially] tended to encourage the freedom of the slave."[1] In short, Mecklin indicates that the evolutionary account of Le Conte, as well as the provincial logics deployed by Royce regarding the Negro, are in fact erroneous interpretations of evolutionary science used to justify the political subjugation of the Black race in an effort to assimilate this group. The previous writings on Royce's race

thinking are more geared toward the exegetical expressions of dearly
held personal assumptions about Royce's ethical character, and the need
to describe him as socially conscious and aware of the racism in his
time, rather than his actual perceptions and sensibilities of racial and
ethnic difference at the turn of the century. In fact, little to no research
explores the evolutionary theories or ethnological assumptions of Royce's
thinking concerning the American race problem. This chapter attempts
to address this gap in Royce scholarship by analyzing the evolutionary
theories behind Royce's philosophy. Royce comes to theorize about race
contact and the practices of the South as an outgrowth of Joseph Le
Conte's theories of evolution and racial development. Insofar as Royce
believes that Blacks and immigrants are impressionable enough to take
on the necessary motifs of white civilization, the means he suggests to
accomplish these ends—assimilation, provincialism, and loyalty—must
account for the racial differences ethnologists were actively debating
during the writing of his racial corpus.

It is my position that the terminology utilized throughout Royce's
writings on race fits into his overarching concerns about national unity.
Clarifying why Royce sees assimilation as that "especial art," and what led
to Royce's development of a race theory, or what I have aptly termed his
development of the *Dark Arts*, is necessary to understanding his idealism
and how this idealist philosophy translates into the social program he
offers throughout his writings on race. In what follows, I intend to show
how Royce's "loyalty to loyalty," his metaphysical idealism, is not only
indebted to Joseph Le Conte's influence, but the evolutionary theodicy
that emerges from race contact. First, I will show that Royce's 1901
article entitled "Joseph Le Conte" is an ignored foundational piece that
discloses why Royce saw his own practice of philosophy to be directly
indebted, or more accurately determined, by the life and thought of
Joseph Le Conte. Second, and perhaps more importantly, I will outline
how Royce's colonial arts are Royce's attempt to resolve the issues raised
by Joseph Le Conte's work entitled "The Race Problem in the South,"
published in 1892, where Le Conte called for an "art of government"
and warned of the dangers that civil unrest poses to America's national
character. And in the last section of this chapter, I will introduce John
M. Mecklin's philosophy of race traits and his argument against Josiah
Royce's proposals for racial assimilation and British colonial administration in the American South.

Exorcising Royce's Racist Spirit:
How Le Contean Evolutionism Manifests as
Royce's Evolutionary (Social) Theodicy

While the primary literature documenting the relationship between Joseph Le Conte and Josiah Royce has been around for over two decades, philosophers have been slow to attend to the implications of this relationship to Royce's thoughts about race. This is strange given the centrality of Joseph Le Conte's philosophy to Royce's idealism and social political theory. Joseph Le Conte was born on a plantation February 26, 1823, in Liberty County, Georgia. From a very early age Le Conte had an interest in nature. He often recalled the lessons he learned from nature on his father's plantation, where he came to understand the relation between whites and Blacks, master and slave, as a fundamental expression of natural law. In 1841, Joseph Le Conte completed his Bachelor of Arts degree at the University of Georgia and began his study of medicine at the College of Physicians and Surgeons in New York in 1843. After obtaining his medical degree in 1845, he began an apprenticeship at Harvard University under Louis Agassiz in 1850. Having earned some recognition under Agassiz's tutelage, Le Conte took a position as a professor of chemistry and geology at South Carolina College in Columbia. However, it would not be until 1868 when he was called to a philosophy position at UC Berkeley that he would have the opportunity to meet and mentor the young Josiah Royce.

Royce held an admiration for Joseph Le Conte that could not be rivaled. In 1901, Royce wrote a tribute to his recently deceased mentor and credited Le Conte (d. July 6, 1901) not only for his scientific acumen but his metaphysical idealism. From Royce's nostalgic remarks about Le Conte during his freshman year, where he "looked forward to the time when I should reach the level of work where Joe's lectures would form part of my task,"[2] to his reflections on the life of Le Conte as a seasoned scholar and admits, "[I had] always been conscious . . . of an effort to think in Le Conte's spirit, whatever it has been about which I have been thinking. His wealth of knowledge, his instinct for order and lucidity of reflection, have, indeed, always remained my hopelessly distant ideal,"[3] it is clear that Royce sought to emulate various aspects of Le Conte's thought and outlook upon the world. This ideal may not have been as distant as some may think. Royce explicitly speaks of conjuring Le Conte in his idealist philosophy. Royce writes, "I believe in the world's unity and by indirect proof feel sure of it. But the world of concrete facts will never seem to my unaided thought, as perfect or as clearly visible a union of the One and Many, of harmonious principles and of multitudinous empirical illustrations, as it seemed to me while I listened to his lectures. But his spirit was contagious, was compelling, was enduring in effect."[4] So enduring, in fact, that in December 1915 (eight months before his death), Josiah Royce referenced Joseph Le Conte's teachings, and his subsequent reading of J. S. Mill and Herbert Spencer, as being the major views from which he articulates the idea of community amid World War I.[5]

These passages offer substantial evidence that Royce is orienting his philosophical idealism toward various principles found in his study of Le Conte. According to the late sociologist Stanford Lyman, "much of the social philosophy that Josiah Royce developed was derived from his undergraduate studies with Le Conte at Berkeley. Le Conte, who had been a prominent slave owner and a chemist for the Confederate Nitre Bureau, found refuge from possible trial as a war criminal at Berkeley where he assumed the mantle of a gentle prophet of evolution."[6]

> Royce born amidst what he recalled as a morally bereft gold rush California that had all too easily acquiesced to the style, manner, and racial ideas of the Southern cavalier, sought religio-philosophic guidance and scientific grounding for the restoration of an ethical social order from his studies with Le Conte. Appalled by the violent character, corrupt politics, and social disorder that he saw on the Pacific and assumed to be widespread in the rest of America, Royce, always more religious than his revered but complacently deistic mentor Le Conte, adopted the latter's evolutionism to an elaborate theory of the social system, harmonizing both mind and society with the will of God.[7]

Dwayne A. Tunstall's excellent work on Royce, entitled *Yes, but Not Quite: Encountering Josiah Royce's Ethico-Religious Insight*, has already demonstrated the weaknesses of Royce's absolutist conception of God against George Holmes Howison's critique,[8] but the inadequacies of Royce's reflections on God, community, and individual autonomy can be pushed even further when read as a continuation of his attempts to synthesize the scientific evolutionism of Joseph Le Conte, who was not only mentioned as the inspiration of Josiah Royce's reflection on God in his 1895 essay, "On the Conception of God," but was a respondent to Royce's paper at the Philosophical Union at the University of California.

At the beginning of "On the Conception of God," Royce pays a special tribute to Joseph Le Conte. One could think such a tribute to be misplaced given Le Conte's notoriety as a scientist rather than a philosopher or theologian, but as will be revealed in the course of the replies by Le Conte and Howison, evolution—the struggle between life and death—is in fact a motivating logic of Royce's thinking about God. For Le Conte, "Nature is the womb in which, and evolution the process by which, are generated sons of God."[9] Howison is not far removed from Le Conte's framing of the problem. Because "human nature pours forth all its commingled, doubt and faith,"[10] Howison sees evolutionism as the existential notation to the existence of selves that resist total consumption by the overarching absolutism of Royce's view of God. Howison continues,

> as Dr. Le Conte has so eloquently and so forcibly shown, it does seem clear, through the long and agonizing path of evolution—through struggle, and death, and survival—that a rational, a moral, a self-active being is on the way toward realized existence, and *it is true* that unless there is immortality awaiting it, this long and hard advance through Nature will be balked, and the whole process of evolution turn futile.[11] (Emphasis added.)

Tunstall's argument that the "Conception of God" debate caused Royce to make explicit his ethico-religious insights in 1898 is confirmed,[12] albeit for different reasons. The catalyst for Royce's idea of community is pushed beyond the ontological, not only by Howison's criticism of his relationship between the individual and God, but also by the case made by Le Conte (and confirmed by Howison) regarding how the evolutionary process (individual, social, and communal change) makes the individual existentially resistant to a deterministic and absolutist conceptualization of God.

Remember, in 1915, Royce tells us that his academic and intellectual history starts with Le Conte, tends toward Spencer, and that he returns to these lessons in 1878–1882 during his time at the University of California. In this same piece, Royce explicitly claims that he is not a

Hegelian, while confessing that his "deepest motives and problems have centered about the Idea of Community."[13] In previous works, philosophers have mentioned the relationship between Josiah Royce and Joseph Le Conte in name only. There is much to be learned, not only by Royce's dedication to Le Conte, but Le Conte's response to Royce. Though Le Conte does chastise Royce for his failure to explicitly acknowledge evolutionary thinking in his method, Le Conte nonetheless agrees with Royce's conclusions. Le Conte's support for Royce is so overwhelming that he goes so far as to claim that Royce merely articulates the same conclusion he reaches in his book, *Evolution and Religious Thought*. Remember, Le Conte is clear to point out despite their taking different paths to prove the existence of God, the seeming difference between them is "more apparent than real."[14]

The last chapter of Le Conte's *Evolution and Religious Thought*, "The Relation of Evolution to the Problem of Evil," makes explicit the evolutionary heritage Le Conte claims he and Royce share. According to Le Conte, "the course of human development, whether individual or racial, is from innocence through more or less discord and conflict to virtue."[15] "In all evil," says Le Conte, "the remedy, which not only cures it but transmutes it to good, is knowledge of law and conformity of conduct thereto—a true science and a successful art—in a word, knowledge of the laws of God and obedience to these laws."[16] In a similar tone Royce indicates that

> every time we are weak, downcast, alone with our sin, the victims of evil fortune or our own baseness, we stand as we all know, not only in the presence of besetting problems. . . . We are beset by questions to which we now get no answers . . . such problems, I say, could only be answered if the flickering ideas then present in the midst of our darkness shone steadily in the presence of some world of superhuman experience, of which ours would then seem to be only the remote hint.[17]

This suffering at the individual level sparks the civilized person to think about the purpose of his or her disdain. This is what pulls one to the superhuman level in Royce and is the same formulation that pulls communities toward truer ideas. In our modern categorizations of philosophical thought, it is all too easy and anachronistically inaccurate to presuppose that our canonical divisions between disciplines necessarily correspond to the interests or extent of interrelationship between metaphysics and ethics or practical philosophy, or ontology (God) and the anthropology of now-existing communities. Royce says:

> Do you ask, then: Where in our human world does God get revealed?—what manifests his glory? I answer: Our ignorance, our fallibility, our imperfection, and so, as forms of this ignorance and imperfection, our experience of longing, of strife, of pain, of error, yes, of whatever, as finite declares that its truth lies in its limitation, and so lies beyond itself. These things, wherein we taste the bitterness of our finitude, are what they are because they mean more than they contain, imply what is beyond them, refuse to exist by themselves, and, at the very moment of confessing their own fragmentary falsity, assure us of the reality of that fulfillment which is the life of God.[18]

It is important to remember that the "philosophy of loyalty was and is intended to be a practical philosophy,"[19] which is "naturally interested in pointing out a road to the spiritual world, if, indeed, there be such a world—a road . . . which has a plain relation to our everyday moral life."[20] In short, in attempting to understand how the "evolutionary theodicy" of Royce works, we cannot separate the ideal that foments itself through this evolutionary existential strife, and as such takes form through commune and throughout community, and the suffering, discord, and the presence of alien races, which through contestation pulls the local toward the national—to truth, to the eternal—to enlightened loyalty. The human world is in totality, where the attainment to the ideal held in God is reflected by the choices, the ethics, and the religious and social organizations within communities, to bring that community and the nation forward to a higher morality and spiritual plane.

This view is explicitly articulated as *social theory* in Royce's reflections on evolutionary theory, evolutionary pedagogy, and the legacy of Herbert Spencer. In *Herbert Spencer: An Estimate and Review*, Royce presents an elongated history of evolution starting with the Greeks and extending to the present as an account of what is now popularly referred to as dialectical change. For Royce, the synthesis of the dialectic is explained as the difference between Spencer's prioritization of integration as the primary motivation of evolution and his belief in a cyclical contest between integration and dissolution. Like Le Conte before him, who held that "its [the idea of evolution's] extension by Spencer to every department of Nature has revolutionized the philosophy and methods of every department of thought, especially sociology,"[21] Royce admires the lifework of Herbert Spencer for extending the process of evolution to every sphere of human life.[22] In expressing his admiration for Herbert Spencer, Royce makes an extended commentary on Spencer's life and works and is particularly attracted to Spencer's conclusion, which holds that the process through which Nature births progress in society is evolutionary. Evolution then for the philosopher describes this "process of the knowable universe, or at least some aspect of that entire process."[23]As Stanford Lyman pointed out over decades ago:

> Royce's evolutionism conceived of America as a self-enhancing moral community that would achieve its ultimate integration through the dialectical workings of its own philosophy of loyalty. The latter was an ever deepening faith that reached its apex in loyalty to fidelity itself. Racial antipathies—which Le Conte had treated as an unfortunate consequence of premature emancipation that could be remedied by eugenically sound and scientifically controlled interbreeding—had positive function in Royce's metaphysic. Loyalties to one's own racial group and opposition to others—the ubiquitous process entailed in what William Graham Sumner designated as ethnocentrism—would ultimately move America toward its telos, a racially synthetic and ethically higher moral community. In Royce's adaptation of Le Conte's cyclical evolutionism, the dialectic of conflict would always lead—ultimately—to a positive result. In effect, Royce provided a social theodicy for American social philosophy, a theory of process and change that converted virtually all human conflicts into episodes that moved society toward the realization of ideal social harmony.[24]

The evolutionary teleology of Royce that manifests as—"the resulting doctrine of life and of the nature of truth and of reality which I have tried to work out, to connect with logical and metaphysical issues, and to teach my classes, now seems to me not so much romanticism, as a fondness for defining, for articulating, and for expounding the perfectly real, concrete, and literal life of what we idealists call 'spirit' in a sense which is indeed Pauline"[25]—brings the reader to ask, just as William R. Jones decades before, "Is God a white racist?" This query is brought to the forefront of the discussion by Royce's belief that the ethico-religious community and the place of Blacks, Indigenous peoples, and immigrants in those communities demonstrates the "real," "concrete," and "literal" certainty of God's will. The community's maturation into a moral (Beloved) entity is extant with God. Royce's social philosophy not only evokes a teleology of empire where alien races are absolved of evil by the extent to which they help build toward the Anglo-ideal, but "recognizes that God functions like a weaver in that God weaves the irreducible particulars who act in time and weaves the temporal threads that are their acts into a single tapestry."[26] In this sense, Royce's philosophy depends (as LeConte notes)on an evolutionary theodicy suggesting that the development of social community constitutes these communities such that they tend towards harmony and unity.

Le Conte's Southern Problems: The Ethnological Foundations of Royce's Administrative Strategy

At the beginning of any real attempt to understand Royce's race theory outlined in "Some Characteristic Tendencies of American Civilization" (1900), "Provincialism (1902), and "Race Questions" (1906), there must be an acknowledgment of its indebtedness to his mentor Dr. Joseph Le Conte's evolutionary thought presented in his 1892 book, *The Race Problem in the South*. For Le Conte, "the struggle for life and the survival of the fittest" was the natural law of social contact—be it between animal species or human races. The ethnological concern he articulates as "The Laws of Race Contact" is evidence of the transition of race theory from ethnology to sociology and anthropology.[27] According to Le Conte, "All the factors of organic evolution are carried forward into human evolution, only they are modified by an additional and higher factor, Reason, in proportion to the dominance of that factor—i.e. in proportion to civilization."[28] Whereas organic evolution requires the extinction of the weaker race, human evolution requires the subjugation of the race thought to be inferior in civilization, intelligence, and morality. "The inevitable result of this race contact, will be, must be, ought to be, that the higher race will assume control and determine the policy of the community. Not only is this result inevitable, but it is the best result for both races, especially the lower race."[29] This is virtually the same conclusion he reaches in his 1898 magnum opus. According to Le Conte,

> All evolution, all progress, is from a lower to higher plane.
> From a philosophic point of view, things are not good and evil,
> but higher and lower. All things are good in their true places,

each under each, and all must work together for the good
of the ideal man. Each lower forms the basis and underlying
condition of the higher; each higher must subordinate the
lower to its own higher uses, or else it fails of its true end.[30]

Subjection—rule by the higher civilization—is required by eternal law for
Le Conte's system of evolution to have social and theological relevance,
thus explaining for Le Conte the natural progress given in any civilized
society in the antipathies of race contact. As a social theory, the lower
race must be ruled to spur evolution toward their capacity for democratic
citizenship, according to Le Conte.

More specifically when dealing with race evolution—the condition
whereby the lower race is plastic, docile, and imitative—subjection evolves
the lesser race into the panorama of America society. Le Conte maintains
that slavery developed the character of the Negro, and as such has been
developed beyond slavery. Le Conte is adamant that "slavery was probably
at one time the only natural or even possible relation between the two
races, and was therefore right. The evils were not in the institution, but
its abuses."[31] Slavery had taken the race evolution of the Negro as far as it
could, so "freedom," says Le Conte, "in some form or degree was necessary for its further evolution."[32] Le Conte is especially careful to qualify
freedom. As he says, "the Negro has been educated up to the right to
some measure of freedom, but not as a race to complete freedom. Some
form or degree of control by the white race is still absolutely necessary."[33]

Race evolution is a Lamarckian endeavor, the development and
spiritual elevation of lower races is gradual, whereby "a small part of
improvement of each generation is carried over by inheritance to the
next,"[34] where the small deviation of the race from one generation to the
next endows a civilizational inheritance to its progeny. Le Conte takes
as given that the curricula of race evolution belongs not to the formal
education of the Negro, be it in industry or liberal arts, but informal
education—the education "which comes by contact with higher individuals
and higher races—and is the most important developmental catalyst for
the character, capacity for self-government and citizenship of the lower
races."[35] This informal pedagogy must be sustained, because "whenever
the support is withdrawn he [the Negro] relapses again to his primitive
state . . . rapidly falling back into savagery, and resuming many of their
original pagan rites and superstitions."[36]

Royce and Le Conte's test of a race's vitality is practically the
same in this regard. For Royce, the true test of a race's mental differ-

ence and capacity for civilization rests upon their response to meeting civilization. "Do they show themselves first teachable and then originative? Then they are mentally higher races. Do they stagnate or die out in the presence of civilization? Then they are of the lower type."[37] Le Conte determined the results of the aforementioned test to be that the Negro was the most plastic, much like the Japanese, whereas the Native Indian and the Chinese where much too rigid and hence responsible for their own decline under the weight of contact with white men, the same taxonomy utilized by Royce throughout his writings on race, and the centerpiece of his ethnological example of the Japanese in his essay on "Loyalty to Loyalty."

It is in this sense that Royce's suggestion for colonial administration must be understood. Le Conte calls for a state policy in the South where the policies that control the community still manage the former Black slave. Le Conte is extremely clear in this regard, "I mean not personal control, but control of state policy. There can be no doubt that some device by means of which the policy of the community shall be substantially under the control of those alone who are most capable of self-government is the absolute condition of civilization there."[38]

Le Conte believed the South was the testing ground of Anglo-Saxon culture during the late 1800s. The South represented the most visible colonial achievement of white Americans and in many respects was looked toward as an indication of the larger destiny of the white race. Joseph Le Conte explains:

> It is impossible to exaggerate the importance to the South of this problem, for the very existence of a civilized community there is conditioned on its successful solution. But it is also a problem of widest application, affecting all the races on the face of the earth. Everywhere the white race is pushing its way among lower races. Everywhere, now that slavery is inadmissible, the result is gradual extinction of the lower race. And this tendency to destroy lower races is steadily increasing with the increased energy of modern civilization. Is this result inevitable? If not, how is it to be avoided? Nowhere are the opportunities for the successful solution of this question so favorable as at the South to-day. In the first place, the problem is a more pressing one there than anywhere else; it must be solved, and that speedily. In the second place, the Negro is the very best race that could be selected for the purpose.[39]

Again echoing the meaning of perils common in the late nineteenth century, Le Conte explains that the managing of alien races so that they do not become extinct in their contact with the superior white race is the ethnological conundrum of the day. To gauge how the white race should deal with this newly emergent reality—the enduring existence of inferior races—Le Conte argues that the Negro is the perfect experimental population. Le Conte suggests that the nature of the Negro race makes them amenable to assimilation and imitation. Much like the social ethics presented by Royce as a strategy of Southern administration, anti-Blackness and the particular inferior tropes of Black people were assumed and asserted as the basis engaging other inferior races the world over. This aspect of Le Conte's thought cannot be overlooked as it parallels the specific themes and discussions reflected upon by Royce throughout his racial corpus. The parallels between Le Conte's and Royce's thought are uncanny in this regard.

For example, Le Conte suggests that inferior races can be divided into two groups—"those which are inferior because undeveloped, and those which are so because developed, perhaps highly developed, in a limited way or in a wrong direction."[40] Le Conte asserts that nonwhite races (Negroes, the Chinese, the Japanese, Indigenous Americans) should be assessed on their likelihood to survive their engagements with the white race. He explains, "Races of the first group may be called generalized; they are plastic, adaptable to new conditions, and therefore easily molded by contact with higher races. Those of the second group are specialized; they are rigid, unadaptable to new conditions."[41] The quality of being plastic or being rigid—generalized or specialized—determined how a group would be colonized. Like the theories of Adolf Bastian, Le Conte's theories suggests that one can learn about races, their temperaments, their psychology, to better rule over these groups. The colonial project in the American South was urged to modernize, not dissolve itself in the works of Le Conte and Royce. This is why Royce undergirds his most clearly articulated work on race, "Race Questions and Prejudices," with a recommendation for how to deal with and manage the Negro. Royce was inspired by the ethnological reasoning of his mentor and asserted the racial characteristics outlined by Le Conte to be true, as well as useful for the schematics of his thinking about the growing dilemmas involved with race contact. The Negro and the Japanese were considered plastic races, so greater race contact would civilize these groups. Royce did not simply assert this argument, he inherited it. Describing the plasticity of certain groups and the rigidity of others, Le Conte writes:

The Negro is the best type of the first group, and perhaps the Chinese of the second group. The Chinese are a highly developed race, but extremely rigid under the influence of other races. The Japanese are far more plastic. The Negro has many fine and hopeful qualities. He is plastic, docile, impressionable, sympathetic, imitative, and therefore in a high degree improvable by contact with a superior race and under suitable conditions. It is doubtful if any other race could have so thrived and improved under slavery as the Negro has done. But, although the Negro by means of slavery has been raised above slavery, it would be a great mistake to suppose that he has yet reached the position of equality with the white race—that unassisted he can found a free civilized community.[42]

Le Conte believed that the problem of the Negro in the South was the key to discovering the techniques of resolving the problems of race contact—the perils—the world over. When Le Conte asks, "What is the just and rational relation that should subsist between the two races?"[43] he anticipates the work of his student Royce, who suggests the English model of colonization practiced in Jamaica. The racialist science of Le Conte mirrors the social ethics of Royce not only in how whites interact with Blacks and other racialized groups, but also in the strategies that are thought to be rational and just in dealing with the natures of Black people in the South. Why does Royce appeal to a colonial nation organized by the English to understand the potential strategies to engage Blacks in the South? I would suggest that if Royce is correct, that Anglo-Saxonism is the truest and most efficacious ideal of civilization, then the model of globalization made possible by England would justify an Anglo-American imperial venture to civilize the darker world.

As Le Conte foreshadows, Royce's administrative strategy maintains white control of the community—since the authority of a select few Negroes is only extended over their own and not the entire community. Le Conte and Royce see racial managerialism to be a necessary component of social order and stability in the South. Le Conte's remarks cannot be separated from Royce's preoccupation with the Southern race problem or Jamaica. Royce believes that ethics and philosophy must direct the actions of Southern white communities toward Blacks. Black people emerged from slavery freed but not *free*. In dealing with the Southern problem as outlined by Le Conte, Royce says that a solution will only be realized "when the Negroes themselves get an increasingly responsible part in this

administration in so far as it relates to their own race."[44] As a social pedagogy, "administration works in making the Negro a conscious helper toward
good social order."[45] Reading Royce's call for the Southern states to create
through administration an idealization of Southern life plays a key role in
assimilating the foreign into the familiar. Southern whites showing racial
superiority through deeds and not boasts creates respect and admiration in
the Negro for the law and existing social order, whereby the Negro learns
to not only accept but desire the social organization that defines his or
her Southern community's spirit. Creating acquiescence to the social good
requires the community to make their practices and traditions, which are
aimed at assimilating and repressing their particular racial characteristics,
seem unique, beloved, and deeply founded upon some significant natural
basis,[46] and they "are useful in assimilating to our own social order the
strangers that are within our gates."[47] It is this calling forth of the ideal
of loyalty through enlightened provincialism that causes Royce to invoke
the *Dark Arts*: an invocation rooted in the belief that "it is the especial
art of the colonizing peoples, such as we are, and such as the English are,
to be able by devices of this sort to rapidly build up in their own minds
a provincial loyalty in a new environment."[48]

Developing the Dark Arts: Royce's Race Theory as an Extension of Le Conte's Evolutionary Aesthetic

It may seem peculiar that in the midst of Royce's confession of his fetish
for colonization that he insists on referring to America's technique of
domination as an "especial art." What then does he mean by this term?
To understand the philosophical context and conceptual significance of
this word, we must journey back to Royce's earliest explicit writings on
race, specifically his 1900 treatise on racial assimilationism entitled "Some
Characteristic Tendencies of American Civilization," where he refers to
assimilation not only as an art, but an imperial art. This term carries
with it a heavy philosophical load when placed in context of the race
problems in the South. We must again turn to Le Conte to draw the
parallels between his call for a higher social art and Royce's answer to
this call throughout his corpus. According to Le Conte, "art is the material embodiment of certain underlying rational principles."[49] This means
that art, rather than being an aesthetic reflective of higher truths, is in
the Le Contean purview an ideal, the conceptual impetus that brings

about science to explain actual practices and the function of concretized ideas like the pulley, or pottery, or healing techniques that are not yet explained scientifically. Art, rather than being the embodiment of fixed and verifiable principles that are physically and mathematically relevant to their era, is the catalyst behind such principles. This is true of both kinds of art in Le Conte's mind: the rational or scientific art that seeks to embody the science it comes after and empirical art that is art created by genius or the spontaneous creation of the mind purely from intuition.[50] But how do these two types of art give us insight into the meaning of America's special art—its imperial art inherited from Britain?

The aforementioned categories of Le Conte give us a real clarity into Royce's utilization of these concepts. "All art, by evolution, passes through the two stages,"[51] the empirical and rational. This is the evolutionary path of even the most complex and determinative social art that concerns the early race work of Royce—"namely the art of government, of politics, of social organization."[52] The race problem of the South is of central concern for Le Conte,[53] and it comes to occupy the same position for Royce as evidenced by his extended reflection on how the South should deal with the Negro and how the social thinker should think about this newly emancipated population in need of moral and spiritual uplift in his 1905 pamphlet on "Race Questions." Le Conte thinks that "social art has advanced in a blind, blundering, and staggering way, feeling its way in the dark."[54] The thrust of Le Conte's critique, much like Royce's over a decade later, suggests that while the Negro has evolved past slavery, science has been lethargic and unable to account for the racial elevation manifested in their newly emancipated condition. As such, there is a "serious danger of retrogression in politics unless scientific methods are introduced,"[55] which focus specifically on marrying the principles of sociology with the art of government. This is much like Royce's criticism of race theory's antiquated determinism, which holds "no race of men, then can lay claim to a fixed and hereditary type of mental life such as we can now know with exactness to be unchangeable. We do not scientifically know what the true racial varieties of mental type really are."[56] There still is for Royce "no doubt [that] there are such [racial] varieties."[57] There is a lack of vision, so to speak, of that overarching ideal and impetus that accounts for the dynamic forces of race evolution underway, which can lead us to understand what these varieties really are.

Le Conte warns that empirical methods alone that cast society into an inadequate past simply will not do without a new concept rooted on the Negro's evolution beyond slavery. Royce recognizes this weakness of "race science" a decade later in much the same regard saying that

> there are, of course, unquestionable physical varieties of man-
> kind, distinguished by well-known physical contrasts. But
> the anthropologists still almost hopelessly disagree as to what
> the accurate classification of these true races may be. Such a
> classification, however, does not concern us here. We are now
> interested in the minds of men. We want to know what the
> races of men are socially good for. And not in the study of
> skulls or of hair, or of skin color, and not in the survey of all
> bewildering complications with which physical anthropology
> deals, shall we easily find an answer to our more practical ques-
> tions, viz., to our questions regarding the way in which these
> various races of men are related to the interests of civilization,
> and regarding the spirit in which we ought to estimate and
> practically to deal with the racial traits of mankind.[58]

This art, the art called for by Le Conte, is not only the necessary condition of sociology, but the necessary requisite of civilization itself. The peculiar-ity of this art that can both account for race evolution and the evolution of civilization itself supersedes the empirical and descriptive constrictions of a social theory seeking to create society mechanistically—in a purely empirical image. "In all other arts the material is foreign to the artist; in this, artist and material are identified. Society makes itself [in which] social evolution is mainly determined by the co-operating will of society itself. Thus it is both a product of art and evolution,"[59] whereby for both Royce and Le Conte there must be a focus and reorientation of science around the artistic technique of American civilization—assimilation.

This is the import of Stanford Lyman's connection between Le Conte's cyclical evolutionism and Royce's social theory—the ideal that moves race science beyond biological determinism to environmentalism change is simultaneously the colonizing ideal, which encircles and nullifies the social, cultural, and political existence of racial difference for natural unity. While it is Royce's position that races can change and evolve that places him against the ethnological and biological determinism that maintains the barbarism of the Negro, Royce nonetheless takes up the imperial tyranny that justifies the white man's burden and colonial domination by ethically demanding that Blacks, Indigenous peoples, and foreigners (alien races) surrender themselves and their cultural heritage to the ideal of a white national unity. Royce is extremely clear on this point. He says:

> The greater lesson of the whole process [the wholesome evo-
> lution of our own national consciousness], is the enormous
> potency of a historical system of ideas—the vast power of
> civilization at the present time to transfer its own treasures to
> new regions, and above all, the power that man has to bring
> over to his own type apparently alien men, if only they are
> not too far from him in race, and if only his work in their
> presence is inspired at once with that general toleration so
> common in our own civil life, and with that determination
> so characteristic of our people—a determination that, despite
> all, our own civilization shall continue its own way and shall
> be paramount.[60]

Racial antipathy is this aesthetic motivation, which is why the South must learn to control the intensity of its "white peril," so that the social organization (administration) of society pulls the community toward higher ideals and sets into motion the moral uplift entailed by the enlightened province. By effect Royce gives us not a philosophy of cultural diversity but the genesis of a colonial dark art—a philosophical posture that moralizes the surrender of the racial other to white communities charged with extinguishing Black, Indigenous, and Asian resistance against the white supremacism of America and Britain.

Some American philosophers, however, adamantly disagreed with Royce's optimism in racial malleability and ignorance of race traits. Though Royce relies on one branch of ethnological research, there are other aspects of race and evolution that remain unconsidered by Royce throughout his corpus. John M. Mecklin, however, sought to remind the Northern philosopher of his naïveté regarding the subject of the Negro in the South.

He Wasn't Even a Little Less Racist: John M. Mecklin's Criticism of Royce's Ethnological Interpretation of Race Traits

John Moffatt Mecklin was a Mississippi-born minister turned philosopher. He was a devout pragmatist and admirer of William James as well as a

Southern segregationist.[61] Mecklin earnestly expresses his admiration for James in his autobiography, *My Quest for Freedom*. He writes, "It is no exaggeration when I say that William James has had a deeper influence upon my mental evolution than all other thinkers, ancient and modern, combined."[62] While most of his historical recognition comes from his defense of academic freedom, Mecklin was also a well-known and somewhat respected scholar of the race problem in the South. His book *Democracy and Race Friction* was reviewed in James E. Gregg's *Southern Workman* in 1915, and his essay "The Evolution of Slave Status in American Democracy" was published in Carter G. Woodson's *Journal of Negro History* in 1917.[63] He authored one of the first socio-philosophical investigation of the KKK, entitled *The Ku Klux Klan: A Study of the American Mind* (1963), which is a text still widely cited on Klan history and activity. Mecklin's writings provide a noteworthy contrast to Josiah Royce's philosophy and assimilationism, because his work not only demonstrates a familiarity with the race (racist) science of his day, which he advocated in varying degrees, but also the writings and debates of Black scholars and journalists concerning the race question. Throughout *Democracy and Race Friction*, he challenges not only the assimilatory tendency of Northern liberals, but he indicts the expectations that Blacks can have equality within America's racist democratic system. Though Mecklin holds on to an ethnological science of race that maintains that there are fundamental hereditary differences between racial groups, he nonetheless maintains that each group has a right to develop its own natural gifts or capacities. Similar to Edgar Murphy, Mecklin believes the law, rather than being a repressive *law of absolute equality* that forces the alleged inferior to appeal to the standards given by the superior race, should embrace the South's policy of segregation, since it allows for a more equitable and just *law of consideration* to take place where "equality before the law can only mean for an individual or a group the impartial guarantee of the law's protection, in the development—in their own interest and that of society—of the capacities with which they are endowed."[64]

Being a white Southerner, John M. Mecklin expressed a skepticism toward the possibility of democracy in the United States given its racial history. Starting his analysis from the Declaration of Independence to the Constitution, Mecklin argues that the present system of democracy cannot deal with much less adjudicate equality given the severity of its race problem. America is dedicated to the ultimate assimilation of the Negro, something Mecklin believes is impossible. Mecklin argued that the

North insisted on the racial complacency of the Negro and a surrender of the race's racial gifts. Like Du Bois in his *Suppression of the African Slave Trade 1638–1870*, Mecklin argues that the North was not driven to abolish the American slave trade because of its idealist commitment toward humanity. He writes, "it was not loyalty to inalienable human rights in the abstract that brought about the abolition of slavery in the North, but rather the gradual expansion of the idea of liberty through the free give and take of a vigorous democracy in which economic and social conditions militated against slavery."[65] Slavery, its development as a system of labor, and the conflicts that emerged over its practice between the Northern and Southern states were economic in nature, not moral. Mecklin argues that the Northern states' abolition of slavery was not the result of a shared altruism or humanitarian concern for Blacks, but the economic sustainability of slavery given the climate of the North. He explains, "In the trading colonies of New England and the farming colonies of the Middle States the occupations in which slave labor could be profitably made use of were limited in number. The climate was too cool, especially for freshly imported slaves. Slave labor was ill adapted to the kind of crops the soil demanded."[66] This however was not the case for the South.

> The conditions in the planting colonies from Virginia southward were different. Here was an unlimited supply of fertile lands which lent themselves readily to the unskillful and exhausting methods of slave labor. Here too was a warm climate congenial to the [N]egro, though enervating and often unhealthful for the white. The staples, such as the sugar cane, rice and later the cotton plant, were such as the unscientific slave labor might easily cultivate. All the conditions of profitable slave labor were present, namely, possibilities for concentration of labor, its absolute control and direction and exploitation. The status of the [N]egro in the planting colonies was the outcome of these economic conditions. He was deprived of the stimulating effect of personal intercourse with the white, enjoyed by the slave at the north. His status was fixed by a certain position in an industrial system, the tendency of which was to attach him more and more to the soil and, especially on the larger plantation, to make of him a "living tool." He became, as time went on, the economic unit.[67]

It is this difference between the North and South that determined their commitment to the institution. Neither believed in the equality of the Negro; their position on slavery was merely a question of their dependency the respective region had on the exploitation of Negro labor for their economic livelihood. As such, Mecklin insists that the North was driven by economic necessity, not a reformation of values, to abolish slavery. This economic account of Northern abolitionism also explains why many Northern slaveholders supported the creation of the domestic slave trade, the practice of selling their slaves to Southern states to maximize their profits.[68] This historical claim situates Mecklin's suspicion of Royce's strategy specifically, but also the North's approach to race relations more generally.

Mecklin argues that the "race question belongs to this class of essentially insoluble problems . . . because it springs from those deep-lying and slow-moving forces that make for ethnic solidarity or ethnic diversity."[69] Race antipathy emerges from the same forces that breed racial solidarity. It comes from a natural disposition of a people to commune and reproduce itself. Mecklin contends this is simply an obvious and observable rule of nature. *Democracy and Race Friction* is written as a philosophical inquiry into the problem of race antipathy during a time when, according to its author, "the masses of both races at the South are so occupied with the immediate exigencies of the social situation that they have little time to philosophise upon it."[70] Mecklin concerns himself with the same scenarios of racial contact as Josiah Royce. His book's analysis was primarily drawn from "from the relations of the whites and blacks in the southern states . . . and data in connection with the relations of whites and blacks in the English colonies, especially in Jamaica and South Africa."[71] The results from Mecklin's book however allowed him to make far more global claims about race antipathy, especially after his analysis of white attitudes toward the Chinese and Japanese on the Pacific coast.[72]

Mecklin argues that race traits are hereditary and responsible for instincts that are "undoubtedly the most primitive and powerful factors in all forms of social solidarity."[73] These instincts "constitute in man, as well as in the gregarious animals and insects, the hereditary equipment which makes possible the various forms of social activity."[74] These traits are the "cosmic roots of the social life of man."[75] Before the reader errs in his or her reading of Mecklin, let me say that he should not be read as a strict biological determinist. He in fact argues for the spiritual and intellectual cultivation of these base racial instincts, not a group's submission to centuries of evolution. Mecklin believed that the moral and social self emerges when "rational interpretation and direction have been given to original instinctive impulses," so there is always a need of reflection and philosophical intervention in those behaviors that are thought to be determined by these deeply rooted racial traits.[76] Said differently, hereditary racial traits do not consciously influence group action, but shape general actions. It is only in the midst of race friction that these group tendencies increase and are explained solely as the result of heredity.

According Edward Ross's *Sin and Society*, "Our social organization has developed to a stage where the old righteousness is not enough."[77] The prevalence of greed and profit throughout America meant that "the reality of this close-knit life is not to be seen and touched; it must be thought."[78] While philosophy has little use for history, or historical contextualization, Mecklin's engagement with Ross's text shows that Royce's idealist social philosophy was not at all novel. In fact, Mecklin actually recognizes the rising popularity of idealism and suggests that philosophers ascertain the effect of such thought regarding America's burdening race questions. Whereas Royce was fraught with worry over the possible splintering of provincialism into sectionalism, Mecklin views social stability as a question of political efficiency. He explains:

> the measure of efficient democracy is found in the extent to which the rank and file of citizenship make the ideals embodied in democratic institutions real in actual life. This is difficult when race differences encourage ignorance and group antipathies. Efficient democracy is practically impossible of attainment where we have present a large group, differing fundamentally in race traits, to a large extent illiterate, lacking in the sober sense of responsibility that comes with the possession of property, often devoid of patriotism local or national, and with no clear ideas on social or political issues.[79]

Like Royce, Mecklin understands the problem that confronts the rank and file throughout America, however, he differs in that he does not believe idealism, which takes all racial and cultural difference to be dissolvable, is a panacea offering social stability. Royce's loyalty to loyalty gives the individual who is without guidance on political issues or patriotism purpose. His idealism gives them a shared destiny that stands in for their substantive understanding. In other words, Royce replaces democracy with (moral) duty and ideas with the ideal. However, such a system of efficient democracy can only work with small homogeneous groups, according to Mecklin. America is much too diverse and racially different to sustain itself through an idealism that is ultimately incompatible with the various race traits of the population.[80] This realization by Mecklin may offer some insight into Royce's hope that provincial homogeneity can be achieved through assimilation.

Given the status that Mecklin affords to race traits, one might ask what exactly does Mecklin believe constitutes a race? Mecklin explains, "when, as a result of natural selection operating upon a segment of the human family, there arises a group similar in origin, similar in offspring, reacting by virtue of similar endowments in the same way to external forces and guaranteeing through common hereditary characteristics the persistence of the general type it embodies, we have what may be called a race."[81] This understanding of race is why Mecklin can say that "race is therefore both fixed and changeable, theoretical and real."[82] It is theoretical as to its origins, and real due to its consequences. It is this realness of race that makes race friction a peculiar social, not individual, problem.[83] A problem with the organization of society, not simply its collection of individual wills. Following the ethnological consensus of his time, Mecklin believes that four great races have emerged through the process of evolution. He explains that "the great race types such as the Australoid, the Negro, the Caucasian, and the Mongolian are the result of age-long selection under definite conditions so that the characteristics of the group are relatively permanent."[84] These races have lost their plasticity and are almost immune to environmental change. Mecklin's conceptualization of race means that Royce's administrative strategy, which depends on the moral impression of white character—the impression of their quiet white racial superiority—overestimates the power of assimilation on the Negro race given their racial traits. Within the confines of ethnology, assimilation supposes the malleability of a race—either the nonexistence or the plasticity of a race's hereditary traits. This is simply not possible regarding the Negro.

Royce's theory of race development asserts that there is nothing in the race, no racial characteristics that are unchangeable and solidified by nature (or God) over the centuries, except for the superiority of the white race. Royce assumes that savage races are more backward and consequently more childlike and savage. Mecklin simply does not believe this is the case with the Negro. He explains that this tropical exuberance of temperament which makes the Negro extreme in joy or grief, in anger or affection, together with his strongly sensuous nature are his greatest handicaps in meeting the stem demands of a stable civilisation. They make him an alien in many respects in the midst of a highly ratio- nalized social order. Furthermore, they can hardly be ascribed to his immaturity, for the [N]egro is not a child race. Such traits are hereditary, the result of ages of fixed group life.[85]

Mecklin argues that the persistence of these race traits, these dispositions that condition how races interpret and creatively engage reality, are neces- sary to our understanding of the social and political relations between whites and Blacks and "indicate the psychological principles involved."[86] Some philosophers will no doubt withdraw from Mecklin's analysis, because it depends on inherited unconscious dispositions of races, but still embrace Royce, who says in "Race Questions and Prejudices" that "we cannot doubt that, just as now we widely differ in mental life, so always there must have been great contrasts between the minds of the various stocks of men. No doubt, if the sciences of man were exact, it would indeed include a race-psychology."[87] While there can be some arguments as to whether Mecklin is drawing from the same sciences Royce aims to indict, which is doubtful given his skepticism to strict biological accounts of racial inferiority, it cannot be denied that Royce just as Mecklin supposes a racial psychology. The difference between their accounts is that Mecklin refuses to believe that the heritage of the Black race that emerged from evolution is any less consequential than that of the white race. This of course does not mean that he believes the white race to be less dominant or superior, just less exceptional in the course that determined its development.

Insisting upon assimilation when the evolutionary impulses of races resists such an approach only serves to ignite race antipathies. "When physical differences of race, as is usually the case, are associated with fixed hereditary differences, they may take on a meaning and import for the social mind entirely independent of their external character. This is especially true where the nature of these differences makes the assimilation of the group a difficult process."[88] Because race friction is in part propagandist, an exemplification of the mob mentality, skin color becomes accentuated. Mecklin explains, in the midst of racial tensions or conflicts, "physical characteristics then become symbols of race and group antipathies of a much more lasting and serious nature."[89] This rule of nature is ultimately why Royce's administrative strategy is doomed for failure.

In chapter 2, I introduced some concerns John M. Mecklin had regarding Royce's interpretation of race relations in Jamaica. Here I would like to explain the consequences Mecklin argued Royce's strategy would have on the political destiny of the Negro in the South at the turn of the century. Colonization was a violent and repressive system of rule throughout the world. Its rise in the American South would be no different and arguably of much greater consequence after Reconstruction for Black Americans than Black Jamaicans. Mecklin was adamant that Royce's call for British administration relied on a view of the Negro unaffected by their freedom from slavery. According to Mecklin, Royce dedicated himself to rationalizing a strategy toward Blacks that would revert the Negro to his condition prior to Reconstruction. It was a strategy that appealed to the most uncultivated sentiments of the Southerner and their aversion to American democracy and Black progress.

> Nothing would, doubtless, be more agreeable to the southerner with his nine millions of [N]egroes than the establishment in the South of a paternalistic government similar to that in Jamaica. But this would involve the utter repudiation of the spirit if not the letter of the Reconstruction legislation in behalf of the [N]egro and a surrender of the transcendental conception of human rights which it implies and which is to-day the rallying point for the Negro contenders for complete equality and their white supporters. It may be seriously doubted whether Professor Royce is prepared to surrender the orthodox conception of democracy as it is embodied in our political symbols.[90]

Bringing the paternalistic government of Jamaica to the South would not improve the lives or conditions of the Black race. Such a policy would only appease the Southern white racist who is committed to recreating the psychology of the slave in free Black citizens and revert the minute political and economic power gained during Reconstruction to nil. Freed Blacks would no longer be pursuing constitutionally guaranteed human rights, instead they would be committed to appeasing the white ruling class in an effort to demonstrate their position on the rungs of civilization.

Given the progress and advance of the Black intellectual class, Mecklin is probably correct that "the period in the relations of the two races when English administration and 'English reticence' could have been cultivated successfully belongs in all probability to an irrevocable past."[91] While the close of the Civil War offered some evidence that the South could reinstate de facto slavery under the auspices of colonial rule, and did in fact attempt to fashion such a regime with Black codes and its institution of Jim Crow, Mecklin's insistence that "the Reconstruction period and the years that have intervened have built up totally different relations between the races, and have instilled into the black political and social ambitions which it is idle to expect that he can be easily induced to forego,"[92] cannot be ignored by advocates of Royce's program. Mecklin considered that the condition of political freedom has changed the aspirations of the race; Royce had not. As evidenced by the rise of organizations like the Afro-American League, the American Negro Academy, the Atlanta Sociological Laboratory, anti-lynching activism, and a rising Black middle class during the late nineteenth century, Mecklin was correct.[92] Even considering self-deprecating Black thinkers like William Hannibal Thomas who believed in the inferiority of the Negro in the late 1800s, there is no historical Black figure intimating the desire to return to slavery or colonial rule.[94] Black intellectuals were looking toward Black self-determination, not the nostalgia of servitude.

The work of John M. Mecklin interestingly complicates the normative view of racial progressivism at the dawn of the twentieth century. Many scholars and fields assume that the North was naturally more progressive than the South regarding racism. This premise is often asserted simply based on a shared presumption that it was the American South, not the North, that was committed to white supremacy and slavery. Little attention is paid to the complex histories of Northern slavery, the domestic slave trade, and the racialist sciences behind progressive education and assimilation in urban centers like Chicago or New York.[95] Mecklin, who is a known segregationist, liberal, and pragmatist, demonstrates two things: first, there was much variety among Southern and Northern thinkers, and second, none of these theorists were unaffected by racism. All white theorists of race, be they ethnologists, or emerging sociologists or anthropologists, failed to meet any recognizable standard of anti-racism. No white thinker's position was necessarily more liberating for Blacks than the other. They all existed in a world where racial equality was theorized as differing degrees of Black inferiority. Mecklin was no different, he was simply more correct in this instance given Royce's anti-Black and imperial commitments.

Conclusion

Wise provincialism, the commune of individuals under the ideal of loyalty to loyalty, though born of necessity, is contingent upon the erasure of a peoples' racial and/or ethnic culture. A nonwhite culture risks the loss of unity, which is what Royce sees as the ongoing failure of British colonization. This is the lesson of the Civil War and the fragmentary strife of the British empire. As such, disunity plays a catalytic role in the social idealism of Royce's provincialism. Many philosophers interested in Royce cite the beginning of Royce's "Race Questions," asking, "is it a yellow peril, or a [B]lack peril, or perhaps, after all, is it rather some form of white peril, which most threatens the future of humanity,"[96] without understanding the pretext of national unity that the first sentences of Royce's essay highlights—namely, that "the numerous questions and prejudices which are aroused by the contact of the various races of men have always been important factors in human history. Such increasing importance of race questions and prejudices, if it comes to pass, will be due not to any change in human nature, and especially not to any increase in the diversity or in the contrasting traits of the races of men themselves, but simply to the greater extent and complexity of the work of civilization."[97] In this regard, disunity operates as a condition for the growth and extension of provincial loyalty. It is precisely because Royce regards the colonization of aliens (nonwhites) to be the necessary condition of race contact that the work of civilization can continue. Disunity, or rather the potential of disunity demonstrated by the failing arts of British colonialism, creates the synthetic national womb from which assimilation can be born. Royce is extremely clear about this in relation to the ultimate purpose of provincialism (which was demonstrated in chapter 3).

As Royce himself makes clear in his philosophy of loyalty, the national ideal is the practical concern of a philosophy of loyalty, and as such resists revisions that suggest the equal valuing of racial multiculturalism or cosmopolitanism. What we have in Royce, as demonstrated by his admiration for the Japanese, is a building up of the nation that can take the traditions of others and use it to build its imperial power and dominance in service of the white man's burden. The colonizer does not simply become the cosmopolitan by the swipe of the revisionist pen. Royce's philosophical indebtedness to Le Conte's evolutionism, his indulgence of the imperial arts, and his belief in the inferiority of nonwhite races makes him a philosopher of Empire, not its challenger. To suggest otherwise despite the historical record seeks to expend energy defending white supremacist tyranny rather than exposing it—ironically fulfilling Royce's end goal, which is to bring white philosophy, the teachings and curricula of the liberal arts university, in line with the Anglo-Saxon ideal by eliminating the ability of Blacks, Indigenous, and Eastern peoples to challenge it.

Epilogue

Josiah Royce's reflections on race explain turn-of-the century idealism as a philosophy inextricably tied to evolution and ethnology just as well as to nation and empire. These associations are not well understood in philosophy, nor are they part of our discussions of American philosophical thought more generally. As such, the texts and debates presented in this book will be difficult if not impossible for many American philosophers to accept. Unlike previous works on Royce's philosophy of race, this book has not only surveyed the historical debates Royce had with other scholars over his proposal for British administration, but the various materials available to show how Royce's thoughts were understood within his own time. It is not an imagining of Royce, but rather a genealogical exposition of the ideas and aspirations Royce himself endorsed. This book argues that Royce unapologetically develops a philosophy dedicated to empire. This imperial inclination, the supposition of white racial superiority, is not external to his system of thoughts, but at the very core of it. For philosophers who pride themselves in the possession of the spirit and personality of the figure, it is sometimes difficult to imagine their historical figures, or themselves for that matter, driven by such racial motivations. Philosophy almost mandates a dehistoricization of an author. Perhaps it is necessary for the reader to pause here to think of the premises he or she will be inclined to impose upon this study to explain Royce's relationship to empire.

As philosophers, and liberal arts scholars more generally, there is a tendency to protect the theorist. We protest historicization and intellectual contextualization. As theorists, we dedicate ourselves to theory—the sole productions of the individual and our intimate intuitions of their text. To methodologically protect this approach, we are taught to cast criticisms of our interpretations into various aspects of irrelevance—this objection is history, or that critique is ideological, these concerns are political, not philosophical. These are not substantive retorts to the multiple engagements with text, but the tendencies we are taught to justify theory. It is the manifestation of these scholars' repertoire, so to speak, aimed at protecting the legacy of the theorist we dedicate our philosophical interest toward. It is not uncommon to suggest that racism or imperialism was a personal predilection of a thinker, a set of attitudes, rather than a desire for specific institutions, or a societal organization empowering white individuals or white culture to be recognized as superior and dominant over other groups.

This book resists such a reduction. Royce, like many turn-of-the-century white intellectuals, is arguing for a world in which the white race and the values that have emerged from this racial group the world over are enabled to remain dominant. This requires the philosopher to think beyond his or her disciplinary customs toward a view of philosophy as a set of questions and concerns relating to the undoubted superiority of the white race. Given this supposition, the idealism of Royce, as well as the progressivism of John Dewey or Jane Addams, attempt to extend and expand the conditions of their day, because it is this milieu that they believe offers the ability to further democracy and civilization.[1]

Josiah Royce's "Some Characteristic Tendencies of American Civilization" offers a bridge between his idealism and his race theory—two aspects of his thinking previously assumed to be quite distant. Royce's reflection on imperialism and assimilation anticipates the worry he has concerning America's instability and the great loss America endured during the Civil War in his later essay on provincialism. America, now repaired from the division and conflict of the Civil War, must find a new destiny and fitting cause to which it must now aspire. Empire is that cause and the white man's burden is America's step toward this destiny. For some, no amount of evidence, be it Royce's own words or the testaments of those from his own time, will convince them of Royce's allegiances to white supremacy, imperialism, or racism. For some, this association is simply not possible—it will remain unfathomable. For others, those compelled to look deeper because of the evidence, this book will clarify the ambiguity of Royce's proclamations. It will illuminate the terms and debates shrouded within the vagueness of historical reference and enable many scholars for the first time to see both the complexity of Royce's system of racial domination and the very real dangers of American assimilation.

Royce articulates an intricate idealist system where white citizens transcend their individuality toward a heritage of global superiority. (w)hite Americans are compelled toward history and empire, toward Europe to reclaim the origin of their racial greatness. They are told that their values, and ideas, the creed that makes them American, is of noble and imperial birth. They are told they are the inheritors of the right to rule and conquer. They are the divine explorers of the world—the guardians of Europe's legacy of civilization. (w)hite Americans are given the task to spread this racial pride and inculcate it within every visitor and occupant of their communities. They are told that their racial pride is providence. There is little room for cultural exchange in Royce's configuration of the nation. It is a public driven by its obsession with order and its synonymity with the one true idea. This is the Anglo-Saxon ideal carried by every white American and every white community. Those who do not belong to the white race are subjugated by this will, not the inheritors of it. For racialized groups, for Blacks, Royce's America was apartheid. It was an America dedicated to their oppression and impoverishment, not their improvement as newly freed persons and citizens.

Is the Debate about Royce's Racism a Historiography of Redemption? The Apologetic Exegesis of Royce's Imperial Aspirations

The ethics of Josiah Royce has emerged as a yet another American philosophical figure's premonition that comes to anticipate, around the turn of the century, the post–civil rights moment and the agenda of integrationism developed from the 1960s forward. Perhaps I am the only one who finds it strange that no matter the thinker, no matter the time period, and no matter the limitations of their own scientific or cultural views, every American philosopher from John Dewey to Jane Addams agrees with W. E. B. Du Bois and anticipates and ultimately comes to endorse the civil rights policy of integrationism, and multicultural, multiracial, multiethnic communities associated with the dream of Martin Luther King. It appears to be the case that there is a predetermined answer to race problems and the study of race in American philosophy that ultimately under-specializes the study and investigation of the actual thinking, be it philosophical, anthropological, sociological, or historical,

concerning American racism.² Royce's provincialism and his philosophy
of loyalty is just the most recent incantation of this civil rights dogma.
Is it not possible that American philosophers engaged the world from
the perspective of the colonizer, and as such did not seek integrationism
with Blacks, but instead sided with the growing imperial call of Western
nations? Is it not possible that the thoughts and justifications for white
supremacy and Anglo-Saxonism in Josiah Royce's thought from 1900
forward tells the reader a different story, a story where Western nations
fearful of instability, and the chaos that befell colonial lands established
under Pax Britannica, sought to solidify national ethos rather than plu-
ralize racial and ethnic traditions?

　　This is the question that American philosophy has avoided in an
effort to sanitize its thinkers and pretend a relevance to contemporary
racism through isolated and deeply flawed—deeply racist—texts. As
scholars interested in pursuing Royce's theories, be it for historical insight
or as normative guidance, we find the text oriented oddly by the mandates of our time. In this age, we often find thought to be determined
by the consensus of the scholars invested in a figure, rather than the
evidence as it presents itself to us. In the case of Josiah Royce, they seem
to gift to him the ideas of a time far removed from his own. Because
he utilized a term, the Beloved Community that would become affixed
to the work of Dr. Martin Luther King, there has been a tendency to
interpret King's proclamations in the 1960s as evidence of Royce's virtue
and benevolent intentions toward the Negro in the 1900s. In this way,
Royce's text becomes sacred and ahistorical—the product not of his
thinking about the world before him, but a commodity of this world,
this time, the need of today's scholars for closure, a need to maintain
purity throughout the works of the figure. While this articulation may
seem extraneous and unneeded, it is important nonetheless to offer
a lens, or rather an unveiling commentary on the issues that remain
unannounced in these debates over Royce's provincialism. Stated differently, despite the words of Royce, his articulations of imperialism,
and repression of Blacks in the South, there is a need to write a text, a
chapter, an article that demonstrates concretely that Josiah Royce know-
ingly participated in constructing a racist colonial apparatus as his basis
of thinking about Blackness and foreignness in America. Royce was an
adamant supporter of the white man's burden, a duty whites believed
they had to spread their civilization throughout the world. This view
explicitly endorses imperialism by the West and advocates imperialist

conquest for America. Because this idea and characterization of Royce runs counter to how Royceans see Royce, there is a tendency to dismiss such research as purely historical and outside of Royce's philosophical register, so to speak. These disciplinary confinements are suggested to be sufficient to warrant dismissal of the specific history and ideas Royce is deploying in his work, and seen as a necessary apologetic accompanying the demand for Royce to be canonized.

While I am generally skeptical of the type of identity politics that assume a predetermined individual disposition toward race, there is something striking in the seemingly unified position taken up by scholars of Royce who have concluded that Royce's support for imperialism, colonialism, and his proposal to colonize Black people in the American South as the British do in Jamaica are not motivated by racism or the presumption of the racial superiority of whites. While racial identity is certainly not determinative, it seems oddly unified regarding Royce's position toward Black Americans and immigrants more generally. Perhaps such consensus is merely the reflection of the practices of academic philosophy, the product of a learned apologetics that justifies this kind of defense of Royce and the symbols deployed to conjure up ideas and a consensus-based narrative supporting him as a racially progressive thinker. Regardless, the debates concerning Royce remain instructive of American philosophy's general perception and handling of racism historically, since many of the assumptions this book identifies in Royce are common among many of American philosophy's white historical figures. I must admit however that it seems somewhat regressive to write a book that has to argue that creation of colonial zones in the American South, or proposals for the assimilation of foreign groups, are racially oppressive in the twenty-first century.

Some scholars have gone to great efforts to defend Royce from his racial proclamations. Mathew Foust goes to great lengths to suggest to the reader that an editorial omission from *The Pluralist* printing saves Royce's entire project from its very clear endorsement of racism, assimilation, and his advocacy of colonization in the South. Foust, for example, makes no effort whatsoever to address any of the new historical and archival material my work introduces to Royceans on the race question, but despite this glaring want in his analysis, he represents to the reader that this editorial/textual omission in the *Pluralist* printing is not only enough to convince the reader that my reading of Royce is in error, but that a mere twenty words overwhelms my discovery of Royce's Aberdeen speech, his various endorsements of racialist science from Adolf Bastian and James Frazer, his insistence upon assimilation, and his endorsement of the white man's burden. Shannon Sullivan on the other hand has continued to frame the conversation around a critical moment in Royce that she interprets as Royce being pensive, and critical, of the white peril. Elizabeth Duquette's interpretation of Royce celebrates Royce's stance against lynching, while ignoring Du Bois's criticism of Royce's understanding of lynching and the contrast between Du Bois's political demands and Royce's political alternative to Southern lynch law. Jacquelyn Kegley continues to read Royce as racially progressive despite his ethnological commitments and his own statements concerning race and empire. These passages continue to remain absent in her engagements with Royce and race. These positions all are legitimate creative renderings of Royce's philosophy. I say this not as an attempt to dismiss any of the authors' previous works, but to suggest that Royce scholars are avoiding the actual debates of key essays and passages in Royce. These aforementioned positions represent any number of interpretations scholars can have of aspects of Royce's thinking, however, they are not engagements with what Royce actually says or is debating among scholars in his own time regarding race.

To some, all things are merely interpretations, all equal and all valid. To those thinkers, I ask: *what then is the distinction between research and opinion.* Is there ever any need for Royce scholarship? Can there even be Royce's thought, or is it all merely "interpretations" of what he said. Of course not. Philosophers overwhelming believe there are truths beyond opinion, yet when it comes to issues of race, racism, or empire, these comments to truth and actual fact seem all to fleeting. There is a historical reality and facts surrounding Royce's texts, and our investigation of these real aspects of his thinking reveal Royce's dangerously racist and imperial motivation for dealing with American racism and the effects of race contact on allegedly inferior racial populations.

This need to *save Royce*, and to *defend Royce*, against his own endorsement of colonization as a means to preserve the nation, remains an obstacle to a serious investigation into white figures and their philosophical heritage more generally. At some point, the historically minded textual scholar runs up against the localized consensus of those dedicated to the figure, and when race and racism are involved, such a response is usually virulent and unified. As is traditionally the case in these types of arguments concerning the racism of white philosophical figures there is a spin placed on their thought to emphasize the need for their cherished ideas. In the case of Royce these ideas are usually associated with the ideals of "unity," "community," "loyalty," where the liberal-progressive sentiments of the philosophy are used to define such terms, rather than the manuscripts, events, and cultural meanings available to Royce and used by him to achieve such conceptualizations of social beings and his social program.

Even if contemporary scholars do begin to engage the "myth of Royce's racial progressivism," there is a way in which Royce scholars, dedicated to the apotheosis of Royce's reflections on race, will continue to enforce the adamant political motif that ultimately it is simply better to interpret Royce to be an anti-racist, despite the historical and philo-sophical record of his blatant white supremacy and rampant colonialism, since it is this interpretation that will achieve his canonization as a major American philosophical figure. Because this challenge to Royce's current uses in American race theory is just as political and ideological as it is scholarly and philosophical, I feel confident in asserting that his theo-ries, insofar as they actually deal with the question of racial and cultural communities in the United States, are fundamentally useless. Since Royce conceptualizes racial and cultural diversity as a threat to the spiritual foundations of the American nation that must be eradicated to make way for the true realization of America's true Anglo-Saxon birthright, his philosophy has *absolutely no* theoretical merit in regard to the race problem. This is not to say that Royce may not be a useful historical reference for the convergence of idealism and ethnology, but to suggest Royce must be anti-racist because of an at-large consensus is contrary to the mission and consequence of scholarly research. There must be some distinction between what Royce actually says and means by his work and what philosophers creatively intend for their work as their own.

For philosophers like Shannon Sullivan, Mathew Foust, and Jac-quelyn Kegley, Royce becomes useful for dealing with racism because of the lessons they believe he teaches white America. Lessons like the value of community or the nonbiological origins of race seem to be profound ideas given the history of anti-Black racism and white supremacy in this country. This praise however is rooted in an assertion that Royce is useful for dealing with racism, without much explanation as to how one might actually reach such a conclusion. Royce did suggest that race was not biologically determined, so to speak, but he was adamant that it was the historical and cultural legacy of Anglo-Saxon reign globally that proved the superiority of the white races. What answers do these authors provide to the reader and/or scholar confronted with the questions that arise from this contention? Is Royce simply mistaken? Do scholars revise his philosophy to fit their twenty-first-century sensibilities so that Royce can be praised as racially progressive? How then does one revise his insistence upon the colonization of Black people in the American South and his insistence upon the subjugation of Black, Indigenous, and immigrant peoples? How does one utilize Royce's account of whiteness, where Anglo-Saxon heritage makes white Americans a colonizing people, for anti-racist and anti-colonial resistance?

There Is Another (Du Boisian) King: The Irreconcilable Difference between Martin Luther King Jr. and Josiah Royce's Idea of the Beloved Community

How do Black scholars, Brown scholars, Indigenous scholars reconcile Royce's view that they are fundamentally a threat to the stability of the nation? How do these people reconcile the desire for their groups to not exist, but only mirror the tropes of the white race? How does one utilize Royce's view that racial and ethnic difference is a destabilizing force in America, or mobilize such a conceptualization of racial and ethnic social being given the boom of the Latino/a population and steady increase of Black peoples in this country? If one takes Royce seriously, then Black self-determination movements would threaten not enhance national unity. How would these proven Black strategies of liberation be categorized in Royce's philosophy, which asks all members of its province to hold on to, and propagate, the same social habits and mental interests that maintain Anglo-Saxon domination? Should I even explore these questions as a problem in Royce's social philosophy, or must I do as Royceans do and assert that "community is diverse," "community is plural," and maintain despite the actual textual evidence of his anti-Blackness, his white man's burden, that this is how "Royceans read Royce." Are such assertions really using Royce at all, or are they using a post–civil rights integrationist ethos associated with caricatures of Kingian ideals like the Beloved Community as currency (racial street cred) to get the racism of the Roycean project to go down more smoothly?

Charles Marsh notes in "The Civil Rights Movement as Theological Drama" that there is a great distance between Royce's view of the Beloved Community and that of Martin Luther King Jr. Marsh writes, "the dichotomy between the divine and human would be fully overcome in the beloved community, so that the consciousness of God could be seen to be residing in the community."[3] There is little to no distinction between the individuals that comprise community and God. There is God—the cause—and those who embody this sacred creed. Marsh theorizes that "Kant's ethical rationality shapes Royce's own moral admonitions, albeit with a robustly American spin."[4] He continues:

> Kant's imperative—"Act in conformity with that maxim and that maxim only which you can at the same time will to be a universal maxim"—is recast in language suitable for social reform in America: "So act as to help, however you can, and whenever you can, towards making mankind one loving brotherhood, whose love is not a mere affection for morally detached individuals, but a love of the unity of its own life upon its own divine level, and a love of individuals in so far as they can be raised to communion with this spiritual community itself." The result captures the essence of liberal Protestant ethical religion, the location of the divine–human relation in some pleasing modulation of human experience, in this case in a certain moral affection for universal community. Framed against its philosophical antecedents, the term beloved community shimmers with liberal hopes of human progress and perfectibility.[5]

Royce achieves the brotherhood of the Kantian maxim ironically through colonialism, what Kant thought of as a more robust and global cosmopolitanism.[6] For Royce, the loyal self is imbued with the ideal—a concept that becomes synonymous for the idea of God, community, and empire. These concepts are synergistically connected by the nation, nurtured by the community, and the cause of the loyal individual. For Royce, God intends America's rise to empire and the colonial disposition of individuals who enable this advance. It is the unity demanded by loyalty to loyalty.[7] In a universal brotherhood linked by the values inherited from the United Kingdom, like individuality and human freedom, all members loyal to these ideas are enabled to thrive and develop toward the good. Imperialism is the expansion of this community throughout the world. It is the necessary missionary ethic of loyalty so to speak. Remember, in responding to Harnack's liberal view that individuals may gain salvation through loving other individuals, Royce responds, "Not through imitating nor yet through loving any mere individual human being can we be saved, but only through loyalty to the Beloved Community."[8] It is by embracing community that the individual becomes more than merely an individual. It is loyalty—the loyalty to loyalty—created within the community and taken up by individuals aspiring to be more than themselves, a *we* that can see empire alongside God and country.[9]

But how does this parallel the thought of Martin Luther King Jr.? In other words, how can scholars reconcile this revising of Royce as a racial progressive with King's calls for the somebodyness of Black Americans, a suggestion adamantly denied by the colonial administration advocated by Royce to calm America's Negro problem? Noting that scholars have often drawn parallels between King and Royce's use of the Beloved Community, Marsh argues that "King always kept a guarded distance between his own use of the term and its philosophical and cultural formulations," including that of Royce.[10] Marsh explains that unlike Royce, King's philosophy maintains a distinction between God and the community, a theological distinction that allowed him to explain the unrealized racial equality of the world and God's relationship to rightness he aimed to materialize. "King's use of beloved community was always permeated with the raw material of his own formative experiences in the southern black church."[11] It was never simply an importing of Royce's thinking, or an imitation of Royce's theological relationship to the racial order of his day. In contrast to Royce's Kantianism, Marsh writes that

> King's vision of "the camp meeting" trades on this philo-sophical discourse, and it also nicely illustrates the synthetic ingenuity of his theological imagination, his ability to bring into a unified perspective the two dimensions of his civil rights vision: everyday people gathered in fellowship in the free space of divine love. But unlike Hegel's famous synthesis and Royce's version, King preserves the fundamental difference between God and community, as one sees in his sermons and speeches. And how could he not? The Jim Crow South—like the history of the African diaspora—hardly yielded a theod-icy, a cool assimilation of the being of God with the way of the world. Still, a unity exists between God and the world, but a unity sustained asymmetrically from the side of God's majesty—the great camp meeting in the promised land of freedom has been prepared by God.[12]

King believed that the community and God shared in a unity, but he did not believe as Royce did that the community—its ultimate aim—was the embodiment of God himself. The Pauline community was not salvation for King as it was for Royce. There is also another relevant distinction to note in King's thought, namely, it was thoroughly anti-imperialist and anti-colonial.

Martin Luther King Jr. did not see racism as an argument explained purely in terms of morality, personal belief, and democratic amelioration. Like many of the Black thinkers of the sixties, Martin Luther King recognized that racism's reach was global in scope and not singularly dedicated to the destruction of segregation in American society and the integration of Black Americans into the social and moral maladies of American society. Instead of understanding racism as being synonymous to American segregation, King took an anti-colonial perspective, which made imperialism a foundational component of modern-day racism. This perspective by King, initially conceptualized as the internationalist extension of Du Bois's analysis of the color line, became the basis of the American civil rights movement. "Racism," says King, "is no mere American phenomenon. Its vicious grasp knows no geographical boundaries. In fact, racism and its perennial ally—economic exploitation—provide the key to understanding most of the international complications of this generation."[13]

It is this worldwide focus that provides the conceptual alluvium of King's revolution of values—"All men are interdependent. Every nation is an heir of a vast treasury of ideas and labor to which both the living and the dead of all nations have contributed."[14] So the conceptual changes of America, the sense by which one becomes a person through their struggle against the racist, economic, militarism of the present order, is a transformation, not of the politics advocated, but the human sought to be realized in the world. Toward the end of his life, King recognized that the need for Black solidarity and independence did not need to trade off with the transcendental aim of a global and shared ethical humanity. King recognized the need to reach the conscience of the people, to appeal to the shared sentiments of the oppressed the world over who aimed for freedom from the constraints of neocolonialism. He also recognized that such goals were arrested through the use of violence. While King acknowledged the aim of Frantz Fanon's call for revolutionary violence was also a call for the creation of a new humanism, King was wary of Fanon's faith that violence could actualize such a grand idea. Fanon maintained that "the new humanism is written into the objectives and methods of the struggle."[15] For King this ethical demand exposed a contradiction in Fanon's program: " 'to work out new concepts' and 'set afoot a new man' with a willingness to imitate old concepts of violence. Is there not a basic contradiction here? Violence has been the inseparable twin of materialism, the hallmark of its grandeur and misery. This is the one thing about modern civilization that I do not care to imitate."[16]

While the Black Power movement emerged as a new call for Black self-respect, it imitated the strategies of old. As King says, "Humanity is waiting for something other than blind imitation of the past. If we want truly to advance a step further, if we want to turn over a new leaf and really set a new man afoot, we must begin to turn mankind away from the long and desolate night of violence."[17] This realization became the impetus behind King's redefinition of Black Power. King knew that Black Power, in order to succeed, had to reject the long-held divisions between power and love, which was understood as weakness. Contrary to Carmichael, King did not see power as simply the ability to actualize an act—a radical Black self-consciousness in society—King held that

> power, properly understood, is the ability to achieve purpose.
> It is the strength required to bring about social, political or
> economic changes. In this sense power is not only desirable
> but necessary in order to implement the demands of love and
> justice. One of the greatest problems of history is that the
> concepts of love and power are usually contrasted as polar
> opposites. Love is identified with a resignation of power and
> power with a denial of love.[18]

Power is needed, but this power, the ability for change, must not come at the expense of love, the sentiment and acuity necessary to guide it toward its ends. It must not become defined by the limits of its time or the resentment beneath the politics of its day. "What is needed is a realization that power without love is reckless and abusive and that love without power is sentimental and anemic. Power at its best is love implementing the demands of justice. Justice at its best is love correcting everything that stands against love."[19] Black Power then is the means by which the humanity of Black people guides, offers to the world, the psychology and moral conscience of political change.

Like Du Bois, King, who initially penned the introduction to the 1969 edition of Du Bois's *Darkwater* published by Schocken Books, saw racism and its resolution residing in the mobilization of the world against American traditions of democracy and economic prosperity.[20] King was adamant in this internationalist and economic critique of racism and stated:

> In one sense the civil rights movement in the United States is a special American phenomenon which must be understood in the light of American history and dealt with in terms of the American situation. But on another and more important level, what is happening in the United States today is a significant part of a world development. . . . All over the world like a fever, freedom is spreading in the widest liberation movement in history. The great masses of people are determined to end the exploitation of their races and lands.[21]

Du Bois took this description to necessitate a normative political analysis. For Du Bois, desegregation and the civil rights movement that followed made Blacks subservient to the capitalist interests of white America that sought to exploit Africa for its raw materials. In an essay entitled "American Negroes and Africa's Rise to Freedom," Du Bois argued, "Negroes slowly turned to a new ideal: to strive for equality as America citizens . . . [they] learned from their environment to think less and less of their fatherland and its folk. They learned little of its history or its present conditions. They began to despise the colored races along with white Americans and began to acquiesce in color prejudice."[22] Much like the argument made in his *Soliloquy*, Du Bois takes the acceptance of African-descended peoples' Americanness to be a complicity in the propaganda of empire appealing to the "distaste and recoil [from Africa], because of what the white world taught them about the Dark Continent," and it is this resentment, born and bred in the United States for centuries, toward being regarded as African.[23] In fact, Du Bois felt such conviction on this point in 1962 that he penned an essay entitled "Whites in Africa after Negro Autonomy," explaining,

> my resentment at the doctrine of race superiority, as preached and practiced by the white world for the last 250 years has been pointed to with sharp criticism and contrasted with the charity of Gandhi and of the colored minister [Dr. Martin Luther King, Jr.] who led the recent boycott in Alabama. I am quite frank: I do not pretend to "love white people." I

think that as a race they are the most selfish of any on earth.
I think that the history of the world for the last thousand
years proves this beyond doubt.[24]

Emphasizing understanding the "white world as a whole," where whites
are judged by their positionality in colonial empires—their complacency
in war, murder, and poverty—Du Bois cuts against the dominate trend
to understand him as a multicultural integrationist. This is especially
relevant given his "Address to a Black Intellectual Community," where he
likens the support of integration to "cultural genocide."[25] The same can
be said of the tendency of philosophy to read Du Bois as a Hegelian,
despite his dismissal of idealism in a letter to Herbert Aptheker in 1956
and his 1904 book review of his book *The Souls of Black Folk*.[26]

In other words, philosophers have deliberately deemphasized the
centrality of white supremacy, racism, and colonialism in Royce's work,
while erasing the dissent of Du Bois to integration and imperialism and
King's support of Black Power and anti-colonialism in an effort to create
caricatures of these Black thinkers' actual positions that can be associated
with Royce. The consequence of this process at its most basic level is the
miseducation of scholars actually interested in the philosophical insights
of the aforementioned thinkers. Over time, the amount of present-day
literature embellishing these distortions becomes historical and determinative—canonical—and consequently buries the *actual* associations and
insights of these Black thinkers under the archives of consensus-based
peer review literature. Our contemporary moment allows us the luxury of
contesting the accuracy of this phenomenon, but the historical relevance
of this debate is irrelevant amid the proliferation of articles in canonical
journals that canonize these distortions and solidify even more so the
erasure of Black conceptual analyses.

It is my hope that this book allows scholars of Royce to better
understand and nuance the conversations of community, individuality,
and race in Royce's corpus. By exposing Royce's dedication to empire, I
hope to inspire future generations to acknowledge the dangers of Royce's
philosophy so that the ideas of white superiority are not reproduced as
synonymous with ideas like freedom, individuality, or community. This
book offers philosophers and theorists of race access to various scholars
and texts written by Black thinkers, some of whom studied and sought to
correct these shortcomings of Royce, without apology. Instead of dedicat-
ing ourselves to disciplinary apologetics that defend Royce, future scholars

now could genuinely learn from his allegiances, to learn the distinctions and debates Black thinkers at the turn of the century engaged in Royce's work. This text provides an opportunity for race theory in American philosophy to advance beyond merely associating white philosophers from the early nineteenth century with historic Black icons. This shift emphasizes the detailed surveys, the racial theories, and the debates Black theorists endorsed and presumed and the distinctions they believed differentiated their work from that of white ethnologists and philosophers in the late nineteenth and early twentieth centuries. This text should remind us that philosophy is intimately involved and determined by the assumptions of its day, a realization that requires more care and understanding of the times we theorize from, not less.

Notes

Preface

1. Tommy J. Curry, "On Derelict and Method: The Methodological Crisis of Africana Philosophy's Study of African Descended People Under an Integrationist Milieu," *Radical Philosophy Review* 14.2 (2011): 139–164, 141.

2. Amir Jaima, "Africana Philosophy as Prolegomenon to Any Future American Philosophy," *The Journal of Speculative Philosophy* 32.1 (2018): 151–67.

3. Louise Newman, "Women's Rights, Race, and Imperialism in U.S. History," in *Race, Nation and Empire in American History*, ed. James Campbell (Chapel Hill: University of North Carolina Press, 2007), 157–179, 173.

4. Elizabeth Cady Stanton, "Women and Black Men," *The Revolution*, February 4, 1869.

5. Stanton, "Women and Black Men."

6. Ibid.

7. Rosalyn Terborg-Penn, *Afro-Americans in the Struggle for Women's Suffrage* (Dissertation: Howard University, 1977), 260.

8. Elizabeth Cady Stanton, "Manhood Suffrage," *The Revolution*, December 24, 1868.

9. Stanton, "Manhood Suffrage."

10. Rosalyn Terborg-Penn, "The Politics of the Anti-Woman Agenda: African Americans Respond to Conservatism," in *Dimensions of Black Conservatism in the United States*, ed. Gayle T. Tate and Lewis A. Randolph (New York: Palgrave, 2002), 64–89, 70.

11. Terborg-Penn, "The Politics of the Anti-Woman Agenda," 70.

12. Terborg-Penn, *Afro-Americans in the Struggle for Women's Suffrage*, 326–336.

13. Belle Kearney, "The South and Women's Rights," *The Women's Journal*, April 4, 1903, 106.

14. Kearney, "The South and Women's Rights," 107.

15. Tommy J. Curry, "Concerning the Under-specialization of Race Theory in American Philosophy: An Essay Outlining Ignored Bibliographic Sources Addressing the Aforementioned Problem," *The Pluralist* 5.1 (2010): 44–64.

16. See Allison Sneider, *Suffragists in an Imperial Age: U.S. Expansion and the Woman Question, 1870–1929* (Oxford: Oxford University Press, 2008); Margaret D. Jacobs, *[w]hite Mother to a Dark Race: Settler Colonialism, Maternalism, and the Removal of Indigenous Children in the American West and Australia, 1880–1940* (Lincoln: University of Nebraska Press, 2009); Kathleen Blee, *Women of the Klan: Racism and Gender in the 1920s* (Berkeley: University of California Press, 2009); and Elisabeth Gillespie McRae, *[w]hite Women and the Politics of [w]hite Supremacy* (New York: Oxford University Press, 2018).

17. A. H. Keane, *Ethnology: Fundamental Ethnical Problems; the Primary Ethnical Groups* (Cambridge: Cambridge University Press, 1909), 2.

18. W. E. B. Du Bois, "Letter to Herbert Aptheker," in *The Correspondence of W. E. B. Du Bois: Volume III Selections 1944–1963*, ed. Herbert Aptheker (Amherst: University of Massachusetts Press, 1997), 394–396, 394–395.

19. Tommy J. Curry, "Empirical or Imperial: Issues in the Manipulation of Du Bois's Intellectual Historiography in Anthony Appiah's *Lines of Descent*," *Graduate Faculty Philosophy Journal* 35.1–2 (2014): 1–29; and "It's for the Kids: The Sociological Significance of W. E. B. Du Bois's Brownie Books and Its Philosophical Relevance for Our Understanding of Gender in the Ethnological Age," *Graduate Faculty Philosophy Journal* 36.1. (2015): 1–31.

20. See Amir Jaima, "Historical Fiction as Sociological Interpretation and Philosophy: On the Two Methodological Registers of W. E. B. Du Bois's *The Black Flame*," *Transactions of the Charles S. Peirce Society* 53.4 (2017): 584–600.

21. See Jacoby Carter, *African American Contributions to the Americas' Cultures: A Critical Edition of Lectures by Alain Locke* (New York: Palgrave Macmillan, 2016); "Between Reconstruction and Elimination: Alain Locke's Philosophy of Race," in *The Oxford Handbook of Race and Philosophy*, ed. Naomi Zack (New York: Oxford University Press, 2017); and "Racing the Canon: American Icon from Jefferson to (Alain) Locke," in *The Routledge Companion to the Philosophy of Race*, ed. Paul C. Taylor, Linda Martin Alcoff, and Luvell Anderson (New York: Routledge, 2018).

22. See Tommy J. Curry, *The Philosophical Treatise of William H. Ferris: Selected Readings from "The African Abroad or, His Evolution in Western Civilization"* (Lanham: Rowman & Littlefield, 2016); and Dwayne Tunstall, "Idealism in Black: Reclaiming William H. Ferris's Philosophy of History," unpublished.

23. Throughout this text, I take on the grammatical practices of Critical Race Theorists in capitalizing the [B] in Black and lowercasing the [w] in white. This practice is linked to the recognition of the difference in history, politics, and our cultural constructions of what Black(ness) means and represents to marginalized, racialized peoples in distinction to the dominant racist group of

white Americans that defines all those not white as inferior because they lack the humanizing quality of whiteness.

Introduction

1. See Emmanuel Eze, *Race and the Enlightenment* (Hoboken: John Wiley & Sons, 1997); Andrew Valls, ed., *Race and Racism in Modern Philosophy* (Ithaca: Cornell University Press, 2005); and Peter K. P. Park, *Africa, Asia, and the History of Philosophy: Racism in the Formation of the Philosophical Canon, 1780–1830* (Albany: State University of New York Press, 2013).

2. See Ronald K. Goodenow, "Racial and Ethnic Tolerance in John Dewey's Educational and Social Though: The Depression Years," *Educational Theory* 27.1 (1977): 48–64; Frank Margonis, "John Dewey's Racialized Visions of the Student and the Classroom Community," *Educational Theory* 59.1 (2009): 17–39, and Frank Margonis, "John Dewey, W. E. B. Du Bois, and Alain Locke: A Case Study in White Ignorance and Intellectual Segregation," in *Race and the Epistemologies of Ignorance*, ed. Shannon Sullivan and Nancy Tuana (Albany: State University of New York Press, 2007), 173–196; and Thomas Fallace, *Dewey and the Dilemma of Race: An Intellectual History, 1895–1922* (New York: Teachers College Press, 2011).

3. Dwayne Tunstall, "Josiah Royce's 'Enlightened' Anti-Black Racism?" *The Pluralist* 4.3 (2009): 39–45, 44.

4. See Tommy J. Curry, "Royce, Racism, and the Colonial Ideal: White Supremacy and the Illusion of Civilization in Josiah Royce's Account of the [w]hite Man's Burden," *The Pluralist* 4.3 (2009): 10–38.

5. Jacquelyn Kegley, "Josiah Royce on Race: Issues in Context," *The Pluralist* 4.3 (2009): 1–9, 8.

6. Kegley, "Josiah Royce on Race," 2.

7. Ibid., 1. Kegley's first footnote also explains that "Shannon Sullivan makes this point in an introductory piece for a manuscript being considered by Fordham University Press, *Josiah Royce's Race Questions, Provincialism, and Other American Problems*, edited by Sullivan and Scott Pratt" (8).

8. Ignas K. Skrupskelis, "Annotated Bibliography of the Publications of Josiah Royce," in *The Basic Writings of Josiah Royce Volume 2: Logic, Loyalty, and Community* (New York: Fordham University Press, 2005), 1167–1226, 1204.

9. Tommy J. Curry, "Concerning the Under-specialization of Race Theory in American Philosophy: An Essay Outlining Ignored Bibliographic Sources Addressing the Aforementioned Problem," *The Pluralist* 5.1 (2010): 44–64.

10. Kegley, "Josiah Royce on Race," 1.

11. Martin R. Delany, *The Condition, Elevation, Emigration and Destiny of the Colored People of the United States* (New York: Humanity Books, 2004 [1852]), 48.

12. Delany, *The Condition*, 48.

13. Antenor Firmin, *The Equality of the Human Races*, trans. Asselin Charles (Urbana: University of Illinois Press, 2002), 443.

14. Firmin, *The Equality of the Human Races*, 443.

15. Martin R. Delany, *Principia of Ethnology: The Origin of Races and Color* (Baltimore: Black Classic Press, 1991), 91.

16. Delany, *The Origin of Races and Color*, 448.

17. See Margonis, "John Dewey's Racialized Visions of the Student and Classroom Community," and Fallace, *Dewey and the Dilemma of Race.*

18. For a description of the racial antipathy in Chicago School assimilation theory and social work, see R. Fred Water, "Assimilation and Cultural Pluralism in American Social Thought," *Phylon* 40.4 (1979): 325–333. For an analysis of racism within the Progressive movement, see Thomas Fallace, *Race and the Origins of Progressive Education, 1880–1929* (New York: Teachers College Press, 2015).

19. Bettina Aptheker, "Introduction," in *Lynching and Rape: An Exchange of Views by Jane Addams and Ida B. Wells*, ed. Bettina Aptheker (New York: The American Institute for Marxist Studies, 1977), 1–24, 11.

20. Jane Addams, "Respect for Law," in *Lynching and Rape: An Exchange of Views by Jane Addams and Ida B. Wells*, ed. Bettina Aptheker (New York: The American Institute for Marxist Studies, 1977), 25–29, 28–29.

21. Maurice Hamington, "Public Pragmatism: Jane Addams and Ida B. Wells on Lynching," *The Journal of Speculative Philosophy* 19.2 (2005): 167–174.

22. See F. E. Daniel, "Castration of Sexual Perverts," *Texas Medical Journal* 27.10 (1912): 369–385; and G. Frank Lydston, "Castration Instead of Lynching," *Atlanta Journal-Record of Medicine* 8 (1906): 456–458. For a full discussion of this debate, see Melissa N. Stein, *Measuring Manhood: Race and the Science of Masculinity, 1830–1934* (Minneapolis: University of Minnesota Press, 2015).

23. See Curry, "Concerning the Under-specialization of Race Theory in American Philosophy."

24. Jean Finot, *Race Prejudice* (London: Archibald Constable, 1906), 316.

25. The works of Black authors are sorely underanalyzed in this regard. See Caroline Bond Day, "Race-Crossings in the United States," *The Crisis* 37.1 (1930): 81–82, 103; and W. Montague Cobb, "Physical Anthropology of the American Negro," *American Journal of Physical Anthropology* 29 (1942): 113–222. These works were selected because both credit the work of Du Bois's Atlanta Laboratory as the basis of the findings or inspiration for the studies. In other words, Black anthropologists were using the work of Martin Delany, Edward Blyden, and W. E. B. Du Bois to continue their attacks on racist biological explanations of Black inferiority and inequality, not Royce or other American philosophers touted as "progressive" today. See Ira E. Harrison and Faye V. Harrison, eds., *African-American Pioneers in Anthropology* (Urbana: University of Illinois Press, 1999).

26. See Earl Wright, "The Atlantic Sociological Laboratory 1896–1924," *Western Journal of Black Studies* 26.3 (2002): 165–174; and Earl Wright and Tom Calhoun, "Jim Crow Sociology: Toward an Understanding of the Origin of Principles of Black Sociology via the Atlanta Sociological Laboratory," *Sociological Focus* 39.1 (2006): 1–18.

27. W. E. B. Du Bois, *The Health and Physique of the Negro American: A Social Study Made Under the Direction of Atlanta University by the Eleventh Atlanta Conference* (Atlanta: The Atlanta University Press, 1906), 13.

28. Herbert A. Miller, "Some Psychological Considerations on the Race Problem," in *The Health and Physique of the Negro American: A Social Study Made Under the Direction of Atlanta University by the Eleventh Atlanta Conference* (Atlanta: The Atlanta University Press, 1906), 53–59, 54–55.

29. See Miller, "Some Psychological Considerations of the Race Problem," 54, for a rich discussion of the inaccuracy of psycho-physics in relation to the Negro.

30. Take Herbert A. Miller's statement at the end of section 6 in *The Health and Physique of the Negro American*:

Finally, class and race as well as sex problems arise from lack of spiritual affinity between the groups or individuals concerned. They lack "consciousness of kind." This phrase resolves itself into consciousness of the same kind of ideals or purposes. A social relation exists as soon as there are common purposes. If the ideals or purposes differ there will be antagonism. The first cause of this difference is due to some superficial accidental condition, such as the customs of the tribe or the color of the skin, which stand as symbols of the sameness of kind. That these external symbols are only accidental is proved by the ease with which they are laid aside when some deeper principle draws men together, bridging chasms that had seemed impassable. Mere propinquity will often do it. This accidental element in the race problem makes it no less real, but the purpose of science and philosophy is not to get the temporal and the accidental, but rather the universal and essential. The purpose of education and social progress is to make the accidental give way to the essential, and to let each individual stand for his true worth to society; then the problems as they now confront us will cease to exist (59).

31. Jacquelyn Ann Kegley, "Is a Coherent Racial Identity Essential to Genuine Individuals and Communities? Josiah Royce on Race," *Journal of Speculative Philosophy* 19 (2005): 216–228, 216.

32. This debate has been extensively documented in African American philosophy. In Anthony Appiah's "The Uncompleted Argument: Du Bois and the Illusion of Race," he concludes:

> Race, we all assume, is, like all other concepts, constructed by metaphor and metonymy; it stands in, metonymically, for the other; it bears the weight, metaphorically, of other kinds of difference. Yet, in our social lives away from the text-world of the academy, we take reference for granted too easily. Even if the concept of race is a structure of oppositions—white opposed to black (but also to yellow), Jew opposed to Gentile (but also to Arab)—it is a structure whose realization is, at best, problematic and, at worst, impossible. If we can now hope to understand the concept embodied in this system of oppositions, we are nowhere near finding referents for it. The truth is that there are no races: there is nothing in the world that can do all we ask "race" to do for us. The evil that is done is done by the concept and by easy-yet impossible assumptions as to its application. What we miss through our obsession with the structure of relations of concepts is, simply, reality. (*Critical Inquiry* 12 [1985]: 21–37, 35–36)

This debate continues as he confirms his racial eliminativism against the criticisms of Joyce A. Joyce and Houston Baker's racial conservatism in "The Conservation of 'Race,'" *Black American Literary Forum* 23 (1989): 37–60, and his 1992 work *In My Father's House: Africa in the Philosophy of Culture* (New York: Oxford University Press, 1992), esp. chapters 1, 2, 3, and 4, respectively entitled, "The Invention of Africa," "Illusions of Race," "Topologies of Nativism," and "The Myth of an African World." While Kegley cites Appiah's work in *The Ethics of Identity* (Princeton: Princeton University Press, 2005), she misunderstands Appiah's stance on race and its relationship to soul making and solidarity. At best, race as a rationally defective term can be used descriptively to assess discriminatory practices in much the same way that Tommie Shelby's *We Who Are Dark: The Philosophical Foundations of Black Solidarity* (Cambridge: Belknap Press, 2005) describes, but it says absolutely nothing about culture as Kegley wishes to maintain in her interpretation of Royce.

For responses to Appiah's claim, see Robert Gooding-Williams, "Outlaw, Appiah, and Du Bois's 'The Conservation of Races,'" in *On Race and Culture*, ed. Bernard W. Bell, Emily R. Grosholz, and James B. Stewart (New York: Routledge, 1996), 39–56, and Lucius Outlaw, "Conserve Races: In Defense of W. E. B. Du Bois," *On Race and Culture* (1996): 15–37, where Outlaw is quite adamant that for Du Bois, in order to understand human history and thus be informed in attempting to structure the making of the future through organized effort, the focus of such understanding must be the racial group, the "vast family" of related individuals. While individuals are, of course, necessary components of social groups, and must never be lost sight of when analyzing and assessing human ventures, they are neither sufficient for accounting for social groups, nor self-sufficing and thus able to account for their own existence and well-being. . . . Survival of individuals is tied inextricably to the well-being of the individual's natal group; and the well being of this group requires the concerted action of its individual members, action, to a significant degree, predicated on and guided by shared, self-valorizing identities defined, to some extent, in terms of the group's identifying bio-social and cultural racial (or ethnic) characteristics. These are both constituted by and constitutive of the group's cultural life world. (31)

Because Kegley is not familiar with the aforementioned debates, her essay reads like a laundry list of associations with whom Royce is claimed to agree about the race problem: W. E. B. Du Bois, Alain Locke, Lucius Outlaw, Robert Gooding-Williams, and Cornel West. This amalgamation of authors is an example of the nonexistence of scholarly standards with regard to the thought of Black thinkers and the traditions these thinkers operate within. Despite the tensions between racial conservationists, racial eliminativists, prophetic pragmatists, critical theorists, and multiculturalists, Kegley adamantly claims that Royce can hold all contemporary Black philosophical views simultaneously.

33. For a discussion of William H. Ferris's position on the race question and his consideration of Royce's alternative, see William H. Ferris, *The Philosophical Treatise of William H. Ferris: Selected Readings from The African Abroad or, His Evolution in Western Civilization*, ed. Tommy J. Curry (Lanham: Rowman & Littlefield, 2016). In Ferris's work, he attributes much of his idealist sensibilities to his study under Royce at Harvard and extensively cites Royce's essay "Race Questions and Prejudices" as evidence of the possibility that Blacks can learn European civilization. The Negro-Saxon, as Ferris calls the Black American, is the result of Royce's assimilation.

34. See William T. Fontaine, *Reflections on Segregation, Desegregation, Power and Morals* (Springfield: Charles C. Thomas, 1967), or the chapter for his 1967 book published as "Josiah Royce and the American Race Problem," *Philosophy and Phenomenological Research* 29.2 (1968): 282–288.

35. What is most disconcerting about Kegley's work is its lack of historical context and its blatant extrication of Southern racism from Royce's 1906 essay

on racism. One example of this occurred in Kegley's defense of Royce as a racial
conservationist at the 2008 Central APA meeting in Chicago when Kegley argued
that Royce was not a racial eliminativist because he says, "If race-amalgamation
is indeed to be viewed as always an evil, the best way to counteract the growth
of that evil must everywhere be the cultivation of racial self-respect and not of
racial degradation" (Josiah Royce, "Race Questions and Prejudices," *International
Journal of Ethics* 16 [1906]: 265–288, 273–274). By disregarding the historical
context of such a statement, she ignores that Royce is presenting a case against
interracial marriage, miscegenation, and supporting the preservation of white
racial purity by claiming that his proposal for colonial administration would in
fact prevent race mixture. By assuming race mixture is an evil, Royce perpetuates
the dominant racist motivations of his time, namely, that white women must be
protected from the sultry desires of Black men to protect the pureness of the
white race. While Kegley's works represent the most extreme example in regard
to Royce, this is a common practice among white scholars who lack the necessary
sensibilities in Black history to situate accurately white thinkers' relationships to
race. In general, there is no method, no standard, of comparison in philosophy.
In many cases, history, sociology, or even texts in tension with an author's desired
interpretation are simply ignored or deemphasized. Such capriciousness can have
deleterious effects with regard to understanding a figure's actual relationship to
the racialist sciences or discourses of their time.

36. Josiah Royce, *Race Questions, Provincialism, and Other American Problems*, in *Race Questions and Other Problems*, ed. Scott Pratt and Shannon Sullivan
(New York: Fordham University Press, 2009).

37. Scott Pratt, "Introduction to *Race Questions, Provincialism, and Other
American Problems*," in *Race Questions and Other Problems*, ed. Scott Pratt and
Shannon Sullivan (New York: Fordham University Press, 2009), 1–19, 8.

38. Ibid.

39. Ibid.

40. Josiah Royce, "Race Questions and Prejudices," *International Journal
of Ethics* 16.3 (1906): 265–288, 274.

41. Royce, "Race Questions and Prejudices," 275.

42. Pratt, "Introduction," 9.

43. Ibid., 16–17.

44. Ibid., 17.

45. Josiah Royce, "Preface," in *The Problem of Christianity: The Christian
Doctrine of Life, Vol. 1* (New York: MacMillan Company, 1913), viii–ix.

46. See Josiah Royce, *War and Insurance* (New York: MacMillan Company,
1914) where he explains that the nation-state, the policy of government and
rule, is not displaced by the Beloved Community.

47. Shannon Sullivan, "Royce's "Race Questions and Prejudices,'" in *Race
Questions and Other Problems*, ed. Scott Pratt and Shannon Sullivan (New York:
Fordham University Press, 2009), 20–34, 21.

48. Sullivan, "Royce's 'Race Questions and Prejudices,'" 26.

49. Ibid., 26–27.

50. Ibid., 31.

51. Ibid.

52. Ibid., 32.

53. For many contemporary thinkers, prior works are no help in situating Royce's thinking on race. On the one hand, John Clendenning, for example, believes that Royce should be commended for his perspectives on race. See *The Life and Thought of Josiah Royce* (Nashville: Vanderbilt University Press, 1999), 305–306. On the other hand, however, he explicitly announced Royce's anti-black racism to the distinguished gathering at Harvard in 2007 by sharing the story of Royce's harsh words and use of the epithet "nigger" in relation to his table service at a Saratoga Springs hotel. There is an ambiguity in Royce scholarship that admits to racism in his personal life, but separates it from his larger intellectual project. Even Marilyn Lake and Henry Reynolds's *Drawing the Global Colour Line: [w]hite Men's Countries and the International Challenge of Racial Equality* (Cambridge: Cambridge University Press, 2008) continues the traditional interpretation of Royce as a racial progressive. It is interesting, however, that these authors point out Royce's insistence on racial homogeneity (42), but still offer a rather flattering account of Royce's thinking on race in chapter 10.

54. Quoted in Elizabeth Duquette, *Loyal Subjects: Bonds of Nation, Race, and Allegiance in Nineteenth-Century America* (New Brunswick: Rutgers University Press, 2010), 179.

55. Duquette, *Loyal Subjects*, 181.

56. Alain Locke, ed., *The New Negro* (New York: Atheneum, 1992), 449–450.

57. Jerome Dowd, *The Negro in American Life* (New York: Century Company, 1926), 117.

58. W. E. B. Du Bois, "Josiah Royce," *The Crisis* 13.1 (1916): 10.

59. Du Bois, "Josiah Royce," 10.

60. Ibid.

61. Ibid.

62. Ibid.

63. Ibid.

64. See Amy Helen Kirschke and Phillip Luke Sinitiere, eds., *Protest and Propaganda: W. E. B. Du Bois, the* Crisis*, and American History* (Columbia: University of Missouri Press, 2014), and Dan S. Green and Edwin D. Driver, eds., "Introduction," in *W. E. B. Du Bois on Sociology and the Black Community* (Chicago: University of Chicago Press, 1978), 1–48, 21–22.

65. W. E. B. Du Bois, *Dusk of Dawn: An Essay Toward an Autobiography of a Race Concept* (New Brunswick: Transaction, 1983), 293–294.

66. W. E. B. Du Bois, *The Negro* (Mineola: Dover, 2001), 154.

67. Dr. Charles Victor Roman was a medical doctor. He was an African North American, a Black American who migrated to Canada, and former president of The National Medical Association.

68. Charles Victor Roman, *American Civilization and the Negro: The Afro-American in Relation to National Progress* (Philadelphia: F. A. Davis Company, 1916), 69.

69. Roman, *American Civilization and the Negro*, 173.

70. Tommy J. Curry, "On Derelict and Method: The Methodological Crisis of Africana Philosophy's Study of African-Descended Peoples under an Integrationist Milieu," *Radical Philosophy Review* 14.2 (2011): 139–164.

71. William T. Fontaine, "Josiah Royce and the American Race Problem," *Philosophy and Phenomenological Research* 29.2 (1968): 282–288.

72. Fontaine, "Josiah Royce and the American Race Problem," 282.

73. Ibid., 282–283.

74. William T. Fontaine, *Reflections on Segregation, Desegregation, Power and Morals* (Springfield: Charles C. Thomas, 1967).

75. E. Franklin Frazier, "The Failure of the Negro Intellectual," in *The Death of white Sociology: Essays on Race and Culture*, ed. Joyce Ladner (Baltimore: Black Classic Press, 1973/1962), 52–66, 53.

76. W. E. B. Du Bois, "An Address to the Black Academic Community," *Journal of Negro History* 60.5 (1975): 45–52, 46.

77. Du Bois, "An Address to the Black Academic Community," 46.

78. Ibid.

79. Hosea Easton, *A Treatise on the Intellectual Character, and Civil and Political Condition of the Colored People of the U. States; and the Prejudice Exercised Towards Them; with a Sermon on the Duty of the Church to Them* (Boston: Isaac Knapp, 1837), 35.

80. Easton, *A Treatise on the Intellectual Character*, 36–37.

81. Ibid., 38.

82. Ibid., 40.

83. Ibid.

84. Ibid., 41.

85. Ibid.

86. F. E. Daniel, "The Cause and Prevention of Rape," *Texas Medical Journal* 19.11 (1904): 452–462.

87. Hunter McGuire and G. Frank Lydston, *Sexual Crimes among the Southern Negroes* (Louisville: Renz and Henry, 1893).

88. Louise Newman, *[w]hite Women's Rights: The Racial Origins of Feminism in the United States* (New York: Oxford University Press, 1999), 161.

89. W. E. B. Du Bois, *The World and Africa: An Inquiry into the Part Which African Has Played in World History* (New York: International, 2003), 19.

90. Du Bois, *The World and Africa*.

91. Ibid.

92. W. E. B. Du Bois, *Darkwater: Voices from Within the Veil* (New York: Schocken Books, 1969), 51.

93. Du Bois, *Darkwater.*

94. Ibid.

95. Charles Mills, *The Racial Contract* (Ithaca: Cornell University Press, 1997), 1–2.

96. Frances Lee Ansley, "Stirring the Ashes: Race, Class and the Future of Civil Rights Scholarship," *Cornell Law Review* 74 (1989): 993–1077, n. 129.

97. Eduardo Bonilla-Silva, *[w]hite Supremacy and Racism in the Post–Civil Rights Era* (Boulder: Lynne Rienner, 2001), 37.

98. See Robert D. Bullord, "The Legacy of American Apartheid and Environmental Racism," *Journal of Civil Rights and Economic Development* 9.2 (1994): 445–474, and Dorceta Taylor, *Toxic Communities: Environmental Racism, Industrial Pollution, and Residential Mobility* (New York: New York University Press, 2014).

99. Barbara J. Fields, "[w]hiteness, Racism, and Identity," *International Labor and Working-Class History* 60 (2001): 48–56.

100. Fields, "[w]hiteness, Racism, and Identity."

101. Tommy J. Curry & Gwenetta Curry, "On the Perils of Race Neutrality and Anti-Blackness: Philosophy as an Irreconcilable Obstacle to Thought," *American Journal of Economics and Sociology* (Forthcoming); Tommy J. Curry "Will the Real CRT Please Stand Up: The Dangers of Philosophical Contributions to CRT," *The Crit: A Journal in Critical Legal Studies* 2.1 (2009): 1–47.

102. Charles Mills, *Blackness Visible: Essays on Philosophy and Race* (Ithaca: Cornell University Press, 1998), 6.

103. Mills, *Blackness Visible.*

104. Ibid., 7.

105. See Josiah Royce, *Pussycat Blackie's Travels: There's No Place Like Home,* ed. Randall Auxier (Bloomsbury: Artemis, 2014).

Chapter 1

1. I often remark that Josiah Royce's "Some Characteristic Tendencies of American Civilization" was a lost speech buried on Google Books. For years, I had been interested in the progression of Royce's thinking on American racism and empire given his language choices in *Race Questions, Provincialism, and Other American Problems,* and insisted that there must be another document or record of his thinking on the subject. On multiple occasions I was told that there was nothing else, and through a random Google Book search I stumbled across this essay in late 2008.

2. Josiah Royce, *California: From the Conquest in 1846 to the Second Vigilance Committee in San Francisco: A Study of American Character* (Boston: Houghton, Mifflin and Company, 1886), vii–viii.

3. Royce, *California*.

4. Ibid., 2.

5. Ibid., 2.

6. Ibid., 30.

7. Ibid.

8. Ibid., 48.

9. Ibid.

10. Ibid., 52.

11. Ibid., 53.

12. Ibid., 54.

13. Ibid., 59.

14. Ibid., 60.

15. Ibid., 66.

16. Ibid., 63.

17. Ibid., 71.

18. Ibid., 91.

19. Ibid., 151.

20. Ibid.

21. Ibid., 156.

22. Ibid., 225.

23. Ibid.

24. Ibid., 226.

25. Ibid.

26. Ibid.

27. Ibid., 368.

28. Ibid., 370.

29. Ibid., 371.

30. Ibid.

31. Ibid.

32. Ibid.

33. Ibid.

34. Ibid.

35. Ibid., 372.

36. Ibid.

37. Ibid.

38. Ibid., 373.

39. Ibid.

40. Ibid., 374.

41. Ibid.

42. Ibid., 315.

43. Ibid., 374.

44. Ibid., 367.

45. Ibid., 277.

46. Ibid., 281.

47. Ibid., 277–278.

48. Ibid., 328.

49. Ibid., 362.

50. Ibid., 281.

51. Ibid., 375–376.

52. Ibid., 501.

53. Ibid.

54. Ibid.

55. Ibid., 500.

56. Vernon J. Williams, Jr., *Rethinking Race: Franz Boas and His Contemporaries* (Lexington: University of Kentucky Press, 1996).

57. See Thomas Huxley, "Emancipation—Black and [w]hite," in *Science and Education* (New York: D. Appleton and Co., 1898), 66–75, and Frederick Hoffman, "Race Traits and Tendencies of the American Negro," *Publications of the American Economic Association* 11.1–3 (1896): 1–329.

58. Josiah Royce, "Race Questions and Prejudices," *International Journal of Ethics* 16 (1906): 265–288, 281.

59. Royce, "Race Questions and Prejudices."

60. "The same feature of an indomitable individualism, which, in political as well as in religious affairs, conduced to the rejection of universalism and to the formation of nations, led to the creation of a new world, that is to say, of an absolutely new order of society adapted to the character, the needs, and the gifts of a new species of men. It was a creation brought about by natural necessity, the creation of a new civilisation, a new culture. It was Teutonic blood and Teutonic blood alone (in the wide sense in which I take the word, that is to say, embracing the Celtic, Teutonic and Slavonic, or North European races) that formed the impelling force and the informing power. It is impossible to estimate aright the genius and development of our North-European culture, if we obstinately shut our eyes to the fact that it is a definite species of mankind which constitutes its physical and moral basis. We see that clearly to-day: for the less Teutonic a land is, the more uncivilised it is." Houston Stewart Chamberlain, *Foundations of the Nineteenth Century* (London: John Lane Company, 1912), 187–188.

61. Royce, "Race Questions and Prejudices," 267.

62. Ibid., 267–268.

63. The digital (Google Books) version of *Ethnische Elementargedanken in der Lehre vom Menschen*, or *The Ethnic Elementary Ideas in the Doctrine of Man*, Vol. 1 (Berlin: Weidmann sehe Buchhandlung, 1895) at Harvard College Library comes from the personal library of Josiah Royce. I believe it is safe to

conclude that Josiah Royce had a robust familiarity of Adolf Bastian's work and perspectives on human variations.

64. Royce, "Race Questions and Prejudices," 285.

65. Ibid.

66. Ibid.

67. Adolf Bastian, "Ethnology and Psychology," in *Adolf Bastian and the Psychic Unity of Mankind: The Foundations of Anthropology in Nineteenth-Century Germany*, ed. Klaus-Peter Koepping (St. Lucia: University of Queensland Press, 1983), 163.

68. Bastian, "Ethnology and Psychology."

69. Ibid.

70. Ibid.

71. Adolf Bastian, "The Folk Idea as Paradigm of Ethnology," in *Adolf Bastian and the Psychic Unity of Mankind: The Foundations of Anthropology in Nineteenth Century Germany*, ed. Klaus-Peter Koepping (St. Lucia: University of Queensland Press, 1983), 170.

72. Royce, "Race Questions and Prejudices," 278–279.

73. Ibid., 278–282.

74. Ibid., 278.

75. Ibid.

76. Bastian, "The Folk Idea as Paradigm of Ethnology," 170–178, 170.

77. Ibid., 175.

78. Ibid., 174. Bastian's examples of folk ideas are things like the bow in Melanesia or the blow-pipe or bola in South America. The folk idea is what is created in the cultural area (historical geography) of a people, and what geographic materials are available to them.

79. Ibid., 170.

80. Ibid.

81. Ibid., 171.

82. Frazer says: "But if in the most backward state of human society now known to us we find magic thus conspicuously present and religion conspicuously absent, may we not reasonably conjecture that the civilised races of the world have also at some period of their history passed through a similar intellectual phase, that they attempted to force the great powers of nature to do their pleasure before they thought of courting their favour by offerings and prayer—in short that, just as on the material side of human culture there has everywhere been an Age of Stone, so on the intellectual side there has everywhere been an Age of Magic? There are reasons for answering this question in the affirmative." James George Frazer, *The Golden Bough: A Study in Magic and Religion* (Auckland: The Floating Press, 2009), 136.

83. Frazer, *The Golden Bough*, 117.

84. Ibid., 118–119.

85. Ibid., preface.

86. Royce, "Race Questions and Prejudices," 288.

87. Frantz Boas, "Human Faculty as Determined by Race," in *A Franz Boas Reader: The Shaping of American Anthropology, 1883–1911*, ed. George W. Stocking, Jr. (Chicago: University of Chicago Press, 1974), 221–242. For a great discussion on Boas's work, see Williams, *Rethinking Race*, especially the introduction and chapter 1.

88. Richard W. Rees, *Shades of Difference: A History of Ethnicity in America* (New York: Rowman & Littlefield, 2007), esp. chapters 1 and 2. For a demonstration of this connection, see William I. Thomas, "The Scope and Method of Folk-Psychology," *The American Journal of Sociology* 1 (1896): 434–445.

89. George M. Fredrickson, *The Black Image in the White Mind* (Middleton: Wesleyan University Press, 1971), 327.

90. Robert E. Park, *Race and Culture* (Glencoe: Free Press, 1950), 280.

91. Fredrickson, *The Black Image in the White Mind*, 320–321.

92. Ibid., 321.

93. Josiah Royce, "Some Characteristic Tendencies of American Civilization," *Transactions of the Aberdeen Philosophy Society* 3 (1900): 194–218, 195.

94. Royce, "Some Characteristic Tendencies of American Civilization," 194.

95. Ibid., 195.

96. Ibid.

97. Ibid., 196.

98. Ibid.

99. Ibid., 197.

100. Ibid., 205.

101. Ibid., 211.

102. Ibid.

103. Ibid., 197.

104. Josiah Royce, "Provincialism," in *The Basic Writings of Josiah Royce: Logic, Loyalty and Community* (New York: Fordham University Press, 2005), 1067–1088, 1085.

105. Royce, "Provincialism."

106. Ibid., 201.

107. Royce, "Some Characteristic Tendencies of American Civilization," 197.

108. Rudyard Kipling, "The White Man's Burden: The United States & The Philippine Islands, 1899," in *Rudyard Kipling's Verse: Definitive Edition* (Garden City: Doubleday & Co., 1940), 321–323.

109. Patrick Brantlinger, "Kipling's The White Man's Burden and Its Afterlives," *English Literature in Transition, 1880–1920* 50.2. (2007): 172–192.

110. Gretchen Murphy, *Shadowing the white Man's Burden: U.S. Imperialism and the Color Line* (New York: New York University Press, 2010), 34.

111. Murphy, *Shadowing the white Man's Burden*, 34.

112. Kipling, "The White Man's Burden," 322.

113. Jacquelyn Ann K. Kegley, "Racism, Race, and Josiah Royce: Exactly What Shall We Say?" in *The Relevance of Royce*, ed. Kelly A. Parker and Jason Bell (New York: Fordham University Press, 2014), 162–189.

114. Kegley, "Racism, Race, and Josiah Royce," 183.

115. Ibid.

Chapter 2

1. Royce, "Race Questions and Prejudices," 265.

2. Ibid.

3. Ibid.

4. Geoffrey Hughes, "Kaffir," in *An Encyclopedia of Swearing: The Social History of Oaths, Profanity, Foul Language, and Ethnic Slurs in the English-Speaking World* (London: M.E. Sharpe, 2006), 280–282.

5. Royce, "Race Questions and Prejudices," 266.

6. Ibid.

7. Ibid.

8. Ibid.

9. Jacquelyn Ann K. Kegley, "Josiah Royce on Race: Issues in Context," *The Pluralist* 4.3 (2009): 1–9.

10. Kegley, "Josiah Royce on Race."

11. Ibid.

12. For a discussion of the "white peril," see William Garrott Brown, "The White Peril: The Immediate Danger of the Negro," in *The New Politics and Other Papers by William Garrott Brown* (New York: Houghton Mifflin, 1914/1904), 103–142, and "The White Peril and the Southern Negro," *The American Monthly Review of Reviews* 31, ed. Albert Shaw (1905): 102–104. William Garrott Brown was the premier Southern historian of his day and recognized as such by Harvard greats like William R. Thayer and Albert Hart (see Wendell H. Stephen, "William Garrott Brown: Literary Historian and Essayist," *The Journal of Southern History* 12.3 [1946]: 313–344).

13. Shannon Sullivan, "Transforming [w]hiteness with Roycean Loyalty," in *Contemporary Feminist Pragmatism*, ed. Maurice Hamington and Celia Bardwell-Jones (New York: Routledge, 2012), 19–41.

14. Sullivan, "Transforming [w]hiteness with Roycean Loyalty," 36 n. 46.

15. Ibid.

16. Ibid.

17. George Lynch, "The [w]hite Peril," *The Nineteenth Century and Beyond: A Monthly Review* 57.340 (1905): 948–957.

18. See Peter J. Breaux, *William G. Brown and the Development of Education: A Retrospective on the Career of a State Superintendent of Public Education of African Descent in Louisiana* (PhD diss., Florida State University, 2006).

19. See the *Harvard Graduates' Magazine* 4 (1895): 339 and *The Quinquennial Catalogue of the Officers and Graduates of Harvard 1636–1910* (Cambridge: Harvard University Press, 1910), 23.

20. *The Quinquennial Catalogue of the Officers and Graduates of Harvard 1636–1910*, 76, 114.

21. Albert Shaw, "[w]hite Peril and the Southern Negro," *The American Monthly Review of Reviews* 31 (1905): 102–104.

22. William Garrott Brown, "The [w]hite Peril: The Immediate Danger of the Negro," *The North American Review* 179.577 (1904): 824–841, 824.

23. Brown, "The white Peril, 825.

24. Ibid.

25. Ibid., 826.

26. Ibid., 828.

27. Ibid., 831–832.

28. Ibid., 839.

29. Ibid., 840.

30. Ibid.

31. Ibid., 841.

32. Ibid.

33. Roderick Jones, "The Black Peril in South Africa," *The Nineteenth Century and After* 54 (1904): 712–723, 712–713.

34. See Gareth Cornwell, "George Webb Hardy's *The Black Peril* and the Social Meaning of 'Black Peril' in Early Twentieth-Century South Africa," *Journal of South African Studies* 22.3 (1996): 441–453.

35. Lynch, "The [w]hite Peril," 957.

36. See "The [w]hite Peril," *The Review of Reviews* 182.31 (1905): 610.

37. Sidney Lewis Gulick, *The [w]hite Peril in the Far East: An Interpretation of the Significance of the Russo-Japanese War* (New York: Fleming H. Revell Company, 1905), 164–179.

38. Even if we accepted Sullivan's narrowing of the term to George Lynch's essay, it would not help her interpretation of Royce, since Royce adamantly disagreed with Lynch, as well as Gulick. Unlike these authors, Royce supports Britain's imperialism and urges America to take up the white man's burden. This is the exact opposite of the sympathetic view adopted by Lynch in his 1905 piece on the white peril.

Perhaps even more shocking is Shannon Sullivan's use of the perils as synonymous to the menacing terrors nonwhite races pose to whites in her new book. Sullivan writes, "whiteness also experiences itself as threatened from without—witness so-called yellow peril, black peril, and all other sorts of 'menacing' forces that other nonwhite races represent. Historically, miscegenation and immigration—the mixing of white and nonwhite 'blood'—probably have served as the two greatest 'threats' to the purity of whiteness" (Shannon Sullivan, *Good [w]hite People: The Problem with Middle-Class [w]hite Anti-Racism* [Albany: State

University of New York Press, 2014], 31). Ironically, Sullivan now takes up the idea of perils in their historical context as well as their association to miscegenation and immigration, yet no citation or credit is given to my previous interpretations of white, Yellow, and Black peril even though Sullivan herself argued against the idea that the perils meant what she now claims they do in her 2014 text. As is often the case, Black scholars' insights are taken up without credit in philosophy despite the scholarly record demonstrating otherwise.

39. Sullivan, "Royce's 'Race Questions and Prejudices,' " 34.

40. Royce, "Race Questions and Prejudices," 266.

41. Ibid.

42. Ibid., 270.

43. Ibid.

44. John Dower, *War Without Mercy: Race and Power in the Pacific War* (New York: Pantheon Books, 1986), 156.

45. Dower, *War Without Mercy*, 156.

46. Yamato Ichihasi, *Japanese Immigration: Its Status in California* (San Francisco: The Marshall Press, 1915), 13.

47. Dower, *War Without Mercy*, 162.

48. Gina Marchetti, *Romance and the Yellow Peril: Race, Sex, and Discursive Strategies in Hollywood Fiction* (Berkeley: University of California Press, 1993), 3–4.

49. Marchetti, *Romance and the Yellow Peril*, 3.

50. H. A. Millis, *The Japanese Problem in the United States* (New York: MacMillan Company, 1915), 24; Sidney L. Gulick, *The American Japanese Problem: A Study of the Race Relations of the East and the West* (New York: Charles Scribner's Sons, 1914), 3–27.

51. Gulick, *The American Japanese Problem*, 226.

52. Ibid., 232.

53. Dower, *War Without Mercy*, 126–127.

54. Ibid., 236.

55. Ibid., 212–213.

56. Ibid., 213.

57. Ibid., 231.

58. Ibid.

59. Reginald Kearney, *African American Views of the Japanese: Solidarity or Sedition?* (Albany: State University of New York Press, 1998), 20.

60. Kearney, *African American Views of the Japanese*, 38.

61. Other less-known Black thinkers also criticized the adoption of Japan as Europe's own as problematic. See Charles Victor Roman, *A Knowledge of History is Conducive to Racial Solidarity and Other Writings* (Nashville: Sunday School Union Print, 1911), 23.

62. Kelly Miller, *Race Adjustment: Essays on the Negro in America* (New York: The Neale Publishing Company, 1909), 36.

63. Okakura Kakuzo, *The Book of Tea* (London: Forgotten Books, 2007/ 1906), 3.

64. A. H. Keane, *Ethnology in Two Parts: Fundamental Ethnical Problems and the Primary Ethnical Groups* (London: Cambridge University Press, 1909), 14.

65. Royce, *Race Questions, Provincialism, and Other American Problems*, 103.

66. Ibid.

67. Ibid., 104.

68. Ibid., 105.

69. Kegley, "Racism, Race, and Josiah Royce," 173.

70. Royce, *Race Questions, Provincialism, and Other American Problems*, ix.

71. In a letter to Henry L. Oak dated September 17, 1885, Royce described Black waiters as "Saratoga niggers swarm[ing] like big black flies, in the vast dining hall of the hotel." (*The Letters of Josiah Royce*, ed. John Clendenning [Chicago: University of Chicago Press, 1970], 179. While this may be the only surviving document expressing such racist attitudes, the casualness of Royce's remark suggests that this utterance was not out of character for Royce. By 1885, Royce had studied in Europe, lived in several US cities, and had become a Harvard professor with two important scholarly books published. He was no longer the bumpkin from the backwater. He had world experience enough to be fully responsible for his remarks, however casual. Robert V. Hine also describes Royce's marginal activism against segregation in chapter 1 of his book entitled *Josiah Royce: From Grass Valley to Harvard* (Norman: University of Oklahoma Press, 1991). While Hine does point to the racial elitism and racism held by Royce earlier in his life (159), he incorrectly assumes that a position that adopts favorable attitudes toward other immigrant groups means that he reversed his stance of anti-black racism. The recent work by Richard W. Rees in his book *Shades of Difference* convincingly demonstrates that the rise of immigration did not change the anti-Black views of many Americans, and in many ways perpetuated anti-Black racism, in an effort to expand the caste of whiteness.

72. Royce, "Race Questions and Prejudices," 270–271.

73. Ibid., 277.

74. Elizabeth Duquette, "Embodying Community, Disembodying Race: Josiah Royce on 'Race Questions and Prejudices,' " *American Literary History* 16 (2004): 29–57.

75. It is also relevant to note that Du Bois speaks against Royce's sensibilities to the problem of lynching, especially given Royce's resistance to Du Bois's articulation of the Southerners' tyranny in a paper given to Royce to satisfy his English requirement. Du Bois says, "naturally my English instructors had no idea nor interest in the way in which Southern attacks on the Negro were scratching me on the raw flesh" (*The Autobiography of W. E. B. Du Bois: A Soliloquy on Viewing My Life from the Last Decade of Its First Century* [New York: International, 1968], 144). In *Against Racism*, Herbert Aptheker identifies the

professor of that class as Josiah Royce and his two assistants, Ernest L. Conant and George P. Baker, Jr. W. E. B. Du Bois, *Against Racism: Unpublished Essays, Papers, Addresses 1887–1961*, ed. Herbert Aptheker (Amherst: University of Massachusetts Press, 1985), 16.

Now Elizabeth Duquette makes a deliberate effort to call my analysis of Royce's position on lynching and Du Bois's support of my interpretation "somewhat simplistic" in her book *Loyal Subjects: Bonds of Nation, Race, and Allegiance in Nineteenth-Century America* (New Brunswick: Rutgers University Press, 2010), 260 n. 73. Duquette claims that Du Bois's statement concerning what he learned from failing Josiah Royce's course changes how we should understand Du Bois's actual statement that Royce did not understand the problem of lynching. The mental acrobatics Duquette performs in order to defend Royce here is an impressive example of how some scholars merely need an assertion of a historic white figure's progressivism rather than any textual evidence of such progressivism to absolve a figure historically wedded to anti-Black racism from condemnation. Now Du Bois does say that he "realized that while style is subordinate to content, and that no real literature can be composed simply of meticulous and fastidious phrases, nevertheless that solid content with literary style carries a message further than poor grammar and muddled syntax" (*The Autobiography of W. E. B. Du Bois*, 144), but this is in response to how Du Bois says he chose to write about lynching, and how in doing so he disregarded literary style and grammar. Recalling the essay he wrote for the class taught by Josiah Royce, Du Bois remembered, "the words and ideas surged in my mind and spilled out with disregard of exact accuracy in grammar, taste in word or restraint in style. I knew the Negro problem and this was more important to me than literary form. I knew grammar fairly well, and I had a pretty wide vocabulary; but I was bitter, angry, and intemperate in my first thesis" (ibid., 144). Du Bois was trying to communicate the anger of being Black and a victim of white mob violence, and it was his personal view that Royce and the other instructors of the course did not "feel" that experience and reality as it affected the Negro.

Duquette's exorbitant exegesis maintains that Du Bois's "emphasis on style anticipates, although in a markedly different register, Royce's eventual argument about the formal problems of embodiment in the discussion of race in the United States" (*Loyal Subjects*, 210). Has Royce now become a postmodernist at the turn of the twentieth century concerned primarily about racial embodiment, the bodies of raced individuals, as separate from the racial groups he believes to be explained by the cutting-edge theories of turn-of-the-century anthropology? Is it appropriate simply to make something up, to invent a historical argument based on one word? At some point there is a limit to what the text establishes as a historical possibility, and Duquette has far exceeded that point, since the text she offers fails to provide any semblance of a warrant or reason for her thinking on this issue. In fact, Du Bois clarifies (offers text to explain) exactly what he meant by his comments. Remember, Du Bois begins his reflection on Royce's class by stating, "I was at the point in my intellectual development when the content rather than the form of my writing was to me of prime importance" (*The Autobiography of W. E. B. Du Bois*, 144), so he is reflecting upon how he sought to convey the great evil of lynching during his time at Harvard. After he received the failing grade in Royce's class, he says, "I was aghast, but I was not a fool. I did not doubt but what my instructors were fair in judging my English technically even if they did not understand the Negro problem" (ibid.). In order to correct his grammar and style, he then enrolled in English 12, "the best course on the campus for English composition" (ibid.). Both before Du Bois offered his opinions of lynching and the Negro problem and after he was graded, Du Bois concludes that his English professors could not understand the problem of lynching in any affective capacity; they only encountered the essay technically. In a last effort to establish some continuity between Royce and Du Bois, Duquette says, "given that Du Bois would have been Royce's student before the composition of 'Race Questions and Prejudices,' it does not seem a huge leap to consider that the philosopher's experience with this brilliant student might have influenced the development of the argument in the essay" (*Loyal Subjects*, 210). Unfortunately, there is *absolutely no text or evidence* offered to support this assertion. In fact, my evidence suggests that Du Bois and Royce would have been of different minds about lynching, since Du Bois, who was an adamant enemy of white supremacy and the white man's burden, would have rejected Royce's suggestion to colonize Black people in the South, a strategy that would have made the projects and research he was conducting at Atlanta University from 1896 to 1924 impossible, especially given Du Bois's advocacy for social equality at the time. It is simply not enough to assert without warrant that Royce was influenced by Du Bois, an assertion never meant to truly establish intellectual lineages and exchanges between the figures, but to serve as a narrow apologetic to defend Royce against charges of racism.

76. Royce, "Race Questions and Prejudices," 271.

77. Ibid., 272.

78. Ibid., 274.

79. Ibid.

80. Ibid., 275.

81. Ibid.

82. Ibid.

83. J. W. Garner, "Problems of Race Friction," *The Dial* 46.541 (1909): 19–20.

84. Thomas Nelson Page, *The Negro: The Southerner's Problem* (New York: Charles Scribner's Press, 1904).

85. Page, *The Negro*, 95.

86. Royce, "Race Questions and Prejudices," 277.

87. Frederick Douglass, *Why Is the Negro Lynched* (Bridgewater: John Whitby and Sons, 1895).

88. Ida B. Wells-Barnett, *Southern Horrors: Lynch Law in All Its Phases* (New York: The New York Age Print, 1892).

89. Ida B. Wells, *Crusade for Justice: The Autobiography of Ida B. Wells*, ed. Alfreda M. Duster (Chicago: University of Chicago Press, 1970), 64.

90. Page, *The Negro*, 117.

91. Ibid., 118.

92. Ibid., 119.

93. Royce, "Race Questions and Prejudices," 271.

94. Ibid.

95. Ibid., 276.

96. Ibid.

97. Ibid., 273–274.

98. Randall Auxier, *Time, Will, and Purpose: Living Ideas from the Philosophy of Josiah Royce* (Chicago: Open Court Press, 2013), 54. Auxier finds Royce relevant to contemporary discussions of ontology because he was not married to a fixed or fundamental ontology. Rationality, according to Auxier, is "based on the structure of possibility and probability, not on the structure of necessity" (ibid., 55). Royce believes that philosophical hypothesis "enables us to begin to connect the hypothetical and general to the real" (ibid., 58), so even from Royce's own viewing of conditional statements there is no basis to suggest that he would reject the antecedent much less the consequent. Royce believes the philosopher asserts hypothetical postulates about the world, it is not his job to verify them, as such it is quite possible that he is communicating a belief he takes to be true, since he in fact concludes that British administration is a means to protect white women.

99. Email to Tommy J. Curry, August 8, 2016.

100. Royce, "Race Questions and Prejudices," 276.

101. There was skepticism of Royce's program even in his day. In *Black and [w]hite in the Southern States: A Study of the Race Problem in the United States from a South African Point of View*, Maurice Smethurst Evans argues: "Professor Josiah Royce of Harvard University, 'Race Questions.' The distinguished author is much impressed with the better way in British Colonies and quotes experience in the West Indies. I do not think he fully realizes the different conditions. Did he visit South Africa he would hardly be so optimistic as regards the future of British administration" (Bombay: Longman's, Green and Company, 1915), 286.

102. For the documentation of this correspondence and Sir Sydney Olivier's subsequent use of parts of Royce's essay in his 1910 book entitled *White Capital and Coloured Labour*, see Josiah Royce's letter to George Platt Brett, July 14, 1908, in *The Letters of Josiah Royce*, 523–525, 524.

103. For a discussion of the white man's burden and the rise of apartheid, see Sydney Olivier, *The Anatomy of African Misery* (New York: Negro University

Press, 1969/1927). It is interesting how Olivier accounts for the rise of apartheid through a type of "white peril" between poor whites and the African natives.

104. It is of the utmost importance to stress that Sydney Olivier is not proposed as another white thinker to surpass current American philosophers. Black thinkers have been criticizing the myth of the "white man's burden" for decades. One of the most astute observations of the myth of Anglo-Saxonism is John Edward Bruce, "The White Man's Burden," in *The Selected Writings of John Edward Bruce: Militant Black Journalist*, ed. Peter Gilbert (New York: Arno Press, 1971), 97–98. Also, it is important to point out that Olivier's thinking is also flawed in the same regard as other white thinkers of his time, because he could not truly embrace a theory of true racial equality. Olivier genuinely believes that the civic mixture of whites and Blacks in Jamaica has civilized the Jamaican Negro in capacity and morality over their savage African ancestors. For proof of this element in Olivier's thought, see "The White Man's Burden at Home," *The International Quarterly* 11 (1905): 6–23, esp. 20, where Olivier describes the morality of the Jamaican Negro. Some readers may also find page 12 of this article worth a read, as Olivier defends why white men should marry Black women, but is apprehensive of intermarriage between Black men and white women. This article is also elaborated upon in greater detail over three chapters in Olivier's 1910 work entitled *White Capital and Coloured Labour* (chapters 4–6).

105. Sir Sydney Olivier, *White Capital and Coloured Labour* (Westport: Negro Universities Press, 1970/1910), 8.

106. Olivier, *White Capital and Coloured Labour*.

107. Ibid.

108. Ibid., 9.

109. Ibid.

110. See Olivier, "The White Man's Burden at Home," 7.

111. Ibid., 6.

112. Olivier, *White Capital and Coloured Labour*, 21.

113. Ibid., 25.

114. For a detailed discussion of Olivier's position, see chapter 4 in *White Capital and Coloured Labour*.

115. Olivier, "The White Man's Burden at Home," 10.

116. Ibid., 13.

117. Ibid.

118. Olivier, *White Capital and Coloured Labour*, 160–162.

119. Walter White, "The Paradox of Color," in *The New Negro: Voices of the Harlem Renaissance*, ed. Alain Locke (New York: Atheneum, 1992), 361–368, 367.

120. Patrick Bryan, *The Jamaican People: Race, Class, and Social Control 1880–1902* (Kingston: University of West Indies Press, 2000), ix.

121. Bryan, *The Jamaican People*, ix.

122. Ibid., x.

123. Ibid., 49.

124. Brian L. Moore and Michele A. Johnson, *Neither Led nor Driven: Contesting British Cultural Imperialism in Jamaica, 1865–1920* (Kingston: University of the West Indies Press, 2004), 241.

125. Bryan, *The Jamaican People*, 110.

126. Ibid., 112.

127. Ibid., 113.

128. Ibid., 113–114.

129. See ibid., especially chapters 11 and 12.

130. Bernard Magubane, *The Making of a Racist State: British Imperialism and the Union of South Africa 1875–1910* (Trenton: Africa World Press, 1996), 124.

131. W. T. Stead, ed., *The Last Will and Testament of Cecil Rhodes* (London: Review of Review Office, 1902).

132. W. T. Stead, "How to Deal with Negroes," *Review of Reviews* 39.109 (1906): 488.

133. H. W. V. Temperley, "The Imperial Control of Native Races," *The Contemporary Review*, June 1906, 804–813.

134. W.T. Stead, "How to Deal with Negroes: An Object Lesson from Jamaica," *Review of Reviews*, May 1906, 488.

135. John Moffatt Mecklin, *Democracy and Race Friction: A Study in Social Ethics* (New York: MacMillan Company, 1914), 160. Ironically, the work of the Mississippi-born philosopher John M. Mecklin is more closely aligned to the current project of white racial conservationists like Jacquelyn Kegley and Shannon Sullivan. Mecklin in fact argues in *Democracy and Race Friction* that Blacks have to create their own racially particular "social heritage," which best allows them to take advantage of American civilization.

However, it is important to remember that no whites at this point in America had really begun to acknowledge the equality of races, so the idea under contestation is over assimilation or racial solidarity (separatism). Mecklin argues that because every race has specific race traits that determine their temperament toward "civilization," every race must find its own course. The best whites can do for Blacks in this view is to assist their race leaders toward their self-defined racial goals. From what Mecklin calls the "equality of consideration," he argues that the race problem, while unsolvable, can be best managed. In other works, Mecklin in fact criticizes Lockean liberalism and the idea of equality that comes from the "North." For a discussion of these criticisms, see John M. Mecklin, "The Evolution of Slave Status in American Democracy I," *The Journal of Negro History* 2 (1917): 105–125, and "The Evolution of Slave Status II," *The Journal of Negro History* 2 (1917): 229–251.

136. See Charles M. Bakewell, "Royce as an Interpreter of American Ideals," *International Journal of Ethics* 27 (1917): 306–316.

137. John Moffatt Mecklin, "Royce as a Social Interpreter," *International Journal of Ethics* 27 (1917): 520–524, 521.

138. Mecklin, "Royce as a Social Interpreter," 524.

139. Mecklin, *Democracy and Race Friction*, 160–161.

140. Mecklin explains, "Whatever may be said of the theoretical justice of such a doctrine, the fact remains that never in the history of the contact of the white and the black races has such an ideal been realised; least of all has England, the champion of freedom, ever made it the basis of practical relations with backward races" (*Democracy and Race Friction*, 161).

141. Edgar Murphy, *The Basis of Ascendency: A Discussion of Certain Principles of Public Policy Involved in the Development of the Southern States* (London: Longmans, Green, & Co., 1910), xii.

142. Murphy, *The Basis of Ascendency*, xii.

143. Ibid.

144. Ibid., xv.

145. Ibid., xvi.

146. Ibid.

147. W. E. B. Du Bois, *The Conservation of Races: The American Negro Academy Occasional Papers No. 2* (Washington, DC: The American Negro Academy, 1897), 8.

148. Murphy, *The Basis of Ascendency*, xvii.

149. Ibid.

150. Ibid., xiii.

151. Lymon Moody Simms Jr., "Josiah Royce and the Southern Race Question," *Mississippi Quarterly* 22.1 (1968/1969): 71–74, 72.

152. Simms, "Josiah Royce and the Southern Race Question," 73.

Chapter 3

1. Royce, *Race Questions, Provincialism, and Other American Problems*, vi.

2. Ibid., vi.

3. Ibid.

4. Royce, "Some Characteristic Tendencies of American Civilization," 213.

5. Royce, *Race Questions, Provincialism, and Other American Problems*, 63.

6. Royce, "Some Characteristic Tendencies of American Civilization," 212.

7. Tommy J. Curry, "Saved by the Bell: Derrick Bell's Racial Realism as Pedagogy," *Philosophical Studies in Education* 39 (2008): 35–46.

8. Gary Peller, *Critical Race Consciousness: Reconsidering American Ideologies of Racial Justice* (Boulder: Paradigm, 2011).

9. Royce, *Race Questions, Provincialism, and Other American Problems*, vi.

10. Ibid., 63.

11. Royce, "Provincialism," 1073.

12. Ibid.

13. Royce, "Some Characteristic Tendencies of American Civilization," 197.

14. Ibid., 198.

15. Ibid.

16. Ibid.

17. Ibid.

18. Ibid.

19. Ibid., 200.

20. Ibid.

21. Ibid., 202.

22. Ibid., 202–203.

23. The edition cited throughout this essay is the 1908 version republished in Royce's larger work on *Race Questions, Provincialism, and Other American Problems.* The 1902 version appeared both as a pamphlet and in the *Boston Evening Transcript,* June 14, 1902.

24. Royce, "Provincialism," 1070.

25. Ibid.

26. Ibid., 1071.

27. Some may think this too strong a statement given the popularity of Sullivan's and Kegley's work (see chapter 2); however, I believe that Royce's actual texts are the best testimonies of his philosophy. In the 1900 essay "Some Characteristic Tendencies of American Civilization," Royce insists that linguistic, cultural, and historical difference should be eradicated through children's education in schools, churches, and universities. He places a special emphasis on philosophy's role in this regard.

28. Royce, "Provincialism," 1073.

29. Ibid.

30. Some may think this is an exaggeration; however, a brief reading of Royce's introduction to "Some Characteristic Tendencies of American Civilization" will remove any doubt about Royce's conviction on this issue.

31. Royce, "Characteristic Tendencies," 205.

32. Ibid., 205–206.

33. Ibid., 206.

34. Ibid.

35. Royce actually says, "When I spoke about academic developments, I necessarily pointed out the close relations that we have had with German Universities, and with the learning and science of the world, in so far as they are not only of English, but also of Continental European origin. But our political and social life is founded unquestionably upon motives that may be easily and directly traced to their sources in these islands" (ibid., 206).

36. Ibid.

37. Ibid.

38. Ibid., 206–207.

39. Ibid., 211.

40. Ibid., 207.

41. Ibid.

42. Ibid., 211.

43. Ibid.

44. Ibid.

45. Ibid.

46. Ibid., 212.

47. Ibid.

48. Ibid.

49. Royce, *Race Questions, Provincialism, and Other American Problems*, 66.

50. Royce, "Some Characteristic Tendencies," 215.

51. Ibid.

52. Ibid.

53. Josiah Royce, *The Philosophy of Loyalty* (New York: The MacMillan Company, 1908), v.

54. Auxier, *Time, Will, and Purpose*, 346.

55. Dwayne Tunstall, *Yes, but Not Quite: Encountering Royce's Ethico-Religious Insight* (New York: Fordham University Press, 2009), 1.

56. Tunstall, *Yes, but Not Quite*, 1.

57. See Auxier, *Time, Will, and Purpose*; Tunstall, *Yes, but Not Quite*; and Jacquelyn Kegley, *Josiah Royce in Focus* (Bloomington: Indiana University Press, 2008).

58. Royce, *The Philosophy of Loyalty*, 9.

59. Ibid., 12.

60. Ibid., 13.

61. Ibid., 15–16.

62. Ibid., 16.

63. Ibid., 16–17.

64. Ibid., 17.

65. Ibid., 18.

66. Ibid., 20.

67. Ibid., 32.

68. Ibid., 34.

69. Ibid., 35.

70. Ibid., 22.

71. Ibid., 108.

72. Ibid., 52.

73. Ibid., 116.

74. Ibid., 121.

75. Ibid., 122.

76. Mathew A. Foust, *Loyalty to Loyalty: Josiah Royce and the Genuine Moral Life* (New York: Fordham University Press, 2012), 116.

77. Foust, *Loyalty to Loyalty.*

78. Ibid., 117.

79. W. E. B. Du Bois, *Darkwater: Voices from within the Veil* (New York: Dover, 1999), 18.

80. Du Bois, *Darkwater.*

81. Ibid., 26.

82. Ibid., 29.

83. Foust, *Loyalty to Loyalty*, 117.

84. Ibid., 116.

85. Quoted in ibid., 117.

86. Ibid.

87. Royce, "Provincialism," 1072.

88. Foust, *Loyalty to Loyalty*, 118.

89. Royce, "Provincialism," 1072.

90. It is puzzling to me how Royce scholars who concern themselves with the problem of race through Royce are able to insist with no additional evidence or context to the quotes they select that their reading of Royce is not only correct, but should be treated as being the most authoritative. Throughout Foust's book, as well as Kegley's various works on Royce, quotations are simply pulled from the pages of Royce, sometimes midsentence, to support whatever political positions can be imagined. With Foust in particular, it seems that an editorial mistake in the printing of a passage, since the sentence was in the original copyedit sent to the publisher, was allowed to serve as the basis of absolving Royce of all previous mentions and suggestions of racism and the threats posed by Blacks and foreigners.

91. Shannon Sullivan, "Whiteness as Wise Provincialism: Royce and the Rehabilitation of a Racial Category," *Transactions of the Charles S. Peirce Society* 44.2 (2008): 236–262.

92. Sullivan, "Whiteness as Wise Provincialism," 237.

93. Ibid.

94. Ibid., 242.

95. Frederick Douglass, "The Word White," in *Frederick Douglass: Selected Speeches and Writings*, ed. Philip S. Foner (New York: Lawrence Hill Books, 1999), 275.

96. Rees's work is profound in the sense that it looks to historic Black authors and their scholarship to interpret and analyze the problems surrounding "ethnicity" in the United States. Though his work does have major blind spots, his scholarship directly addresses Sullivan's concern. For a more in-depth review of his work, see Tommy J. Curry, "Illuminated in Black: A Book Review of *Shades of Difference* by Richard W. Rees," *Journal of African American Studies* 12.3 (2008): 304–307.

97. Sullivan, "Whiteness as Wise Provincialism," 240. It is extremely telling that Sullivan only looks at Brown's "assault" as an instance of wise whiteness,

when there are other white women like Lydia Maria Childs who put the race question above the gender question in works like *The Duty of Disobedience to the Fugitive Slave Act* (Boston: The American Anti-Slavery Society, 1860), or infamous works like Mark Twain's "The United States of Lyncherdom," which can be found at: http://people.virginia.edu/~sfr/enam482e/lyncherdom.html (retrieved September 11, 2008).

98. See W.E.B Du Bois, "John Brown," in *The Oxford W. E. B. Du Bois Reader*, ed. Eric J. Sundquist (New York: Oxford University Press, 1996), 256–264.

99. For a discussion of Douglass's praises and condemnations of Brown, see "Capt. John Brown Not Insane," in *Frederick Douglass: Selected Speeches and Writings*, 374–375; Frederick Douglass's "Letter to the New York Herald, Nov. 4, 1859," in *Frederick Douglass: Selected Speeches and Writings*, 377–378; and his letter "To Helen Boucaster," in *Frederick Douglass: Selected Speeches and Writings*, 379.

100. See the essays entitled "Canada—Captain John Brown" and "Martin R. Delany in Liberia," in *Martin R. Delany: A Documentary Reader*, ed. Robert S. Levine (Chapel Hill: University of North Carolina Press, 2003), 328–335.

101. Sullivan describes the introduction, chapters 3 and 4, and the conclusion as being further development of her previous works on Royce's provincialism, namely, "Transforming [w]hiteness with Roycean Loyalty: A Pragmatist Feminist Account," and "[w]hiteness as Wise Provincialism: Royce on Rehabilitating a Racial Category." See Sullivan, *Good [w]hite People*, x.

102. Sullivan asks, "Can what animates white people be spiritually healthy instead? How might white people's animation constitute them by binding them to rather than allowing them to flee from their whiteness? With her or his critical self-love, the figure of the white ally attempts to offer a psychosomatic alternative both to white supremacy, on the one hand, and to white liberals' relentless attempts to distance themselves from their racial identities and histories on the other (*Good [w]hite People*, 12).

103. For a discussion of the economic basis of lynching, see Wells, *Southern Horrors and Other Writings*, and Tommy J. Curry, "The Fortune of Wells: Ida B. Wells-Barnett's Use of T. Thomas Fortune's Philosophy of Social Agitation as a Prolegomenon to Militant Civil Rights Activism," *Transactions of the Charles S. Peirce Society* 48.4 (2012): 456–482. For a discussion of the sexualized aspects of lynching and Black men, see Martha Hodes, "The Sexualization of Reconstruction Politics: White Women and Black Men in the South after the Civil War," *Journal of the History of Sexuality* 3.3 (1993): 402–417. For a discussion of Klan violence in the American South during Jim Crow, see Robert F. Williams, *Negroes with Guns*, ed. Marc Schleifer (New York: Marzani and Munsell, 1962).

104. For a historical account of white women's lynching of Black men, see Crystal N. Feimster, "New Southern Women and the Triumph of [w]hite Supremacy," in *Southern Horrors: Women and the Politics of Rape and Lynching* (Cambridge: Harvard University Press, 2009), 125–157. For an analysis of the rise of white women's KKK organizations and violence against Black Americans

in the twentieth century, see Kathleen Blee, *Women of the Klan: Racism and Gender in the 1920s* (Berkeley: University of California Press, 2009).

105. Sullivan, *Good [w]hite People*, 45.

106. Ibid.

107. Ibid., 46.

108. Ibid.

Chapter 4

1. Mecklin, "The Evolution of Slave Status in American Democracy II," *The Journal of Negro History* 2.3 (1917): 229–251, 230. Mecklin's second essay deals with the economic motivations behind the abolition of slavery. His first essay deals with the economic foundations and necessities of American slavery, see John M. Mecklin, "The Evolution of Slave Status in American Democracy," *The Journal of Negro History* 2.2 (1917): 105–125.

2. Josiah Royce, "Joseph Le Conte," *International Monthly* 4 (1901): 324–334, 327.

3. Royce, "Joseph Le Conte," 329.

4. Ibid., 329. It is also interesting to note the use of the artistry to describe the works and speech of Le Conte. Royce says, "Many as fascinating lecturers you find may find, but seldom are as thorough workers as he was. Many more productive men of science exist, but few of them are as much artists as was Le Conte" (329). This signifies a very important link between the works introduced by Le Conte and Royce's taking up of this term to describe assimilationism.

5. Josiah Royce, "Words of Professor Royce at the Walton Hotel at Philadelphia, December 29, 1915," *The Philosophical Review* 25.3 (1916): 507–514, 509–510.

6. Stanford Lyman, "Le Conte, Royce, Teggart, Blumer: A Berkeley Dialogue on Sociology, Social Change and Symbolic Interaction," *Symbolic Interaction* 11.1 (1988): 125–143, 128.

7. Lyman, "Le Conte, Royce, Teggart, Blumer," 128–129.

8. Tunstall, *Yes, but Not Quite.*

9. Ibid., 50.

10. Ibid., 51.

11. Ibid., 51.

12. See Dwayne Tunstall, "Haunted by Howison's Criticism: The Birth of Royce's Late Philosophy," in *Yes, but Not Quite*, 28–50.

13. Royce, "Words of Professor Royce at the Walton Hotel," 510.

14. Josiah Royce, "The Conception of God," 44.

15. Joseph Le Conte, *Evolution: Its Nature, Its Evidences, and Its Relation to Religious Thought* (New York: D. Appleton and Company, 1898), 372.

16. Ibid.

17. Josiah Royce, *The Conception of God: An Address before the Union* (Berkeley: Executive Council of the Union, 1895), 44.

18. Ibid., 34.

19. Josiah Royce, "The Philosophy of Loyalty," in *The Basic Writings of Josiah Royce: Vol 2: Logic, Loyalty, and Community*, ed. John J. McDermott (New York: Fordham University Press, 2005), 855–1015, 994.

20. Royce, "The Philosophy of Loyalty," 997.

21. Joseph Le Conte, *The Race Problem in the South* (New York: D. Appleton and Company, 1892), 351.

22. Josiah Royce, *Herbert Spencer: An Estimate and Review* (New York: Fox, Duffield, and Company, 1904), 73–75. It is however important to note that while Royce's admiration for Spencer extends throughout all aspects of Royce's philosophy. He disagrees with Spencer as to the effects that evolution has on the mental and moral development of children. In the second section of Royce's 1904 work entitled "Herbert Spencer's Educational Theories" (121–183), Royce invokes loyalty to loyalty as a corrective of the mechanistic account of Spencer's individualist scientism. Rather, says Royce, "The privilege of making our own blunders, and of learning thereby, is, in respect of such matters, very precious. But there are other respects in which we learn best through imitation, obedience, and whatever else does not leave us to ourselves, but wisely informs us with tendencies to action which we could never have invented if left to ourselves. In general, loyalty—the essence of orderly social morality—is in most of us, in case we attain to loyalty at all, the result rather of an early 'heteronomy' of the will, which can only later reach 'autonomy.' . . . Let us honor him for what he was. But let us be glad that he is not the trainer of our children" (182–183).

23. Royce, *Herbert Spencer*, 13.

24. Lyman, "Le Conte, Royce, Teggart, Blumer," 129.

25. Royce, "Words of Professor Royce at the Walton Hotel," 511.

26. Tunstall, *Yes, but Not Quite*, 39.

27. See A. H. Keene, *Ethnology: Fundamental Ethnical Problems; the Primary Ethnical Groups* (Cambridge: Cambridge University Press, 1909); Juul Dieserud, *The Scope and Content of the Science of Anthropology* (Chicago: Open Court Press, 1908); and Joseph Deniker, *The Races of Man: An Outline of Anthropology and Ethnology* (New York: The Walter Scott Publishing Company, 1904).

28. Le Conte, *The Race Problem in the South*, 359.

29. Ibid., 359–360.

30. Le Conte, *Evolution*, 374.

31. Le Conte, *The Race Problem in the South*, 361.

32. Ibid.

33. Ibid.

34. Ibid., 366.

35. For a further discussion of this principle, see Le Conte, *The Race Problem in the South*, 367. For additional clarification of Joseph Le Conte's view of evolutionary theory and his defense of Lamarckianism, see Joseph Le Conte, "Evolution of Human Progress," *Open Court: A Quarterly Magazine Devoted to the Science of Religion* 5.191 (1891): 1, where he says, "but the use of reason of the Lamarckian factors as already shown . . . all our hopes of race improvement, therefore, are strictly conditioned on the efficacy of these factors, i.e. on the fact that useful changes in each generation are to some extent inherited and accumulated in the race" (1).

36. Le Conte, *The Race Problem in the South*, 367. It is also important to understand the relationship and significance between what Le Conte calls character and (Christian) religion. In *Evolution*, Le Conte argues that "the uncultured savage sees a separate god in every object. As culture advances, his gods become fewer and nobler, until in the most advanced states, man recognizes but one infinite God" (347). Like most ethnological research in the mid-1800s and even theories of sociology at the turn of the century, religion and the beliefs of "primitive" peoples were used as a measure for or against their barbarism. This is also part of the debate used by Royce to question the biological determinism of race theory, which fails to address the dynamic progress of races from this lower theology to a higher monotheism.

Later in that work, Le Conte also maintains that "as organic evolution reached its goal and completion in man, so human evolution must reach its goal and completion in the ideal man—i.e. the Christ. . . . It is not necessary that the ideal man—the Christ—should be perfect in knowledge or power; on the contrary he must grow in wisdom and in stature, like other men; but he must be perfect in character. Character is essential spirit. . . . Character is the attitude of the human spirit toward the divine spirit" (360–361).

37. Royce, "Race Questions and Prejudices," 1105.

38. Le Conte, *The Race Problem in the South*, 361.

39. Ibid., 362.

40. Ibid.

41. Ibid.

42. Ibid.

43. Ibid.

44. Royce, "Race Questions and Prejudices," 1100.

45. Ibid., 1098.

46. Royce, "Provincialism," 1072.

47. Ibid., 1073.

48. Ibid.

49. Le Conte, *The Race Problem in the South*, 351.

50. Ibid., 353.

51. Ibid., 352.

52. Ibid.

53. Ibid., 353.

54. Ibid.

55. Ibid.

56. Royce, "Race Questions and Prejudices," 1107.

57. Ibid.

58. Ibid., 1101.

59. Ibid.

60. Josiah Royce, "Some Characteristic Tendencies of American Civilization," *Transactions of the Aberdeen Philosophy Society* 3 (1900): 194–218, 213.

61. John M. Mecklin, *My Quest for Freedom* (New York: Charles Scribner, 1945), 145, 258.

62. Mecklin, *My Quest for Freedom*, 145.

63. See W. A. A., "Democracy and Race Friction," *The Southern Workman* 44.2 (1915): 179–181. It is relevant to note that James E. Gregg was the principal of Hampton University and advocate of the industrial program advocated by Booker T. Washington; see his article "Industrial Training for the Negro," *The Annals of the American Academy of Political and Social Science* 140 (1928): 122–127. See Mecklin, "The Evolution of Slave Status in American Democracy," *Journal of Negro History* 2.2 (1917): 105–125.

64. Mecklin, *Democracy and Race Friction* (New York: MacMillan Company, 1914), 257.

65. Mecklin, "The Evolution of the Slave Status in American Democracy," 105.

66. Ibid., 108.

67. Ibid., 109.

68. See Damian Alan Pargas, *Slavery and Forced Migration in the Antebellum South* (New York: Cambridge University Press, 2015); and George William Van Cleave, *A Slaveholder's Union: Slavery, Politics, and the Constitution in the Early American Republic* (Chicago: University of Chicago Press, 2010).

69. Mecklin, *Democracy and Race Friction*, vii.

70. Ibid., viii.

71. Ibid., ix.

72. Ibid.

73. Ibid.

74. Ibid., 2.

75. Ibid.

76. Ibid.

77. Edward Alsworth Ross, *Sin and Society: An Analysis of Latter-Day Iniquity* (Boston: Houghton Mifflin Company, 1907, 40).

78. Ross, *Sin and Society*, 40.

79. Mecklin, *Democracy and Race Friction*, 6.

80. Ibid., 6–12.

81. Ibid., 23.

82. Ibid.

83. Ibid., 16.

84. Ibid., 24.

85. Ibid., 48.

86. Ibid., 49.

87. Royce, "Race Questions and Prejudices," 279.

88. Mecklin, *Democracy and Race Friction*, 132.

89. Ibid.

90. Ibid., 161–162.

91. Ibid., 162.

92. Ibid.

93. For a discussion of the Afro-American League, see Tommy J. Curry, "The Fortune of Wells: Ida B. Wells-Barnett's Use of T. Thomas Fortune's Philosophy of Social Agitation as a Prolegomenon to Militant Civil Rights Activism," *Transactions of the Charles S. Pierce Society* 48.8 (2012): 456–482; and Emma Lou Thornbrough, *T. Thomas Fortune: Militant Journalist* (Chicago: University of Chicago Press, 1972).

For a discussion of the American Negro Academy, see Alexander Crummell, "Civilization: The Primal Need of the Race" and "The Attitude of the American Mind toward the Negro Intellect," in *The American Negro Academy Occasional Papers 3* (New York: Arno Press, 1969); and Alfred A. Moss, *The American Negro Academy: Voice of the Talented Tenth* (Baton Rouge: Louisiana State University Press, 1981). For a discussion of the Atlanta Sociological Laboratory, see Earl Wright II, "The Atlantic Sociological Laboratory 1896–1924: A Historical Account of the First American School of Sociology," *Western Journal of Black Studies* 26.3 (2002): 165–174; Earl Wright and Thomas C. Calhoun, "Jim Crow Sociology: Toward an Understanding of the Origin and Principles of Black Sociology via the Atlanta Sociological Laboratory," *Sociological Focus* 39.1 (2006): 1–18; Earl Wright, "Beyond W. E. B. Du Bois: A Note on Some of the Lesser Known Members of the Atlanta Sociological Laboratory," *Sociological Spectrum* 29.6 (2009): 700–717; and Aldon Morris, *The Scholar Denied: W. E. B. Du Bois and the Birth of Modern Sociology* (Oakland: University of California Press, 2015).

Concerning the rise of an aspiring Black middle class, see Michele Mitchell, *Righteous Propagation: African Americans and the Politics of Racial Destiny after Reconstruction* (Chapel Hill: University of North Carolina Press, 2004); Glenda Gilmore, *Gender and Jim Crow: Women and the Politics of [w]hite Supremacy in North Carolina, 1896–1920* (Chapel Hill: University of North Carolina Press, 1996); and Kevin K. Gaines, *Uplifting the Race: Black Leadership, Politics, and Culture in the Twentieth Century* (Chapel Hill: University of North Carolina Press, 1996).

94. William Hannibal Thomas, *The American Negro: What He Was, What He Is, and What He May Become: A Critical and Practical Discussion* (New York: The MacMillan Company, 1901). Also see John David Smith, *Black Judas: William Hannibal Thomas and the American Negro* (Athens: University of Georgia Press, 2000).

95. G. Stanley Hall, *Adolescence: Its Psychology and Its Relations to Physiology, Anthropology, Sociology, Sex, Crime, Religion and Education*, Vols. 1–2 (New York: D. Appleton & Co., 1904). For an explanation of recapitulation theory, see Robert E. Grinder, "The Concept of Adolescence in the Genetic Psychology of G. Stanley Hall," *Child Development* 40.2 (1969): 355–369. For an explanation of recapitulation and Progressive Era education reforms and assumptions, see Thomas D. Fallace, *Race and the Origins of Progressive Education, 1880–1929* (New York: Teachers College Press, 2015).

96. Royce, "Race Questions and Prejudices," 3.

97. Ibid., 2–3.

Epilogue

1. For a discussion of John Dewey's racism, see Goodenow, "Racial and Ethnic Tolerance in John Dewey's Educational and Social Thought"; Margonis, "John Dewey's Racialized Visions of the Student and the Classroom Community"; Margonis, "John Dewey, W. E. B. Du Bois, and Alain Locke," 173–196; and Fallace, *Dewey and the Dilemma of Race*. For a description of the racial antipathy in Chicago School assimilation theory and social work, see R. Fred Water, "Assimilation and Cultural Pluralism in American Social Thought," *Phylon* 40.4 (1979): 325–333. For an analysis of racism within the Progressive movement, see Fallace, *Race and the Origins of Progressive Education, 1880–1929*.

2. See Curry, "Concerning the Under-specialization of Race Theory in American Philosophy."

3. Charles Marsh, "The Civil Rights Movement as Theological Drama: Interpretation and Application," *Modern Theology* 18.2 (2002): 231–250, 237.

4. Marsh, "The Civil Rights Movement as Theological Drama," 237.

5. Ibid., 237–238.

6. See Emmanuel Eze, "The Color of Reason," in *Postcolonial African Philosophy: A Critical Reader* (Cambridge: Blackwell, 1997), 103–131; and Robert Bernasconi, "Kant as an Unfamiliar Source of Racism," in *Philosophers on Race: Critical Essays*, ed. Julie Ward and Tommy Lott (Malden: Blackwell, 2002), 145–166.

7. Royce in fact articulates a similarity between his previous use of the universal community and the Beloved Community. He writes, "And the community to which, when grace saves him, the convert is thenceforth to be loyal,

we may here venture to call by a name which we have not hitherto used. Let this name be 'The Beloved Community.' This is another name for what we before called the Universal Community. Only now the universal community will appear to us in a new light, in view of its relations to the doctrine of grace" (*The Problem of Christianity: The Christian Doctrine of Life* [New York: The MacMillan Company, 1913], 172).

8. Royce, *The Problem of Christianity*, xxv.

9. Royce sees significant overlap between the loyal community and the role grace plays in enabling loyalty. He writes:

> The realm of grace is the realm of the powers and the gifts that save, by thus originating and sustaining and informing the loyal life. This realm contains, at the very least, three essentially necessary constituent members: First, the ideally lovable community of many individuals in one spiritual bond; secondly, the spirit of this community, which is present both as the human individual whose power originated and whose example, whose life and death, have led and still guide the community, and as the united spiritual activity of the whole community; thirdly, Charity itself, the love of the community by all its members, and of the members by the community. To the religion of Paul, all these things must be divine. They all have their perfectly human correlate and foundation wherever the loyal life exists. (*The Problem of Christianity*, 192)

10. Marsh, "The Civil Rights Movement as Theological Drama,"237.

11. Ibid., 239.

12. Marsh, "The Civil Rights Movement as Theological Drama," 239.

13. Martin Luther King Jr., *Where Do We Go from Here? Chaos or Community* (Boston: Beacon Press, 1967), 173.

14. King, *Where Do We Go from Here?*, 191.

15. Frantz Fanon, *The Wretched of the Earth* (New York: Grove Press, 2004), 178.

16. King, *Where Do We Go from Here?*, 68.

17. Ibid.

18. Ibid., 37.

19. Ibid., 38.

20. This essay was originally published by Martin Luther King Jr., as "Honoring Dr. Du Bois," *Freedomways* 8.2 (1968): 104–111.

21. King, *Where Do We Go from Here?*, 179.

22. W. E. B. Du Bois, "American Negroes and Africa's Rise to Freedom," in *The World and Africa* (New York: International, 1965), 334–338, 338. It is relevant to note that Black scholars have also made this argument. For a popular

article making this argument, see Paul C. Taylor, "What's the Use of Calling W. E. B. Du Bois a Pragmatist?," *Metaphilosophy* 35 (2004): 99–114.

23. Du Bois, *The Autobiography of W. E. B. Du Bois*, 343.

24. W. E. B. Du Bois, "Whites in Africa after Negro Autonomy," in *The Oxford W. E. B. Du Bois Reader*, ed. Eric J. Sundquist (New York: Oxford University Press, 1996), 667–675, 669–670.

25. Du Bois, "An Address to the Black Academic Community."

26. W. E. B. Du Bois, "Letter to Herbert Aptheker," in *The Correspondence of W. E. B. Du Bois*, Vol. 3, ed. Herbert Aptheker (Amherst: University of Massachusetts Press, 1978), 394–396.

For Du Bois's view of his own writing in *The Souls of Black Folk*, see his book review entitled "On *The Souls of Black Folk*." Du Bois claims that

> *The Souls of Black Folk* is a series of fourteen essays written under various circumstances and for different purposes during a period of seven years. It has, therefore, considerable, perhaps too great, diversity. . . . On the other hand, there is a unity in the book, not simply the general unity of the larger topic, but a unity of purpose in the distinctively subjective note that runs in each essay. Through all the book runs a personal and intimate tone of self-revelation. . . . In its larger aspects the style is tropical—African. This needs no apology. The blood of my fathers spoke through me and cast off the English restraint of my training and surroundings. The resulting accomplishment is a matter of taste. Sometimes I think very well of it and sometimes I do not. (In *The W. E. B. Du Bois Oxford Reader*, ed. Eric J. Sundquist [New York: Oxford University Press, 1996], 304–305, 305)

It is interesting to see the clarity with which Du Bois approaches his previous work, but what is most important here for philosophical discussions is how Du Bois clearly and deliberately argues that the book be understood as a work of African style, unquestionably distanced from the current interpretations of his work that bind him within the very European constraints that Du Bois himself claims "the blood of his fathers allowed him to cast off."

Index

Aberdeen speech. *See* "Some
Characteristic Tendencies of
American Civilization"
abolitionism, 150–151
activism, anti-lynching, 179
Addams, Jane, ix, xi, 2, 10, 18
with Black men and white women,
149
integrationism and, 185
legacy, 7, 184
racism and, 9, 14, 28
"Address to a Black Intellectual
Community" (Du Bois), 196
African Americans
philosophy, 204n32
Royce and Page debate on, 98–108
African Life and Customs (Blyden),
11, 116
Afro-American League, 179
Agassiz, Louis, 157
Aiken (Dr.), 53–54
amendments, fifteenth, xv
American Civilization and the Negro
(Roman), 23
American Negro Academy, 179
American philosophical canon, viii, xi
*The American Japanese Problem: A
Study of the Race Relations of the
East and the West* (Gulick), 93
anachronism, 14, 34

Anglo-Saxonism, 42. *See also* white
supremacy
assimilationism and, 70, 131
conformity and, 125–126
imperialism and, 116
support for, xvi, xix, 38, 165, 185
"Annotated Bibliography of the
Publications of Josiah Royce"
(Skrupskelis), 6
Ansley, Frances Lee, 31
anti-Black racism
paradigms of, 28–30, 37–38
of white philosophers, 1–2
anti-lynching activism, 179
anti-racism. *See also* anti-Black racism
racism and, 77–79, 151
racist concepts revised as
philosophy of, 35–40
anti-suffrage movement, whites with,
xv–xvi
apartheid, 39, 74
ideo-racial, 6–14
Appiah, Anthony, 15, 204n32
Aptheker, Bettina, 9
Aptheker, Herbert, xix, 196
art
assimilation as social, 41–42, 70,
75, 156, 168
dark, 168–171
of government, 156

237

gmo1ccd

Index

239

Boas, Franz, 11, 66
Bonilla-Silva, Eduardo, 31–32
Brantlinger, Patrick, 75
Brown, John, 150–151
Brown, William G. (1832–1883), 85
Brown, William Garrott (1868–1913), 214n12
   at Harvard University, 85–86
   white peril and, 83, 84, 88–89
Brown v. Board of Education, 26–27, 35
Bruce, John E., 9, 221n104
Bryan, Patrick, 113–114
burden. *See* white man's burden

California
   assimilation and provincialism in, 46, 47–52, 55
   with domestic colonization, 71–72
   Downieville lynching (1851), 53–58
   gold, 51, 158
   politics, 49–50
   social order in, 56–57, 71
   violence and, 48–51
   as wise provincialism model, 51–52, 135
California: From the Conquest in 1846 to the Second Vigilance Committee in San Francisco: A Study of American Character (Royce), 47–48
Canada, 150
Cannan, 53
Caribbean, 150
Carmichael, Stokely, 194
castration, lynching and, 10, 38
Castro, José, 49
Catholic Church, 137
Central American Philosophy Association conference, 3
Chamberlain, Houston Stewart, 211n60. See also *The*

Foundations of the Nineteenth Century
   biological determinism and, 59–60
   Royce and, 59–61
character, religion and, 230n36
Chicago School, 11
children
   with employment, 114–115
   evolution and, 229n22
   in Jamaica, 114
Childs, Lydia Maria, 226n97
China
   immigration and, 92
   as inferior race, 167
   Yellow peril and, 92
Chinese men, white women and, 92
Citizens Councils, xvii
civil rights movement, 190–191
   Du Bois and, 195–196
   King and, 193, 195
Civil War, US, xiv, 21, 32, 41, 71
   loyalty to loyalty as doctrine in post-, 138–142
   slavery and, 127–128, 179
"The Civil Rights Movement as Theological Drama" (Marsh), 190–191
Clendenning, John, 207n53
Cobb, W. Montague, 11
colonialism, 20–21
   assimilationism and, 67–76, 126–132
   conformity and, 146
   genocide and, 37
   ideal with wise provincialism, 132–138
   Jamaica and, 16–17, 113–121
   with Jamaica and Negrophobia, 108–112
   justifications for, 30
   with provincialism as tool for assimilation, 126–132

with whites and contact with other
races, 82–83
race theory
biological determinism and, 230n36
transitions in, 163–164
race traits
ethnology and, 171–180
as hereditary, 174–175, 177
race-psychology, 177
*The Races of Europe: A Sociological
Study* (Ripley), 12
The Race Problem in the South (Le
Conte), 156, 163–164
*The Race Traits and Tendencies of the
American Negro* (Hoffman), 58
racial managerialism, xix, 102, 167
racism. *See also* Anglo-Saxonism; anti-
Black racism; white supremacy
Addams and, 9, 14, 28
anti-racism and, 77–79, 151
concepts revised as anti-racist
philosophy, 35–40
defined, 29, 31–34
dehumanization and, 34, 39
democracy and, xvii–xviii
employment and, 86–88
hate crimes and, 152
in historical context, 28–30,
37–38, 40–43
ideo-racial apartheid and, 6–14
with immigration, 217n71
institutionalized, xx–xxi
integrationism and, ix
King and, 193, 194–195
philosophy and, xvii
prejudice and, 29
race and, 33–34
of Royce, xi, xvi, 1–2, 14–21, 32,
39–40, 45–47, 143, 155–156,
185–190, 202n25, 205n35,
207n53, 209n1
segregation and, 35

suffrage movement and, xiv–xvi
violence and, 55
rapists, Black men as, 9–10, 30, 103,
149
Rassentheoretiker, 60
Reconstruction, 85
benefits of, 40, 45, 102–103
economy and, 86, 178–179
Negrophobia during, 32
Rees, Richard W., 150, 217n71,
226n96
*Reflections on Segregation,
Desegregation, Power and Morals*
(Fontaine), 26
religion, 138–139, 160, 163
character and, 230n36
God and, xviii
schools and, 137
"Respect for Law" (Addams), 9
*Rethinking Race: Franz Boas and His
Contemporaries* (Williams), 58
Review of Reviews, 90, 115–116
Rhodes, Cecil, 115
rights
civil rights movement, 190–191,
193, 195–196
for women, xiii
Ripley, William Z., 12
Roman, Charles Victor, on Royce,
23–24, 208n67
Ross, Edward, 175
Royce, Josiah, viii, ix, xii, xix, 37,
211n63, 215n38, 224n35
with assimilation and
provincialism, 47–52, 55
Bastian and, 60–62
with Beloved Community, 186,
190–197
Chamberlain and, 59–61
with colonial assimilationism, 67–76
with colonial strategy rejected,
113–121